To Beverly on her birthday 1969.

Jesus of the Spirits

Jesus of

STEIN AND DAY/*Publishers*/New York

the Spirits

PEDRO McGREGOR

in association with T. STRATTON SMITH

First published in the United States of America by
Stein and Day/*Publishers*, 1967

Copyright © 1966 by Pedro McGregor and T. Stratton Smith
as *The Moon and Two Mountains*

Stein and Day/*Publishers*/7 East 48 Street, New York, N.Y. 10017

TO MY PARENTS

Contents

Illustrations

CHAPTER ONE

The Adventurers Who Liked Dark Ladies

T H E woman didn't scream until her clothes caught fire. Even then, the husband still hovered fearfully outside the tense circle of faces lining the ring of flaming gunpowder surrounding her. But when, as the drums reached a crescendo, flames licked her hair and she screamed shrilly again, he shouldered his way brusquely into action.

To his horror, the closely packed worshippers turned on him as he tried to push his way through, clawing at his clothes, hanging on to his arms and barring the way. " No, no," they cried urgently, " you must not interfere. Let her be : *they* will look after her; the spirits will not permit her to come to any harm . . ."

Outside the shuttered suburban drawing room, Cadillacs and Chevrolets swished past and the sun beat down on the wide pavements of Belo Horizonte—capital of the state of Minas Gerais, a modern, architect-designed city in the geometric patterns of whose carefully planted avenues mineral workers returning from the siesta can be assured always of walking in the shade. But however specialised in urban development the planners are, however agreeable the mountain air, however beautiful the horizons which give the place its name, those who live in it will be bound to have problems. And some of the 700,000 citizens of Belo Horizonte are likely to seek strange ways of solving them.

Ways strange to the rest of the world, that is, for this is Brazil. And the blazing lady had sought the aid of an association where advice from spiritual spheres could be found. Most helpful they had been, too: evil spirits were haunting her, she had been told, and these were the cause of her suffering. They must be expelled; they had to be exorcised —and this could only be done by fire . . . Thus the chanting, thus the drums and the gunpowder. And thus the right uppercut and the left jab the husband was forced to employ before he could reach his wife, drag her from the flames, smother them by rolling her on the floor, and then rush her —badly burned but fortunately still alive—to the nearest hospital . . .

The woman was white, her husband " tanned," the worshippers black, mulatto and white.

Only in Brazil could this have happened, because only in Brazil is miscegenation accompanied by intermixed religious rites throughout the country. In this vast territory of twenty states whose land area adds up to a total as large as the whole of Europe, races and cultures, mentalities and beliefs, civilisation and barbarism, religion and primitive cults mingle to form an amalgam unique in the world.

This situation was brought about by the type of colonisation to which the country was subjected, the kind of people responsible for it, and also the very size of the place, colonisation being spread over regions differing highly in climatic and geographical characteristics, separated by huge distances. The first colonisers, the Portuguese, landed in Brazil in 1500, mixing with the original inhabitants, the Indians, and later adding African Negroes from many tribes whom they brought to the newly discovered country as slaves. These three races, and their disparate yet strangely similar beliefs, constitute the basic ingredients which were to form, in the melting pot of Brazil, a spiritualist movement as varied as the country's landscapes, as vital as its progress and as generous as the nature of its people. The meeting of Portuguese Catholicism with Negro and Amer-Indian religious cults was to result in a national psychology forming the background to this movement—generically termed Spiritism to distinguish it from the spiritualist beliefs of other countries—whose main trait was determined by the religious syncretism that followed: a rare aptitude of accepting antagonistic religious beliefs and concepts.

It is the purpose of this book to show that Brazil does not harbour—in Kardecism and Umbanda, the two main denominations of spiritism—the world's most powerful movement of this kind just by chance, nor that the mysticism and inclination towards the magical of its average citizen is a phenomenon without due cause.

*　　*　　*

The Portuguese who colonised Brazil were far from ethnically or culturally "pure." Alexandre Herculano's *History Of Portugal* defines them as "an indeterminate population in the midst of two contending groups (the Nazarenes and the Mohammedans), half Christian, half Saracen, with relatives and friends in each group and having sympathies with both on the grounds of belief and custom." Count Hermann Keysering exclaimed that it was "in vain that one looked for a unified physical type" among the Portuguese, adding that he found "individuals with an air of the Scandinavian about them, and Negroid types," both Portuguese, living together in the same land "in a state of profound unity."

The reason for this lies in Portugal's ethnic and cultural connection with Africa throughout its history. Arabs, Berbers, Capsitanians and Lybo-Phoenicians were among her forefathers; Muslim and Christian, in spite of their wars, influenced each other there—the former certainly implanting a number of character traits, not least a tendency towards polygamy.

One of Brazil's most distinguished citizens, the internationally famed social anthropologist Professor Gilberto Freyre, sums it up in his definitive work on his homeland, *The Masters And The Slaves**: "The singular predisposition of the Portuguese to the hybrid, slave-exploiting colonisation of the tropics is to be explained in a large part by the ethnic or,

---

*Originally published in 1933. English language edition translated by Samuel Putman and published by Alfred A. Knopf.

better, the cultural past of a people existing indeterminately between Europe and Africa and belonging uncompromisingly to neither . . . with the African influence seething beneath the European and giving a sharp relish to sexual life, to alimentation and to religion; with Moorish or Negro blood running throughout a great light-skinned mulatto population, when it is not the predominant strain, in regions that to this day are inhabited by a dark-skinned people . . . and with the hot and oleous air of Africa mitigating the Germanic harshness of institutions and cultural forms, corrupting the doctrinal and moral rigidity of the mediæval church, sapping the bones from Christianity, feudalism, Gothic architecture, canonical discipline, Visigoth law, the Latin tongue and the very character of the people. It was Europe reigning without governing: it was Africa that governed."

Miscegenation, in other words, did not start in Brazil, between the colonisers and, first, the Indian, later the Negro: it had started long before, between the Portuguese and the African, the Portuguese and the Moor, the Portuguese and the Negro. Thus there could not have been a people better suited for the colonisation of Brazil, more inclined to miscegenation, abler to adapt to the circumstances that they would find there. The extreme mobility of the Portuguese, bestowed on them by a mixture with races of semitic origin, the "abundant means of maritime transport that Portugal possessed as did no other nation in the first decades of the 16th century" (historian C. Malho Dias), combined with their miscibility—capacity to miscegenate—which "no colonising people of modern times has exceeded or so much as equalled" (Freyre)—these things made it possible for the Portuguese, so ridiculously small in number, to colonise such vast and distant regions as Brazil and Africa.

Among these factors, miscibility played an overwhelming part. "Wherever they might settle, in Africa or in America, the Portuguese made up for the scarcity of manpower by taking wives and begetting offspring with a procreative fervour that was due as much to violent instincts on the part of the individual as it was to any calculated policy stimulated by the State

14

for obvious economic and political reasons," Freyre comments. "For this they had been prepared by the intimate terms of social and sexual intercourse on which they had lived with the coloured races that had invaded their own peninsula or were close neighbours to it, one of which, of the Mohammedan faith, was technically more highly skilled and possessed an intellectual and artistic culture superior to that of the blond Christians . . . Long contact with the Saracens had left [them] the idealised figure of the ' enchanted ' Moorish woman, a charming type, brown-skinned, black-eyed, enveloped in sexual mysticism . . . The brown-skinned woman was in fact preferred by the Portuguese for purposes of love, at least for purposes of physical love," Professor Freyre concludes.

In Brazil, this preference is reflected in an old saying: White woman for wedding, mulatto woman for whoring, black woman for working.

The colonisers were thus hereditarily disposed towards sexual intercourse with those whom other Europeans would consider greatly inferior (to the point of making sexual intercourse with Africans a crime, as in South Africa today); they were, after all, used to it at home—with this difference, that the brownish Moors had been the conquerors, and they the defeated. It was therefore " chique," as we say today, to have sexual relations with coloured women. In Brazil, therefore, " miscegenation and the interpenetration of cultures . . . tended to mollify the inter-class and interracial antagonisms developed under an aristocratic economy," says Freyre.

They also mollified religious differences and brought about the long and still-developing process of what we might term " religious miscegenation." Since the " doctrinal and moral rigidity " of the Church in Portugal had already been " corrupted " by African and other influences, the Portuguese had themselves developed a theological " flexibility " unknown in the other Catholic countries of Europe. Once in South America, at an enormous distance from the organised Church, with only local priests to handle, surrounded by easy-to-get women slaves and innumerable *mestizo* children begotten through this total promiscuity, the colonisers became even more tolerant towards the religious beliefs of their concubines. And the doors of their private lives were thus thrown open to religious beliefs, concepts and practices that would have been labelled as barbarous and simply discarded by any other European colonisers.

The Castilians, for instance, more Gothic and " European," had always maintained their distance from the invading Moors and were thus little inclined towards miscegenation in the New World (Pizzarro may have mated with some Inca women, but he formed no families, nor did he build a patriarchal society founded on miscegenation). The apparent pattern of Castilian colonisation was always aristocratic and caste-forming, allowing little or no confraternisation—a trait discernible today among the military of the Spanish-speaking Latin-American countries, especially in Argentina. The officers of the Brazilian army, in contrast, coming mainly from the lower, miscegenated strata of the population, are essentially democratic and non-aristocratic in feeling and attitude, as witness the revolution of April, 1964.

Belgian, Dutch, French and German colonisers, though less aristocratic, tended to form an administrative elite whose relations with native populations, when they were not furtively licentious, were autocratic in the extreme—to say nothing of the British empire-builders who insisted on dressing for dinner in the middle of the jungle " to keep up appearances " and perpetuate the Establishment!

With those brave souls who crossed the Atlantic in the *Mayflower,* no comparison is possible. A persecuted religious minority, they arrived with a Bible in one hand and a shovel in the other, ready to work and fight to build a country where they could practise their religion freely. Since they had a strong community feeling and had brought their wives with them, the question of miscegenation did not arise, and in any case it was unthinkable: the Bible was interpreted in a different way so far as " natives " were concerned and strong racial barriers were erected from the start (the whole world is a witness to the hard time the Rev. Martin Luther King is having, trying to tear them down at last).

But the 16th century Portuguese, striding the poop of his frail ship on the lookout for the newly discovered land of the Southern Hemisphere, was a different proposition. Avaricious and lustful for the wealth of a land that seemed to have more riches than the Indies, he waded ashore to find the satisfaction of the latter sin easier than the former. On the beaches and a few miles inland, he found women " of beautiful features and a delightful briskness and vividness " whose habits and naked physique much resembled the Moorish beauties he had learned to adore in eight centuries of Saracen domination. They had loose, flowing, dark hair, dark eyes and fat little bodies painted red and, like the Moorish women, they loved to bathe in the river " to refresh their ardent nudity " and frequently combed their hair. Above all, for a piece of mirror or a small toy, the Indian nymphs " would give themselves, with legs spread far apart, to the *Caraibas* [Europeans] who were so gluttonous for a woman " (Freyre).

Agreeable though this was, it was not what the Portuguese had come for, however. They had come to find riches, they had hoped to find another India " with which to carry on trade in spices and precious stones; or a Mexico or Peru from which they might extract gold and silver," the paramount ideal of the get-rich-quick adventurers of the time. But things did not turn out like that: " the discoverers of Brazil did not encounter either kings of Kananor or chieftains of Sofala with whom they might trade and barter. Nothing but . . . savages, wild men, running about naked, sleeping here and there, in hammocks or on the ground, and feeding on manihot flour, jungle fruit and game or fish, devoured raw or roasted in the embers of a fire. On their hands gleamed no pearls of Cipango, no rubies of Pegu; neither gold of Sumatra nor the silks of Kata embellished their copper-coloured bodies, however bedecked with feathers they might be. And in place of Persian rugs, their feet trod the uncarpeted sands," says Gilberto Freyre in one of his more elegiac passages.

Instead of cloves, pepper, sandalwood, cinnamon, ginger, ivory or amber, things of value to a European standard of taste, they found " an infinite number of Brazilwood trees

17

and pipe reeds," says Amerigo Vespucci in a letter quoted by a Brazilian historian; "a land full of groves of trees everywhere . . . waters, many and endless," adds Pero Vaz de Caminha, the chronicler of the discovery. The Portuguese dream of "making a fast buck" dwindled in the cold light of realisation that an export list comprised chiefly of Brazilwood, birds and a few items of less importance, was hardly going to make the merchants of the Northern Hemisphere queue up at the dockside to welcome them home. As the only way to obtain, and maintain, steady economic activity, they were forced into agriculture . . .

But in the formation of an agrarian society in the new land, the coloniser had almost everything against him. The climate, for example, was "irregular, swampy," leading to digestive disturbances in those working under it; it was unfavourable in relation to the soil; and, unlike the English in North America and the Spanish in Argentina, both of whom found a climate and a soil similar to those at home, the Portuguese encountered a soil and a climate which in no way permitted "the profitable cultivation of those alimentary plants to which the European had been accustomed for centuries" (Freyre). Apart from which, man, plants, animals, houses, books, clothes, all were at "the mercy of larvae, worms and insects, gnawing, boring, corrupting. Grain, fruit, wood, paper, flesh, muscles, lymphatic glands, intestines, the whites of the eyes, the toes of the feet, all were a prey to these terrible enemies."

To these unfavourable conditions physically must be added the lack of men prepared to suffer them (for Portugal's population was little over a million at that time), a similar scarcity of state aid (Portugal was "always niggardly in this respect," says Freyre)—and of course the total absence of white women.

Thus the coloniser, brave in the face of adversity, by ethnic tradition a compromiser and an improver, made of things the best he could—and, taking full advantage of the Indian woman's priapism, surrounded himself with as many as possible and started a patriarchal family!

The Indian woman was not only active at night as a mate and during the day about the house: she was also indispensable to the new agriculture, for she would work in the fields with her child wrapped on her back. Not unnaturally, such a paragon was able to influence, as well as being influenced by, the eclectic-minded coloniser. " From the *'cunhã,'* the Tupí-Guaraní woman, has come the best in our indigenous culture," says a paragraph in *The Masters And The Slaves.* " Personal neatness. Bodily hygiene. Corn. The Cashew. Mingau or porridge. The Brazilian of today, a lover of the bath, always with a comb and a mirror in his pocket, his hair gleaming with lotion or coconut oil, is reflecting the influence of his remote grandmother . . .''

Surprisingly little has been written of the influence on the Portuguese of Indian religious beliefs. Yet in their essentials many of these could be considered basically spiritistic in character, differing only in form from some of the Umbanda rites today!

Harald Schulz, the expert who has travelled extensively in the Matto Grosso in search of Indians who have never had any contact with " civilisation," told the writer that each tribe has its own set of beliefs and practices, though there is a commonalty of traits running through them. Among the latter can be counted belief in the supernatural, the cult of the dead, the belief that illness is caused by evil spirits, and the ever-present figure of the *Pazé* (*Pajé* in Portuguese), the medicine-man and high priest. Although we have no detailed descriptions of the (widely varying) practices of the Indians at the time of the discovery of Brazil, we can perhaps, because of these common denominators, use as a symptomatic example Charles Wagley's study of the Tenetehara Indians—those natural recluses living deep in the interior state of Maranhão who throughout the four and a half centuries since the discovery have steadfastly maintained their distance from progress and the coloniser. Wagley, an anthropologist from Columbia University, found that " despite the contacts the Teneteharas have had, and still have, with civilisation, they have maintained their traditional creeds practically unaltered." The constant and frustrated efforts of the Catholic missionaries to change them lends the Tenetehara cults an especial piquancy, an even greater aura of authenticity.

The Tenetehara, who speaks Tupí-Guaraní, the language of the majority of tribes first contacted by the Portuguese, attributes difficult situations—in hunting, childbirth, illness or harvest—to the actions of *Azang*, the errant spirits of the dead, to *Ywan*, the owner of water and those dwelling therein, and to *Marana Y'wa*, the owner of forest and the animals. The man who can control or placate these powerful agents is the *Pazé*, who exerts his own power not through prayer or invocation but through his own magical qualities, which he himself has developed.

Both men and animals are believed to have spirits which live on after death. Man's is called *Ekwê*, and if he dies naturally, it abandons the body to dwell eternally in " The Village of the Supernaturals," called *Karowara-Nekwahawo*, where abundance is overall, work unnecessary and death non-existent. But the Ekwê of those who die " an ugly death," those who have transgressed the laws of incest or are victims of witchcraft, transforms itself into an *Azang*, to wander the forest or inhabit a graveyard. There is nothing a Tenetehara fears more than a cemetery at night. (Cemeteries play a leading part in many magic dogmas, of course, and *Exú*, one of the important spiritual entities in African witchcraft, dwells there.)

Illness, the Tenetehara believes, is caused by a specific object, *Ymaé*, that the supernatural being introduces into the body of the victim—varying in form and substance through fruits, seeds, bones, spines, etc., in accordance with the nature of the being employing it. Each supernatural being has its specific *Ymaé*, and only the *Pazé* has the power to identify which is which. Moreover, only if the particular spirit causing the illness is one of his own " familiars " is he able to " withdraw " the *Ymaé* from the victim's body and effect a cure. Thus the *Pazé* able to " call " or " work with " the greatest number of supernaturals, the one with the greatest number of familiars, is the most popular and the most powerful. Each supernatural has its own song and dance which have to be used to " call " it, but before this the *Pazé* draws heavily on an Indian cigarette obviously possessing hypnotic qualities (a fore-runner, presumably, of LSD or Lysergic Acid) until the supernatural enters him, or, in other words, he falls into a trance.

Wagley quotes the case of a *Pazé* blowing the smoke from one of these cigarettes on to his hands and then on to the body of the patient (precisely as the Indian spirit guides command their mediums to do in Umbanda, though here smoke from an ordinary cigar is used). " He then massaged the patient's chest and neck, directing ' it ' to a certain spot and . . . put his chest against the patient's in an attempt to pass the *Ymaé* of the patient to his own body. As he did not succeed, he started sucking with his mouth . . . until finally he extracted the *Ymaé*, which however was not shown to those present." Some Indians say that the *Pazé* gave them the extracted *Ymaé* as a souvenir, though this is difficult to prove. Another case quoted reports two *Pazés*, each having pressed an ill child to his breast, falling to the floor unconscious after successfully extracting its *Ymaé*. This seems analogous in purpose and technique to the exorcisms of evil spirits in Kardecism and Umbanda, about which more later. One difference between the two, however, is the fact that the *Pazé* can also use his powers for nefarious means (although today most will deny this). For this purpose he would use a wooden object variously called *Ywirá-Maíra, Maíra-Pazé* or simply an *Ywirá*-wood, which can be transferred to the victim, even if far away, with the help of the supernatural in such a way as to kill him. Professor Wagley's informants told him that if one *Pazé* " tied up " the foetus of a pregnant woman in this way, the child would assuredly die in the womb if another *Pazé* did not " free her from the noose."

Thus the Portuguese coloniser, " intimately " connected as he was with the Indians, certainly received his share of their religious beliefs, magic and all. Indian influence on the whole was nevertheless limited from the point of view of time, the Indian male proving unfit for agricultural work and the female in the long run less satisfactory than the Negro in the household. But they had set the scene, established the pattern of cultural and sexual miscegenation which was later to rise to such a peak with the Negroes.

The importance of the Negro in Brazil's ethnic, cultural, social, economic and religious formation cannot be over-emphasised. "Without Negroes, Brazil would not have existed," historian Oliveira Martins wrote in his famous *Brazil And The Portuguese Colonies.* "Every Brazilian, even the light-skinned and fair one, carries about with him in his soul, when not in body and soul alike, the shadow, or at least the birthmark of the aborigine or the Negro, chiefly the African," Freyre adds. "In everything that is a sincere expression of our lives we almost all of us bear the mark of this influence: of the female slave or ' mammy ' who rocked us to sleep, who suckled us, who fed us, mashing our food with her own hands; the influence of the old woman who told us our first tales of ghost and *bicho* [animal]; of the mulatto girl . . . who initiated us into physical love and, to the creaking of a canvas cot, gave us our first complete sensation of being a man; of the Negro lad who was our first playmate . . ."

And, of course, inextricably intertwined as Negro and Portuguese life was to become, closer than in any other recorded case of colonisation, the former naturally passed into the hybrid culture of the latter a great deal of his own cultural and religious value.

Much research into the slave traffic has been seriously hindered by the burning of all existing files in 1891, ordered by Ruy Barbosa as a gesture of rupture from the past by the new Brazilian republic. Unfortunately the gesture, well meant as it was, also broke precious ties with the past in the matter of historical, sociological and genealogical data on the Negroes. Portuguese historian Ernesto Ennes, however, puts the date of the first arrival of Negro slaves at 1570, and the establishment of the first sugar-mills as 1533. Pedro Calmon, another historian, believes that the sugar-mills, which were to establish the patriarchal agrarian structure of the new country in its first centuries, were supplied with slave labour before that, however. He puts the earliest arrivals as far back as 1548.

The slaves were obtained in a number of ways—Portuguese traders bribed their own headmen to round up likely candidates in exchange for rum and cheap merchandise; they manipulated hereditary enemies so that one tribe would ensnare another and hand it over captive in its entirety; they even employed anthropophagous tribes on occasion, such as those hunting dogs of men, the *Jagas*—though this was not an unqualified success insofar as the hunters " ate many of the prisoners they had rounded up, this being their ordinary food," according to Ennes, quoting documents from the Archives of Colonial History in Portugal itself. (It is interesting to note that there was a considerable difference in the selection of slaves destined for British and for Portuguese colonies. The requirements were different: in addition to pure brute labour, Brazil had two other factors to consider— the shortage of white women and the technical needs in connection with the working of metals as the mines were opened up. Thus Negroes of the superior Mohammedan culture were brought to Brazil on a much larger scale than to the United States. The British naturalist George Gardner, who was in Brazil in 1836, wrote of the slaves in Bahia that " both the men and the women are not only taller and more handsomely formed than are those from Mozambique, Benguela and the other parts of Africa, but have a much greater share of mental energy, arising perhaps from their near relationship with the Moor. Among them are many who can both read and write Arabic." Contrary to the Bantu, who may be considered, as a large ethnic mass, among the most characteristically " Negro " with their kinky hair and flat noses, these races with Halmitic and even Berber blood have straighter hair, a more shapely nose and a gentler temperament. Sociologist Oliveira Vianna reports finding, in the state of Minas Gerais, Negroes " with a delicacy of feature and a relative degree of beauty." In fact, you don't have to go that far: just take a stroll any sunny day to the Copacabana beach . . .)

Nothing is more barbarous than slavery. With this premise kept firmly in the forefront of the mind, it is nevertheless possible to argue that slavery in Brazil was perhaps less bad than in other countries, a point of view corroborated by the large-scale miscegenation whose softening effect followed the first transportations. This started only after the Africans had arrived, however, and slave transport from Africa to Brazil remains one of the darkest corners of the country's history. To be fair the Portuguese government had promulgated strict rules pertaining to the safety, health and welfare of the slaves aboard ship. There were no government inspectors, though, and the laws (as a distinguished contemporary wrote) were honoured more in the breach than in the observance. The infamous slave ships could be identified from afar by the stench arising from the foetid holds and from the packed bilges where the sick and dying were piled in their hundreds. Amazingly, despite the rigours of the voyage and the privations of treatment worse than that accorded to beasts, the Negro survived the ordeal and whole tribes and even nations were transported *en masse* to Brazil.

More than thirty different races found themselves working as slaves in the New World—different in degree and amount of culture, different in language, different in physical and anthropological characteristics, and, of course, different in religious habits, cults and practices. One historian identified members of the Yorubas, Egbas, Gêges, Daomeianos, Ijejas, Minas, Angolas, Hausás, Krumanes, Filánios, Timinis, Bengos, Galinhas, Effans, Ashantis and Cabindas, coming mostly from the coast of Sierra Leone, Angola and the Gulf of Guinea. They fell into two main groups, culturally: the Sudanese and the Bantu. The latter, from the Congo and Angola, were good for general labour but of a less advanced mental state than the Sudanese. Those that came from Cape Verde, Guinea and Sierra Leone, according to a work of Gaspar Barleus written in 1660, were " slack and lazy, but delicate and graceful in form, especially the women."

Women from the kingdom of Ashanti in Western Sudan, also called Mina, were especially in demand and are believed to have been the first lawfully married to Europeans. Luis Monteiro, governor of Rio de Janeiro in 1730, wrote that there was not a citizen from the state of Minas Gerais " who

24

can live without a Negro Mina, for they say that it is only with them that they are lucky." These female ideals, who were "wholesome, ingenious, sagacious and affectionate," came from a region where the highest Negro culture and that of the Mohammedan intermixed, which is no doubt why their culture prevailed over the others in Brazil, especially that of the Yoruba.

The Sudanese came mainly to Bahia at first, later spreading to other states, whereas the Bantu were mainly concentrated around Rio. For the Portuguese were always very careful to distribute the various tribes in such a way that there was never a large concentration of tribes friendly to each other in any one region, thus minimising the risk of a general uprising. Even so, occasional outbursts were suffered —the ill-fated rebellion in Minas Gerais, for instance, or the Mohammedan revolt of 1835, led by slaves whose culture was superior even to that of the Portuguese. Then, too, there was the "Republic of Palmares"—one of several breakaway "states" formed in the mountains by fugitive slaves. This one—which even had its own king, called Zambi, the Bantu word for God—was established in 1630 in the area now known as the state of Alagoas, and required several costly expeditions before it was finally suppressed.

Talking of miscegenation in Brazil, one normally thinks of an intermixture of Portuguese, Indian and Negro peoples, but it must be remembered that, once in South America, the Negroes themselves were subject to intermixtures of all these races, a fact that makes the resulting society far more exuberant in racial, cultural, social and religious elements than is generally realised.

" Brazil not only took from Africa the topsoil of a black people that was to fertilise its cane fields and coffee groves, assuage its parched lands and round out the wealth offered by patches of *massapé* [clayey soil suitable for sugar cane]; there were to come to it also, from the same source, 'mistresses of the house,' for its colonists were without white women; technicians for its mines; ironworkers; Negroes versed in cattle raising and the pasturing of herds; cloth and soap merchants; schoolmasters, priests and praying Mohammedans," writes Gilberto Freyre.

During the first two centuries of colonisation, the lack of white women led to the large scale formation of families based on the coloured mistress—later frequently taken by the Portuguese as lawful wives, in particular after the initial crossings had produced the sought-after mulatto type. As a result of this—and of the belief commonly held by the colonisers that the flower of virginity should be plucked as early as possible—the white women, when they came, were married off as early as twelve or thirteen years of age. *La Fleur de la Virginité doit se cueiller . . . dans les premières années, afin qu'elle ne se flétrisse pas,* wrote the 17th century traveller François Coreal, and this virginity mystique persists today in the Brazilian civil code, which provides that a man may demand his marriage to be annulled within forty eight hours if his bride should prove not to be a virgin.

As a result of such marriages at the very onset of puberty, the young brides, though Von Steinen might describe them as late as 1885 as being " enchanting and ensnaring with their flowerlike beauty," had become withered matrons by the age of twenty. If, indeed, they had survived motherhood that long. But whether the child bride survived or not, her offspring were customarily given to wet-nurses to feed not, as some historians would have us believe, because it was the custom of wealthy mothers in Portugal to refuse to suckle their own children, but because she was physically unable to do it herself.

Fortunately for Brazil, the Negro wet-nurse, the " milk-mother," was very well suited for this important role: she flourished under the tropical or sub-tropical climate while the white mother withered away. Or, as Dr. Imbert writes in his 1843 *Medical Guide For Mothers,* " they acquire a power of breast nourishment that the same (tropical) region generally denies to white women." [This is only applicable to the child bride, left a " mere shred of a human being " after continuous pregnancies in what Freyre calls a " grievous and continuous effort to multiply the species." For today, and the climate has not changed, the white woman of normal age in Brazil is perfectly capable of feeding her own child.]

The " black mammies," the *mucamas,* thus held a position high above their theoretical status, far superior to that of a common slave. " These women," Freyre writes, " were given their way in everything: the young ones of the family would come to receive their blessing, the slaves treated them as ladies, the coachmen would take them out in the carriage. And on feast days anyone seeing them, expansive and proudly self-possessed among the whites of the household, would have supposed them to be well-born ladies and not by any means ex-slaves from the *senzala* [slave house]."

Maybe they were not all as fortunate as that. But the trend they set, along with the beautiful mulatto girls whom the masters and their lieutenants took to bed, was to have far reaching effects, as we shall see in succeeding chapters, on the social history of their country.

And the slave girls themselves? How did they fare with the masters? Trajano Galvão, the 19th century poet, sums it up like this:

> *A captive girl am I. Who cares*
> *That in black slavery I languish?*
> *An overseer I've found who dares*
> *To ameliorate my anguish.*
>
> *How gentle is this man at dusk*
> *By roadside bushes calling,*
> *' Oh, nigger girl, come here, come here! '*
> *As the warm, damp night is falling.*
>
> *How exquisite my flirt's delight*
> *To say,' No, Senhor, not tonight! '*

27

CHAPTER TWO

Negro Religion in Africa

I N 1760, the French savant De Brosses published *Du Culte Des Dieux Fetiches,* a work that was to become a landmark in the study of world religions if only for the fact that in it he coined the term " fetichism " as descriptive of the form of religion, practised by African Negroes, which attributed paranormal properties to material objects. De Brosses derived his term from the Portuguese word *feitiço*—the *" chose fée, enchantée "* or enchanted object which the colonisers found the Negroes endowing with magical properties and making the subject of worship and adoration.

The fetich (or fetish) to become a " gris-gris " or instrument of magic can be any material object, from trees, mountains, the sea, to fragments of wood, pebbles or shells, etc., any of which, after preparation and consecration by a priest, thus become the object of a cult.

De Brosses believed that fetichism lay at the origins of all religions and that the Negro, dwelling in the most primitive and barbarous fetichism, was " at the very beginning " of his religious development. This simple concept prevailed for a long period until, in fact, more sophisticated techniques of anthropology coupled with a more detailed knowledge of Africa and its peoples revealed a complexity and variety of cultures until then unsuspected.

The German scientist Leo Frobenius asserts in his *Kulturgeschichte Afrikas* that the description of fetichism as a symbol of *African* religion was a purely European invention, as indeed was the concept of the " barbarous Negro " itself, both being intended indirectly to justify the oppressions of colonisation.

A Brazilian anthropologist, basing his conclusions on the concept of cultural areas embodied in the study of Africa by the American, Melville J. Herskovits, has described the so-called " dark continent " as " a great cultural mosaic where varied and complex patterns of culture mix in unpredictable combinations."

To say that the Negro rites enriching this mosaic were brought to Brazil is as true as saying that European culture was transferred to the United States of America; but to state that these forms of religion consist simply of fetichism is no more true than to say that Western civilisation consists only of Christianity.

Certainly the fetich plays an important role in most African Negro religions. But it does not synthesise their existence. And, as in Europe, there are different cultures and degrees of cultures.

We are not concerned here with Negro religions in general, however: only with those transferred to Brazil or influencing the religious practices of Negroes in Brazil and thus forming a significant factor of the religious anastomosis there.

As a starting point, these may conveniently be divided into two large, general groups: the Sudanese and the Bantu.

Of the former group, it was the Yoruba culture that prevailed over the others, even in regions where the Bantu were more numerous, as happened in Cuba, for instance. This was largely because of " their more advanced theology, their intensively expansive force, the great density of their population and the expansion of their language, spoken by over three million Negroes " (Fernando Ortiz in *Los Negros Brujos*, Madrid, 1904).

It was the Yoruba theogony that chiefly influenced Negro religious practices and rites in Brazil therefore; and it is the Yoruba theogony that still forms the backbone today of Umbanda spiritualism (or spiritism) and the religious practices in Bahia called Candomblé*—both of which are wrongly referred to as Negro fetichist practices . . .

It is the Yoruba religious culture, therefore, that interests us most in the determination of the origin of the largest part of Negro influence in Brazil's religious melting pot.

The great linguistic and cultural conglomerate of the Yorubas developed in the region known today as Southern Nigeria: three million people organised into powerful states and kingdoms at one time, each with its own ministries, priesthoods, armies and systems of taxation—a complex included in the Western Sudan in the Herskovits "cultural area" classification. The region, Herskovits said, was marked by the interpenetration of Negro and Mohammedan cultures and has at one time or another included the kingdoms of Benin, Dahomey, Ashanti, Hausa, Bornu and Yoruba itself.

Of these Benin was the most famous. In 1485, the Portuguese traveller Alonso d'Aveiro brought home a breathtaking vision of a Great Benin whose legendary king boasted " marvellous insignias of bronze." And Dutch explorers at the beginning of the 17th century were describing "a city larger than Amsterdam, with sumptuous palaces and wooden colonnades set with bronze plaques depicting battle scenes." That the Benin civilisation at one time attained great splendour can be proved by the collections of statuettes in bronze and ivory, masks, and other *objets d'art* still to be seen in European museums. And Benin was no isolated example: Southern Nigeria was also the home of such flourishing Yoruba kingdoms as Oyo under the rule of Prince Alafin, Prince Oni's kingdom of Ifé, and—the last of the Yoruba kingdoms, extinguished by the British in 1914—Abeokuta, with Prince Alaké.

The main Yoruba tribes (some of which adopted the names of their kingdoms or their chief cities) are listed by anthropologist Arthur Ramos as: the Egba or Euba from Abeokuta; the Ilesha or Ijesha; the Ijebu; the Ketu; the Ondo; the Eko from Lagos; the Oyo from the kingdom of the same name; the Ifé; the Ibadan; and the Benin. The French gave the

*See Chapter Four.

30

name " Nagôs " to the Yoruba Negroes of the " slave coast," and this was the name by which they became generally known in Bahia also. The word was used, in addition, as one of the names by which their language was called. (Alternatives, according to Delafosse, Havelocque and others, were Yariba, Ayo, Egba, Ayazi, and Aku. But historians disagree about whether these were in fact different names for the same language or separate names for different dialects. The consensus appears to be that they were a collection of related dialects, not differing greatly, with the Nagô predominating.)

Yoruba mythology is extremely complex; a pantheon of gods, a cult administered by priests and priestesses, organised ceremonies of worship and a systematised ritual.

Olorun is generally accepted as highest among the gods, though there are other names to identify what we might call the Supreme God—Eleda, the Lord of Creation; Alaye, the Lord of Life; Olo-Dumaré, the All-powerful; Elemi, the Spirit; Oga-Ogo, and others, according to Ramos and to the studies of the Yoruba made by C. Stephen Farrow.

Olorun is unrepresented by any totem or concrete object of the cult, though sometimes he is identified with the roof of heaven and thus turns into a sky god. But his name frequently occurs in common terms of speech, such as *Olorun-shanu* (Thank God!), *Olorun-ni* (It is God), *Olorun Yia Busi I Fun O* (God bless you!). Having no cult dedicated to him, however, Olorun cannot communicate directly with men but only through intermediaries, secondary divinities called, according to Yoruba beliefs, Orishas. A British missionary named Bowen, who studied the Yorubas in Africa at the end of the last century, saw in this concept an analogy, on the religious plane, of that civil organisation in which the king never contacts his subjects direct but only through his protective buffer, the administrative side of the court.

Bowen believed that the term Orisha, a word of uncertain origin, derived from *Asha,* which means a religious ceremony. Others have seen it as a composite of *Ri,* meaning " see " or " find," and *Sha,* meaning " choose " or " select." Nobody has assigned any finite number to the amount of Orishas available for intercession with Olorun. Some authorities identify more than six hundred.

The theogony originates in Odudua, the Earth or female principle, endowed with reproductive functions, and Obatalá, the "great Orisha" or male principle, representing the sky. Both of them appeared as a result of Olorun's reluctance personally to interfere in the affairs of men. Obatalá signifies "the king of whiteness" or "the king of purity" (*Abati—Ala*), or sometimes the "king of greatness" (*Aba—Tinla*). An alternative title is Orixalá (*Ori—Sha—Nla*), meaning, again, "the great Orisha." In Brazil this form became Oxalá, who is dressed in syncretism to stand for Jesus Christ (see section on Umbanda and the following chapter). Predictably enough, Obatalá was created by Olorun from clay.

Among the Yoruba themselves, the Orisha Obatalá had a civic nature. The protector of cities and of temples, he was generally represented in paintings as a cavalier with a lance. His worshippers customarily dress in white and wear white ornaments.

Odudua, the Earth, is also the subject of differing theories as to her origins. In contrast to the white purity of Obatalá, some say, she is the "black goddess" (from *Dudu,* meaning black, and *Uwa,* meaning existence). Another school stresses the female principle in attributing the derivation of her name to *Odu Ti O Da Wa* ("The One Who Creates Existence").

In Yoruba mythology, Odudua is of course Obatalá's wife, a symbolic union of heaven and earth. She possesses the qualities (and the drawbacks) of a love divinity. As a kind of mythological Venus, her amorous adventures range far and wide and many are the legendary tales relating her prowess. The temple built to her homage in Adô, near Badagry, remains a living testimony to some of these legends.

Obatalá, the masculine god, and Odudua, the feminine, naturally have children; a son, Aganjú, and a daughter, Yemanjá.

The children also married (Yoruba mythology permits itself to be a trifle more explicit than the Bible on the subject of Adam and Eve) and begat a son, Orungan, whose name means " midday " or " the sun is at its zenith." Aganjú means simply " desert " or " waste land."

As though laying a foundation for Freud's postulation of the Oedipus Complex, the Yorubas then have Orungan fall in love with his mother, Yemanjá. One day he decides to take advantage of his father's absence and give full rein to this passion. He succeeds in raping his mother, who then flees from him in horror, pursued by her erring boy, in whom the flame of lust still blazes brightly, until finally Yemanjá collapses, exhausted, and falls on her back. After that . . . a lyric occurrence: her body begins to expand, two streams of water gushing from her breasts to form a great lake and the womb itself bursting to give up a band of the most cherished Yoruba Orishas—Shango, the god of thunder; Ogun the god of war; Olokun, god of the sea; Oyá, goddess of the River Niger; Oshun and Obá, goddesses of the rivers of the same names; Orishako, the god of agriculture; Dada, the god of vegetables; Oshossi, god of the hunters; Okê, the mountain god; and Ajê Shaluga, the god of wealth.

The sun (" Orun ") and the moon (" Oshú ") also came forth from the womb of Yemanjá. But neither of them is considered to be an Orisha and no cult is dedicated to them.

The name Yemanjá (only in Portuguese is the final syllable accentuated) derives from *Yeye,* meaning mother, and *Eja,* meaning fish. Thus " mother of fish," the " water-mother " of all the Orishas. The actual site of the lady's aqueous catastrophe became, according to the myth, the city of Ifé, a town built as the sacred city of Yemanjá. Today in Africa she remains the goddess of the river Ogun, but in Brazil she has developed to become the goddess of the whole sea.

Shango (Xangô in Portuguese) is perhaps the most cult-favoured deity in Yoruba theology. The god of lightning and thunder, he is also known by the names of Jakuta or Shango-Djacuta, the " stone-thrower." There are a number of myths relating to his origin.

Most of the legends suggest that he came from the womb of Yemanjá, but some say that he is the son of Obatalá, and therefore her brother. In the ·former myth, he marries his three sisters, the river goddesses Oyá, Oshun and Obá. One day (according to this legend) he is given a very powerful wishbone by his father (it is never clear whether this is Obatalá or Orungan, the African Oedipus). Having tested its powers and also permitted his wife, Oyá, to try it out, he speaks the next day before an assembly of tribal chiefs in the palace. Immediately he opens his mouth, flames come roaring out, spreading terror and dismay among all present, who take to their heels and vanish into the jungle. Convinced that he must be a god, Shango summons his three wives, stamps his foot on the ground violently, and watches aghast, as it opens to swallow up his three wives and himself!

Since when, they say, he has been regarded as an Orisha . . .

In a rival version of the story, Shango does not fare so well. His wife gets away with the wishbone and hides in the hut of a fisherman called Huixi. Pursued and tormented by her husband, Oyá transfers the powers of the wishbone to the fisherman. Huixi and Shango then engage in mortal combat, the husband being defeated through lack of the charm and disappearing once more into the earth.

Yet another story culled from the Yoruba's treasurehouse of mythology places Shango as king of Oyô, a man become so cruel and so much the tyrant that his continued presence was a burden too heavy for his subjects to bear. When they demand that he and his wives should quit the palace, he attempts to defy public opinion but is defeated and forced to flee at night to the land of his mother, in Tapa, accompanied only by one of his wives. Soon, she too has abandoned him, leaving him alone but for a single slave. One day, hunting in the forest, he eludes this servant and commits suicide. At the tragic news, the chiefs of Oyô hasten to the forest to seek his body, but it has disappeared into the earth, whence the chiefs can hear his cavernous voice talking to them. They build a temple to mark the place of his transubstantiation and go home, broadcasting the great news to all the people: " Shango has not died! He has become an Orisha! "

But, probably because of his former reputation, many people do not believe this story, so Shango becomes enraged

34

and visits upon the city a dreadful tempest, heavy with thunder and lightning.

An alternative version of this story says that Shango was a remarkable monarch as well as a most powerful medicine man who could decimate his enemies by "vomiting" fire from his mouth. According to this myth he had two ministers of whom he was very jealous. In the hope that they might destroy each other, he engineered a fight between them, but one of the ministers was smarter than he had anticipated and succeeded not only in winning the duel but also in deposing the king! Shango is forced to flee to the forest, accompanied by his wives and a handful of faithful subjects. As in the other versions of the story, he is gradually abandoned by them until none is left except his loyal wife, Oyá. Desperate, the ex-king decides to hang himself. When Oyá discovers his body swinging from a tree, she cries out in horror and runs from the place, running, running, running until finally she transforms herself into the goddess of the River Niger. Travellers subsequently passing the scene of the tragedy also observe the body of Shango and spread the news in the city: " Oba So— the king has committed suicide!" Shango's remaining friends then decide to avenge his death and set fire to many houses in the city, shouting " Oba Ko So—the king did *not* commit suicide!" If his spirit is not appeased, these friends say, Shango will punish the city and all its inhabitants. Sacrifices are therefore made—an oxen, a sheep and birds are killed and offered up with oil, special foods and so on—and Shango's wrath is appeased.

The expressions Oba So and Oba Ko So are still used in the cult today to recall this mythological event.

In Nigeria, the Orisha next in importance to Shango is Ogun, the god of iron and of war. Ogun, who is also the god of hunters, is represented customarily by pieces of iron or stone. He is another of the Orishas originating from the womb of Yemanjá as a result of her son's persecution and incestuous lust. Ogun, the legend says, taught men how to hunt, and also thoughtfully showed them which trees were the most suitable for consecration to himself! The altar to this Orisha

35

is therefore habitually set up in front of trees. The animal used in sacrifices to Ogun is the dog.

Such offerings are indispensable preliminaries to any war, expedition or hunting party, and even today the skulls of dogs can often be seen in the houses of blacksmiths, hunters and others who worship Ogun as a testimony of past sacrifices to their Orisha.

After Ogun, the next in the long progression of Orishas is Eshu (Exú in Portuguese), whose name appears to derive from *Shu* (Darkness). He is also called Elegbara or Elegba. Even before his cult had reached Brazil, Catholic missionaries in Africa had identified Eshu with the Devil, but the Yorubas themselves make no such distinction, paying him tribute simply as an Orisha. To his worshippers he is not evil, just powerful, with the ability to do evil *if necessary*. The Yoruba represent Eshu with a cone of clay encrusted with conches and pieces of iron to stand for eyes, mouth, etcetera. Roosters, dogs and goats may be sacrificed to him, but in the thirteenth century he was a phallic divinity requiring human sacrifices on special occasions.

Due to his enormous knowledge, his wisdom and his mastery of the arts of divination, Eshu is much consulted on the handling of day to day affairs, either directly or through priests. In the latter case, these functionaries "read" the message from the Orisha through the use of sixteen special conches, also called Cawries or Kawris. Eshu, whose cult is usually separated from those of the other Orishas, is not, however, considered to be "Number One" in the art of divination. This position is held by Ifá, a special and very high entity considered to be above all the Orishas, and for that reason considered separately here.

An Orisha whose temple may be seen in many African villages is Orishakô (Orixacô), the god of agriculture. His cult is followed with especial fervour by women, possibly because they see qualities of fertility in it. Within the cult, women form secret societies which command a great respect and it is considered an honour for a family to have a daughter initiated into one of these. The cult of Orishakô forms one of the very few exceptions where women are used as priestesses among the Yoruba. (Among the tribes of Dahomey, the Gegês, also called Ewes, permit their womenfolk to participate as priestesses of the cults to a considerably greater degree.)

Since Òrishakô is the god of agriculture, symbolising the fertility of the earth, he is also the god of harvest and his cult is celebrated at every new moon—and of course at the harvest proper, when there is a true festival with singing, dancing, processions and sexual freedom for the worshippers.

After the feast comes the reckoning, and the next Orisha on the list is Shapanan, spelled Xapanan in Portuguese, the god of smallpox! He is also called Shapono, Shapana, or Shankpana in Africa. In one version, the philology of the name, which is of Dahomey origin, relates to *Shon* (to take in small quantities), *Pa* (to kill) and *Enia* (a person). Thus the name of the Orisha of smallpox, Shapanan, stands, appropriately enough, for " the one who kills slowly."

According to his mythical history, Shapanan was a cripple, walking with the aid of a wooden leg and a stick. One day, at a party thrown for all the gods at his palace by Obatalá, Shapanan decided to join in the dancing and merrymaking only, because of his physical handicap, he slipped and fell. The other gods, in a manner regrettably mortal, burst out laughing. And Shapanan, seething in ungodlike resentment against being made fun of, infected the whole lot of them with smallpox! Finally Obatalá was forced to intervene with his magic sword and Shapanan was expelled for ever from the palace and the company of the other gods, since when he has walked alone, with none but his faithful servant Baku for company.

The main, if not the only, reason why he is worshipped is a negative one: he is asked, in his mercy, to keep smallpox away from the worshippers! The Yorubas set up his temple in the forest, at some decent distance from the city or village . . .

An interesting Orisha is Ibeji, the god of twins. In Nigeria (as in other regions of Africa) there are two diametrically opposed attitudes towards the birth of twins: to some, this is an omen of happiness and thus an occasion for rejoicing; to others, the omen is wholly bad. Whichever side of the dichotomy the parents incline towards, the event itself is therefore never received with indifference—thus the cult of Ibeji, to whom is consecrated a black monkey, the flesh of which is tabu to the twins themselves and their parents. Between Lagos and Bagadry, in a place called Erupo, there remains a temple dedicated to Ibeji, where twins and their parents still go once a year to propitiate the god, to ask his protection and to bring their offerings.

Oke, the Orisha of mountains and hills, is popularly supposed to instigate the rolling down of rocks and the beginning of avalanches if not suitably worshipped, and is consequently much revered and specially honoured by those dwelling in mountainous regions. In Nigeria, he boasts a number of temples constructed on rocks, of which the most famous is set up on the sacred rock of Olumo, in Abcokuta. He is also the patron Orisha of the city of Ibadan, which is built between two hills.

To the Yoruba, Oshossi is an Orisha of secondary importance; in Brazil, on the other hand, the name figures today near the top of the list of most popular and powerful Orishas. In Africa, Oshossi inhabits the forest and protects hunters against the attacks of wild beasts, helping them also to catch their prey.

The emblem of Ajê-Shaluga, god of riches, is a cawrie shell, a large one (the conch is used as money among the Yoruba). Whoever finds such an emblem is supposed to receive special protection from the god. Perhaps understandably in a materialistic age, Ajê-Shaluga is also considered to be the Orisha of good luck, rivalling even Eshu in this field. His name derives from the word *Ajê*, which means money.

Yemanjá herself, together with Oya, Oxun and Obá, the three wives of Shango, are all water divinities, as are Olosá and Olokun. The latter (the first part of his name means " sea ") is considered to be the lord of the oceans and is looked upon as protector of sailors and fishermen. He is said to live at the bottom of the sea in command of an enormous phalanx of water spirits. One day, says the legend, Olokun was angry with humanity (it does not explain precisely why!). Indeed, so great was his fury that he vowed to destroy mankind by inundating the whole earth. He was within sight of his objective and had partly succeeded in this unworthy venture when Obatalá intervened, saving the remainder of the earth from a watery grave and forcing Olokun back to his palace in the deep . . .

A change in geographical location, an alteration of names —and the student is reminded irresistibly of another "Orisha" by the name of Jehovah, who saved one Noah from a similar disaster!

At the pinnacle of secondary divinities in Nigeria's pantheic system stands Ifa, the greatest oracle, in a position of honour high above all the Orishas. It is Ifá who predicts great events in the future, good as well as bad; it is Ifá who is consulted before any and every important occasion; it is Ifá who determines to which of the Orishas a new-born baby is to be consecrated; it is Ifá, in times of famine, pestilence or illness, who is asked to reveal which gods, offended, have caused the calamities, and what sacrifices they would accept to enable the Yoruba to redress the unwitting offence, appease the gods, and thus rid themselves of the catastrophe.

All these consultations, of course, are effected through the medium of Ifá's priests.

Several myths attempt to account for the being's origin, none of them entirely satisfactorily, and even with the knowledge gained through the work of Ellis and Farrow, the picture remains obscure.

One of the most popular accounts says that Ifá derives from Obatalá and Odudua, and is thus apparently a brother of Aganjú and Yemanjá. One day, this legend says, Ifá went on an unsuccessful fishing trip before the time of men. Having failed, and being hungry, he asks help from Eshu (which places the supposed event at a time subsequent to the birth of the Orishas, or Eshu would not have been around to ask!). In the event, Eshu promises to teach Ifá the arts of divination, on the condition that he obtains the sixteen nuts from the two palm trees belonging to Orungan, the son of Yemanjá and Aganjú. Following the advice (and presumably still hungry, for the legend makes no mention of food), Ifá seeks Orungan's permission to gather the nuts. This is granted but, the trees being very tall, the nuts have to be gathered by monkeys who, for some reason never explained, throw them down to Orungan's wife, Orishabi . . .

Ifá nevertheless receives the coveted nuts from the hands of Orishabi and hurriedly turns them over to Eshu. The powerful Orisha keeps his promise and thereafter schools Ifá in the arts of divination (though there is still no mention of whether the god finds any fish for the hungry student!). Afterwards, in return for his kindness over the nuts, Ifá shares his newly-found "trade secrets" with Orungan. Which is why, still today, the ceremonial of the Invocation of Ifá begins with the words:

Orungan, Orungan, A Juba O! Orishabi, A Juba O! ("Orungan, we respect you! Orishabi, we respect you! ").

If the foregoing description of the principal Orishas and their attendant myths seems a trifle arid, the writer begs forgiveness, adducing in extenuation the fact that, without a knowledge of their original standing among the Yoruba in Africa, it would be difficult or impossible properly to understand or evaluate the transformations they have undergone in Brazil or the religious practices with which they are now directly related. (In fact these important secondary gods barely scratch the surface of the full list, which runs into several hundreds!)

The Yoruba priests, according to Ellis, are divided into three main orders. Of these, the paramount is the order of the Priests of Ifá, named Babalawos and dedicated solely to the cult of this powerful oracle. (The name derives from *Baba— Li—Awo,* "the Father who has the secret," and is parallelled in the Cuban Babalú, subject of the famous popular song, which derives from the same root.)

A Babalawo has his head shaved and wears clothes only of white. In consulting the oracle, he makes use of sixteen nuts from the special palm tree, the Opelifá, and a special rectangular board with a handle, similar to the Mohammedan writing board, whose name is *Opon-Ifá*. The priest exercises the art of divination by tossing the nuts from one hand to the other, on to the floor, and thence again to the hand, writing all the time notes indecipherable to anyone but himself. The notes, through which are revealed to him Ifá's secrets, he later interprets to the worshippers.

Hierarchically, the order divides in several degrees. The head priest is called Oluwo, his orders being mandatory upon all the others. His assistant is Ajigbona and his deputy Adofin, a kind of " vice-president " who stands in for the head man when he cannot be there in person. Ajigbona, the assistant, also has a deputy, and he is called Aro. The high priest and his three lieutenants share a messenger whose duties are to call the worshippers to the various ceremonies as required. He is named Asare Pawo, and he, too, has a delegate, Asawo. A Babalawo's wife is generally referred to as Apetebi or Awayo.

In olden days, when human sacrifices were made, there was an extra priest, a specialist called Awaro, whose sole function was to effect this rite in the cult of Ifá.

A second category of this first order comprises all those priests who minister on behalf of Orishas specialising in cures —Osanyn and Aroni among them. They are the equivalent of what we should call simply " spiritual healers."

The priests of the Orishas Obatalá and Odudúa form a third category of the first order.

All the members of this order, with the sole exception of those from the city of Ifé, who dress in light blue garments, wear white. As ornaments, the Babalawos may use a bracelet of palm fibre, or one of simple coloured beads, on the left wrist. A Babalawo never neglects to carry an oxen's tail with him.

The second order begins with the priests of Shango, Orisha of thunder and lightning, who comprise the first category. The main or high priests of this second order are called Magbas (from *Emi* and *Gba*, which mean " I receive ") because they are the chosen to receive the messages of the god. All the priests of Shango wear a necklace of red, black and white beads, the worshippers wearing one only of red and white. The " stone of Shango " is the main fetich. Papagori is a bird dedicated to Shango whose calls the Magbas purport to interpret as a symbolic language.

The second category of the second order takes in the priests serving all the other Orishas, each with its special symbols, colours, fetiches and so on, with one single exception: Orishakó, the Orisha of agriculture and fertility. Orishakó, it may be recalled, is the only Yoruba divinity with both priests and priestesses serving the cult. These functionaries, according to Ellis, form, together with the priests of semi-gods and deified men, the third and last category.

Although, with the exception of the priestesses of Orishakó, all religious functions, divinations, sacrifices and practices of medicine among the Yoruba in Nigeria are performed by men, their neighbours in Dahomey (as we have seen) customarily admit girls and women more easily into the service of the gods. Yet in Brazil, where the *mores* of the Yoruba predominated, the converse became true: probably as a side-issue of the conditions peculiar to slavery, it was the woman who took precedence over the man in religious services among the Negroes.

Among the Yoruba, each Orisha has to be specially " prepared " by the priest, and each has his or her specific demands in the way of foods, fetiches, animals, colours, etc. We shall not attempt to describe these tastes in this chapter on the African origins of the Yoruba pantheon: most of the characteristics survived the transplantation to Brazil and can be found in the rites of Candomblé in Bahia or (in a more limited way) in Umbanda (see Chapter Four and Chapter Nine respectively).

One of the most important religious functions among the Yoruba is that known as " the rites of passage," whereby the Orisha to which a new-born child properly belongs is determined. Three days after the birth, the Babalawo is consulted and asked which Orisha should be the object of the child's dedication, what are his duties to be, and what are to be his *Ewos* (an *Ewo* is a tabu which will be respected throughout the entire life of the worshipper). Failing this, the child will inherit the Orisha of his father, the Yoruba social organisation being fundamentally patriarchal. If the Babalawo has been consulted, he will return seven days after the birth of a girl, or nine after that of a boy, to offer sacrifices to Ifá and to Olori, the " lord of the head," in the expectation of obtaining their favours on behalf of the newly born.

The Yoruba week has four days, each consecrated to a chief Orisha: Awo is the day of Ifá, Ogun the day of Ogun, Jakuta the day of Shango, and Obatalá the day of the Orisha bearing that name. Worship of the lesser Orishas may be performed on any of these days.

The spirits of the dead are worshipped in secret societies, which also take care of funeral rites. These take their name from the particular deity to whom they pay homage and play an important part in Yoruba life. The chief secret societies are those of Ogboni, Egungan, Agemo and Oro. Invocation of the latter is the most common at funerals, as a part of the expected lamentations by the family and friends of the deceased. At a Yoruba funeral, the departed is carefully washed, the hair shaved and the body arrayed in the finest garments available. Friends and neighbours are invited to watch over the corpse throughout the night, food and drink being provided for all the guests. If the deceased was an important personage, the feasting and songs may continue for as long as a week. Then, after the burial, an animal is sacrificed and blood spilled over the grave.

Since the subject of Yoruba families has arisen, it may be well to point out here something of the social organisation to which they adhere. The basic family unit, divided into several compounds of the same family, is the *Sib*. In any Sib, status devolves on a strict seniority basis, the eldest member, called Ogbá, being the most respected. The terms *Babá* (Father) and *Iyá* (Mother) are always used by the Yoruba as a sign of respect to an older person. All married women are referred to as *Oya*, and all married men as *Okó*. Since the Yoruba are polygamous, the husband may have " an older wife," called *Iyalê*, and " a younger one," who is called *Iyawó* (the origin

43

of the name *Iyaô* or *Iaô*, given to female initiates in Candomblé, which will be discussed in Chapter Four).

One most important point must here be emphasised: in Yoruba life there is no distinction whatever between religious rites and ceremonies on the one hand, and social, economic and political life on the other. As Edwin W. Smith, a missionary well versed in Yoruba lore, has written: " Religion is not an organised cult separable from the rest of life, but a part and parcel of it, all-pervasive, motivating, controlling, guiding, strengthening . . ."

This may well have some bearing on the fact that, even today, in Africa, though many converts have been made by both Christianity and Islam, the great majority of the people remain animistic in their religious attitudes, believing that most objects in nature are dominated by a particular spirit or god, the sum of whose reactions, good and bad, is responsible for practically everything that happens. Many, too, believe in reincarnation; and most see the world around them as a community of both the living and the dead. Belief in " good " and " evil " magic, curses, tabus, talismans, omens, medicines, divination and witchcraft still prevails throughout the continent. Eighty per cent. of the 8,000,000 population of Kenya, for example, receive their only medical attention from the *M'ganga,* the local witch-doctor, despite a government programme that dispensed 9,000,000 dollars in a single year recently to erect 160 modern medical centres!

The march of progress cannot forever be denied, nevertheless. Two top *M'gangas* recently formed the A.P.A.—the African Physicians' Association.

To become a member? A simple entrance test: candidates are required to divine and recite, to the level of great-grandparents, the complete family tree of someone they have never set eyes on before . . .

Many Africans who leave their tribal environment to live in cities cling there to ancient beliefs in the power of fetiches and charms. College students are known to rely on these to help them pass examinations in some cases—but, after all, is this so very different to the superstition of the Westerner, the black cat and the rabbit's foot?

Deeply inbred though such beliefs are in religion-dominated Africa today, a parallel can be drawn with the strong reliance on charms and fetiches of the modern Brazilian. His somewhat fatalistic attitude towards life, his addition of the phrase " God willing " or " If God wishes " to all statements concerning future occurrences, his generalised belief that mental cases are usually caused by " evil spirits "—all these are evidently traceable to that strong African social and ethnic influence described in the last chapter.

And among such African influences, that of the Yoruba is certainly one of the strongest, which is why their religious customs predominated over those of the other Negro tribes in Brazil.

Until the beginning of the 19th century, the Hausa, Mohammedan tribes from the North of Nigeria, were numerically and sometimes intellectually superior to the Yoruba, at least in Bahia. They were responsible for planning and leading all the insurgent movements against slavery. But after the resounding defeat of the famous revolt of 1835, the Hausa influence disappeared.

The Ewe (or JêJê, as they are called in Brazil), from Dahomey, have much in common with the Yoruba, especially in the hierarchy of their gods, most of the differences between them being at heart simply a matter of semantics. Thus the Dahomey equivalent of an Orisha is a Vodun, and the priest ministering to him, instead of a Babalawo is called a Voduno (the term Voodoo, the generic name popularly used to define witchcraft of the kinds under discussion, derives from the Dahomey word for god. Its use originated in Cuba and other Caribbean islands where the *mélange* of Yoruba and Dahomey terminology had resulted in a hybrid applicable to either).

Legbá (also called Elegbara or Elegba) is the Dahomey equivalent of the Yoruba Eshu—with the difference that, to the Dahomey people, he is in fact a malevolent Vodun. He is regarded as a messenger carrying the thoughts and wishes of

45

the other Voduns to man. In Brazil, this deity is again a trifle *mélangé,* known by the Yoruba name of Eshu but retaining both the Dahomey character of messenger and the Yoruba quality of being able to do either evil *or* good . . .

The Bantu, mostly from the Congo and Angola, brought with them neither the Yoruba pantheon of gods nor the complex mythology and hierarchically organised priesthood. Their influence has thus been correspondingly less.

Theirs was the cult dedicated to the departed.

The Bantu worship a number of Phalanxes, each formed of hundreds and thousands of spirits of the deceased and led by one particular spirit. Most of their religious influence was deployed around Rio de Janeiro, to which at one time they came in large numbers. From it, there developed the cult known as Macumba—which in turn, influenced by spiritism and Candomblé, gave birth to Umbanda.

The chief difference between the Yoruba and Bantu cults, an easy one to remember, is that the former deal solely with divinities while the latter occupy themselves with the spirits of dead mortals.

CHAPTER THREE

Negro Rites in Brazil

M U C H of the astonishing eclecticism distinguishing Brazilian religious life today can be traced to the fact that the prevailing climate during the first centuries of colonisation was one of magic: prayers to the saints, sorcery and exorcism, the Latin formulae of esoteric Catholicism, bogey-men and phantoms—these were the stuff of the supernatural beliefs held by the Portuguese. And the Negroes, for their part, freely imported the spells, potions and fetichism characterising their home life in Africa. The mingling of the peoples in Latin America thus at once produced an interpenetration of Portuguese magic beliefs and Negro magic beliefs, each spiced, to a smaller degree, with Indian myths, which led in time to a situation rich in anomaly. For there was a fundamental, a basic difference between the attitudes of the two races towards magic practices: to the Portuguese, magic and witchcraft, sorcery and spells were rituals on which there was a complete tabu—forbidden practices to be carried out in secret lest a personal foe might register a complaint with the Inquisition; but for the Negro, such behaviour was simply a natural expression of his religion, of the religion of his forebears, of the customs prevailing in his homeland...

And the situation was further complicated by the requirements of Portuguese law and of the Catholic Church. In the days of the slave trade, according to Henry Koster's *Travels In Brazil,* " the Africans that are imported from Angola are baptised in lots before they leave their own shores; and on

47

their arrival in Brazil they learn the doctrines of the Church and the duties of the religion into which they have entered. They bear the mark of the royal crown upon their breasts, which denotes that they have undergone the ceremony of baptism, and likewise that the King's duty has been paid upon them . . ."

Such was the pattern in early Brazil, a country officially Catholic from the beginning of its history and where, therefore, the religion of the slave was automatically a matter of concern to the coloniser, due to the power of that Church (however mitigated by the factors examined in Chapter One). Indeed, it was required that any slaves not so baptised before arrival must be taught certain prayers and so on, the master being held responsible for presenting them at the parish Church to be examined in these within two years of landing in Brazil. This law, though not observed strictly, is interesting as an indication of the way masters tried at least to keep up appearances in favouring the " de-paganisation " of their slaves.

And the slaves themselves, of course, were only too eager to become " Christian," especially as remaining a " pagan " would involve an increasing ostracism, the loss of any chance to enter the master's household service, and so on. " The slave himself wishes to be made a Christian " (wrote Koster) " for his fellow bondsmen will otherwise, in any squabble or trifling disagreement with him, close the string of opprobrious epithets with the name ' pagan '."

To be " made a Christian," however, carried a connotation then perhaps a trifle different to what might seem to be implied.

It meant, above all else, participating in the *external* affairs of that Catholicism practised in Brazil in the first centuries of its history. And it made virtually no demand that the convert should in any sense incline towards the spiritual or moral values professed by his master.

" A mild brand of household religion," stemming from the chapel of the Big House, the seat of the slave-holding farm, was thrown open to the Negro, replete with its family saints, its baptisms, marriages and fête days, all celebrated with banners and flowers and festivities and singing. And this " domestic, lyric and festive Christianity," as Prof. Gilberto Freyre calls it, " became the point of contact and of fraternisation between the two cultures—that of the master and that of the Negro. And there was never any stern and insurmountable barrier between them."

Alongside the observance of Catholic rites and doctrines, the policy of the early slave owners in Brazil was to permit the Negroes (in Freyre's words) " to preserve . . . the forms and accessories of their African culture and mythology." And this *laissez-faire* attitude was for the most part encouraged by the majority of the priesthood. The 18th century Jesuit, André João Antonil, counselled the masters not only to allow, but actively " to aid with their liberality " the natural festivities of the Africans. " Let [the masters] not be shocked when [the Negroes] create their own kings and sing and dance for hours, in a respectable manner, on certain days of the year," he wrote, " nor if they amuse themselves decently one afternoon, after having in the morning observed the feasts of Our Lady of the Rosary, of São Benedito, and of the patron saint of the plantation chapel . . ."

The governors, too, permitted from the early days the continuance of African drum beating. Rather than being an example of " benevolent " tyranny, however, this was a considered policy whose end-product, they believed, would be to encourage the nurturing of tribal differences and thus prevent the unification of the Negroes against their masters (which could have been disastrous, since, possibly until as late as the end of the 19th century, the Negro population outnumbered the white in Brazil). Several uprisings in the slave days failed purely because of the fact that different groups involved wished to be led by different kings, notably the insurrection in Minas Gerais. And the Count of Arcos, writing at the beginning of the 19th century, observed that the government saw this permissiveness as " an act that obliges the Negroes . . . automatically to renew the ideas of reciprocal aversion common to all from the day of birth but which the common disgrace of slavery is slowly smothering." Such ideas, the Count added, could be considered "the most powerful guarantee of the safety of the great cities of Brazil, because once the different nations of Africa forget totally the ire with which nature has disunited them, and those of Agomé become brothers of the Nâgo, the JêJê with the Hausa, the Tapa with the Senitys, and so on, enormous and inevitable danger will threaten Brazil."

(A pragmatic and an interesting application of social anthropology, this! And one which perhaps carries a practical lesson today for the politicians of Nigeria—because until this moment, the Yoruba and the Hausa, the Northern Mohammedans and the Eastern, Mid-Western and Western Orisha-worshippers remain in a state of disagreement, on politics and everything else. Indeed, according to *Time* magazine of 8th January, 1965, Nigeria at the time of its first post-independence General Election was a shambles of violence, threats, boycotts and poll-rigging. The Count of Arcos would no doubt have put it all down to an over-indulgence in drum beating!)

The freedom of the slave thus to preserve religious practices, and even, on special occasions such as Christmas Eve, Epiphany and the New Year, to observe them openly before the master, the priest and the household, made the church (with a small " c," that is to say the chapel which is a dependency of the patriarchal estate of the sugar-mill) a point of contact between slave and owner. Here, where African religion met Western religion, there was a " kind of fraternisation " between Negroes and Portuguese, a meeting centre, a *" place de la concorde "* between the two civilisations (although, as Freyre points out, the concept of a civilising process is an equivocal one, many Negroes possessing far more " culture " than their Portuguese masters!).

Nevertheless, for a number of reasons, the Catholic church did not present the Negro with a rigid, monolithic, superior culture, bound by a set of " superior " values which were unchallengeable. The *Portugales* (as they were called in the 16th century) presented him instead with an organisation whose influence was far more social than ethical, moral or even theological; and with a master possessed of but two primary interests: to get the utmost out of his male slave labour, and to satisfy to the full his raging sexual appetites on the females. Nothing was permitted to stand between him and the accomplishment of these twin goals. Thus so long as he was able to confirm that the slaves participated in the actual *ceremonial* of the church, and so long as this could be demonstrated to church superiors such as bishops or representatives of the Inquisition, then the master was satisfied and was considered to be doing his share.

Up to a point, the same attitudes prevailed among the majority of the clergy. Although few priests relaxed their catechizing efforts in relation to the slaves, in practice these were restricted to the outward observance of liturgical rites and similar external characteristics of the Catholic religion. As long as the slaves kept " Holy Sacraments of the Church," worshipped the saints and asked for the priests' blessings, both eyes were closed to any deficiencies in the Negroes' *spiritual* adherence to Catholicism, as they were to the lustful life of the masters on the one hand, and the continuance of " harmless " pagan religious customs on the other.

It would, after all, have been extremely hard to impose Catholic, or any Christian, ethics where the society could be seen to be based on slave ownership and where the masters were renowned for their sexual depravity and licentiousness.

Not all the priests, of course, meekly accepted this state of things. Such celebrated exceptions as Anchieta and Father Manoel da Nóbrega, the great missionary of the 16th century, raised their voices in protest. " With the Christians of this land," da Nóbrega wrote of Brazil, " there is little to be done, for we have closed to them the door of the Confessional, on account of slaves, with whom they are loath to part, and for the reason that nearly all of them, married and unmarried alike, are living in concubinage withindoors, with their Negro women; and their slaves are concubines, without their conscience troubling them in the one case or the other. And there are priests who are free with their Absolutions and who live in the same manner ..."

The majority of priests, while not living "in the same manner," often because their superiors were aware of the temptations and had warned them against them, were indeed a trifle "free" with their Absolutions. They might heed the church's advice not to succumb to offers of living in the Big House of the plantation. But they could hardly deny that (as Freyre points out) "the powerful voice of the Jesuits was never once raised on the Negroes' behalf as it was on behalf of the Indian women." And, after all, what other course of action was open to them?

To the African of course, after the monstrous and incredible experience of the slave transporting vessel, contact with the church was a ray of light. Although many had in fact been slaves in their native country, nothing there could be compared to the horrors they passed through during the crossing of the Atlantic. And the meetings with the padre, who taught them songs and prayers, introduced them to the many saints, and in particular the patron saint of the farm where they worked, and offered them the opportunity of sharing worship with the lord of the mansion, these represented a softening of the harsh conditions under which they had previously been forced to live.

Becoming, at least in name, a Catholic was therefore an amelioration, a change in the collective tragedy, experienced collectively. The miscegenation which followed must be regarded, widespread as it was, as a personal thing—each example, tragic or otherwise, limited to the partners involved.

The special relationship between master and slave-mistress was in the beginning confined purely to the satisfaction of the animal instincts of the former—a situation which a liberal mind might regard, under the circumstances and in the absence of white women, as "unavoidable." But as time went on the Negro women made themselves respected, as Freyre points out, in two ways: "Through their sexual allure and womanly wiles" on the one hand; and "through the fear inspired by their *mandingas,* or spells," on the other. For of course, as we have pointed out, the *Portugale* was already conditioned by centuries of contact with sorcery, incantations, aphrodisiac potions and magic, both white and black, at home. He had learned, rightly or wrongly, to respect it. And he was therefore in a peculiarly vulnerable position *vis-à-vis* his black mistress. The Negro woman soon realised her master's "weakness" and naturally played upon it and took advantage of it. The nights were no longer restricted to the indulgences of sex: the lady would find ways of letting her master know that the talisman necklace he fingered, the tabus worn on her body, whether they were made from a lion's tooth, an elephant's tusk or a small piece of stone, were powerful . . . When he was tired, she would tell him that she could prepare an effective love potion powerful enough to remedy his insufficiency; if he suffered troubles with his neighbour or was persecuted by the Crown, she would say that she could "fix" matters with the aid of drums, the Babalawo and magic spells . . .

Could the master then later forbid the Negroes such practices, forbid them the uses of fetiches to which he himself had had recourse in secret? Obviously not—and even if he could, he would not.

The master thus joined the priest, the vicar of the plantation, the slaves themselves and even their own priests in an elaborate and complex piece of hypocrisy: all were partners in the same deception. Rather than attempting any genuine "conversion" of the slaves in the proper sense of the word, both parties to the deceit contented themselves with "keeping up appearances"; all parties concerned were participants in a comic-opera whose *leit-motif* was to satisfy the eye . . .

Perhaps in reaction against this, perhaps to render the deception the more convincing, the Portuguese lay colonist, as though eager to quench his burning conscience, feverishly embraced every external form of religious enthusiasm, clung to every outward demonstration of devotion, transforming both his own life and that of his dependants into a continuous sequence of prayers, masses, litanies, sacraments and religious festivities. After the mid-sixteenth century, when sugar prices rose on the European market and life on the Brazilian plantations and sugar-mills became easy, with the slaves doing not most but all of the work, one traveller (quoted by Françoise Coreal in *Voyages aus les Indes Orientales*) commented that the Portuguese were always either " eating, resting, f——g or praying." Gilberto Freyre quotes Coreal further on the subject of Bahia in the 17th century: " On n'y marche point sans un Rosaire à la Main, un Chapelet au Col et un Saint Antoine sur l'Estomac. On est exact à s'agenouiller au Son de L'Angelus au Milieu des Rues."

A century later, a British traveller, Gilbert Farquhar Mathison, was enchanted with the scene he saw on the " fazenda " of Joaquim das Lavrinhas, where the master of the house kneeled in front of the members of his plantation, family, slaves, overseers and all, " to ask for God's blessing and the protection of the Virgin Mary." Another British traveller of the 18th century, Mrs Graham, relates her surprise on hearing litanies sung at nightfall in the streets of Bahia by whites, Negroes, mulattoes, Indians *et al.*

Throughout the period of slavery, in fact, they slept, rose, worked and lay down to sleep with the name of God in their mouths. In the morning it was, " My God, it is thanks to Thy goodness that I again see the light of day. Wilt Thou see that I walk safely, guided by Thy unfailing providence? " (Freyre). At night, as Mathison noticed, the people in the Big House would join slaves of the household and older Negroes from the Senzala, the slave quarters, to pray:

> *With God I lay me down; with God I rise,*
> *With the Grace of God and of the Holy Spirit. May*
>   *Thine eyes*
> *Watch over me as I sleep this night;*
> *And if I should die, then wilt Thou light*
> *Me with the tapers of Thy Trinity*
> *Into the mansion of Eternity?*

Should anyone sneeze, he would invariably be greeted with a " God save you! " or " God bless you! "—a custom prevailing even today, although in the cities the phrase has been transformed into a wish for " Health!," much as the Germans say "*Gesundheit*!" The Negroes themselves took every opportunity of seeking the blessing of their master, saying, "Praised be the name of our Lord Jesus Christ!" to which the master would reply, " Praised be!" or simply " Forever!"

" When it thundered loudly," Gilberto Freyre has told us, " whites and blacks would gather in the chapel or the sanctuary to sing the Benedictus, or intone the Magnificat, and recite the prayers of St. Braz, St. Jerome and St. Barbara. They would light candles, burn holy boughs and recite the Credo. Certain ailments were treated with prayers and anointings with oil as in apostolic times—erysipelas, for example. They would tack up prayer-papers to the windows and doors of houses to protect the family from thieves, assassins, lightning-bolts and tempests . . . On the day on which they began grinding the cane, the priest never failed to be there to bless the sugar mill, and the labour was undertaken with the Church's benediction. Mass was first said, and then they all made their way to the mill, the white males in their sun-hats, slow paced and solemn, and the fat *senhoras* in their mantillas . . . The priest made the sign of the Cross in the air with the hyssop and sprinkled the mill with holy water, many of the slaves taking good care to be sprinkled also. There followed other slow gestures on the part of the priest. Latin sentences. At times, a sermon."

In the words of Father Cardim, back in the 16th century, " they are accustomed, the first time they go to grind, to have the mills blessed, and on that day they do make a great feast, inviting those from round and about . . . The priest, upon being requested to do so, blesses some of those present, a thing that is very much esteemed."

The slaves, it appears, were specially fond of this ceremony, pushing and jostling in their attempts to get nearer to the priest and not miss their opportunity. Then, at night after the blessing, there would be dances, and the slaves would be permitted to have their drum-beating and dance their own Negro dances.

And since the slaves' contact with Catholicism, with Christianity, was restricted to pomp and ceremonial, to feasts and blessings, to commemorations with singing and dancing, and to the exchange of ritualistic phrases, the new religion of the masters seemed to them not at all unlike their own. In Africa, after all, hardly a religious ceremony was complete, or conceivable, without singing and dancing, both of which are part of the very soul of the African, no matter what tribe he belongs to or what religion he professes.

In Brazil, he was met with much the same attitude, plus a great number of saints. Saints? Why not call them Orishas? Are the saints of Catholicism not perfectly within the African's terms of reference and acceptable there in the African conception of hero-worship? Is there not one particular saint for each particular trouble? And is not " tacking prayer-papers to the windows and doors . . . to protect the family " a kind of *Ewo* (obligation) to the powerful Orishas? A different type of fetichism?

What followed was natural and predictable. The African slave felt himself " at home " with the white man's religion, took full advantage of the social betterment it offered, and adapted himself, and his own practices, to the new situation. Similarly, his African priests in the slave quarters (and there were many), quickly realising that they could continue practising their own rites undisturbed so long as *appearances* satisfied the Catholic priest and the master, astutely set up their altars replete with images of the Catholic saints on top while below, concealed from the public eye, they reverently placed the *Itá(s)*, the stones which represented the Orishas, and other fetiches of the African gods.

(Lest we be accused of generalising or over-simplifying, it might be well to say here that when we speak of " the African slave " we are in fact referring to a general trend, tracking a broad climate of development which was to result in the birth later of part of the gigantic spiritualist movement of today; we are following the main stream. This is not to deny the existence of interesting tributaries. The Mohammedan Negroes, for instance, thinking themselves superior to the other Africans, refused to accept Catholicism, adhered to their own religion and maintained a somewhat aristocratic bearing, even in the *senzala*. They led many uprisings until the famous Bahia insurrection of 1835, in which they were completely defeated, partly because they failed to impose their leadership on enough Negroes successfully to face government troops. Their allegiance to Allah was stronger than anything else— and, it was only after this defeat that they succumbed finally to the influence of the white man's religious practices and to those of some of their fellow slaves. There were of course many other trends, many different situations—indeed the very variety of Negro tribes and customs was responsible for the incalculable variety of spiritistic practices identifiable today, when in Nigeria alone over 250 different tribes and as many dialects can still be isolated. Yet we must emphasise that, even within this diversity, there was and is little escaping the influence of the Yorubas. The reason for their vigorous effect upon the religions and customs of their neighbours, which had begun back in Africa, lay not only in the superiority of their culture over all others save the Mohammedan, but also in the singular resemblance between Yoruba theogony and its Catholic counterpart, Olorum and the innumerable Orishas against Jesus and His inexhaustible court of saints. This made the "amalgamation" of Negro and Catholic concepts that much more practicable and undoubtedly lies behind the ascendency of Yoruba influence to the point where it became the basic African ingredient in the religious syncretism of Brazil, and where the Nâgo language, according to Ramos, became the general language of all the Negroes in Bahia.)

With the massive arrivals of Yoruba in the middle of the 18th century, the processes sketched above began to accelerate. The identification of African Orishas with analogous Catholic saints began, without too much effort, to intensify.

Thus Obatalá, also called Orixalá by the Yoruba and Oxalá in Brazil, the "king of purity," the great Orisha, the intermediary between man and the supreme god, Olorun, was easily identified with Jesus. Shango, god of thunder and lightning, was identified with St. Jerome because of his odyssey in the desert and the fact that he dwelt with a lion. Ogun, the god of hunting and of war, became identified with St. George, heraldic knight, Roman officer, patron saint of England—losing at the same time his hunting rights and remaining solely a great warrior, a protector in *demandas* or difficult suits. Oshossi, a secondary Orisha of hunting among the Yoruba, in Brazil took over this function from Ogun and became a first-class and very powerful Orisha, owner of the forest and identified with St. Sebastian, the 3rd century martyr who was also an officer in the Roman army but became a convert to early Christianity.

Yemanjá, mother of the chief Orishas, "mother of fish," the great water mother, in Brazil became equated with the Mother of Christ (the Mother of God instead of mother of the gods). Unlike her role in Africa, she plays here the part of the sea's owner, the queen of the mermaids, taking the position reserved in Africa for Olokun, who is responsible in Yoruba mythology for their version of the biblical deluge. Yemanjá, who is merely goddess of the River Ogun at home, has become a highly respected and venerated entity in South America, the Queen of the Beaches whose importance swelled enormously during the last century. She has taken on several of the Virgin Mary's denominations, too—Our Lady of the Rosary, Our Lady of Piety, Our Lady of the Conception, and so on. The first of these was to become the patron saint of the Negroes.

Oxun, goddess of the river with the same name, became Our Lady of Light. Nanaburuá, or Nana-Buluku in Dahomey, was identified with St. Anne, Yansan and Oyá (Shango's loyal wife) with St. Barbara, Obá with St. Catherine. In this *mélange,* one Orisha can be identified with more than one Catholic saint, and vice versa. Oxun is also equated with Mary Magdalene, for instance.

Eshu, one of the masters of divination, a Yoruba oracle, became the messenger of the Orishas in the Dahomey fashion. And, as before by the missionaries in Africa, he again became identified with the Devil—a classification at variance with

58

his personality, since in fact he may work for Good as well as for Evil. (In the Candomblé of Bahia, however, where they have preserved the Yoruba tradition more purely, Eshu remains untainted by functions similar to those of the Catholic Devil.)

Ifá continued as master of divination and was identified with no saints, possibly because he is not regarded as being in the same category as the Orishas. There are, however, other Orishas and other saints who do feature in this vast canvas of religious syncretism. But they are of lesser importance: the foregoing rank highest on the list.

Such amalgamation of deities permitted the African priests, as we have said, to perform their own rites as an apparent part of Catholic worship " in the African style." These rites were also influenced in time by certain Indian fetichist practices, insofar as these attributed to their gods' daily happenings and accepted the phenomenon of " possession."

In the early centuries of slavery in Brazil, Negro priests frequently gave their flocks news from Africa through their " powers of divination " via the Orishas, in other words through mediumship or extra-sensory perception. " Until a short time ago," says Freyre, " they imported from Africa a number of things for use in their cult: kola nuts, cauris [cawries in Yoruba—sea-shells, porcelain shells used as money on the African coast and also by Babalawos in the complex art of divination and other magic practices], cloth and soap from the coast, and oil of the Dendê palm." (This last is a *sine qua non* for the preparation of popular dishes from Bahia such as the famous *Vatapa,* and the tree, originally transported from Africa, is now happily naturalised in Brazil.)

Nor was the Muslim influence in this sphere of religious activity to be ignored. They, too, according to Freyre, until recently imported from Africa " a number of things for use in their cult: *tecebas* (rosaries); sacred instruments such as the *heré* or *checheré*—a copper rattle shaken in the Shango ceremonies by the ' holy daughter '; and sacred herbs for aphrodisiac purposes or pure pleasure." As Herskovits has pointed out, the Hausa and Fulani, among others, were not

59

pure Mohammedans and their culture resulted from a true interpenetration of Islam with Negro fetichism and animism. The removal of shoes, obligatory before entering a place of worship in most practices of Negro origin today, is an obvious example of what many consider to be a clear case of Muslim influence. The Muslim Negroes, too, were accustomed to import from Africa a special blue ink with which they used to make " cabalistic signs on a blackboard, then wash the board and give the water to drink to the one whose body they wished to charm, or else spill it in his path, and work their magic spells."

Apart from those already mentioned, the Yoruba theogony underwent other changes in Brazil. Olorun, the Supreme Being, for example, all but disappeared from the religious scene. Until the end of the last century, Bahian Negroes spoke of him as " the God of Heaven " and anthropologist Nina Ribeiro, a pioneer in the study of Negro religion in Brazil, once discovered the inscription *Ko Si Oba Kan Ofi Olorun* (" There is no king equal to God ") in an old Bahia butchery. Rodrigues believes that both Muslim and Catholic influences are apparent in this inscription. But you cannot find any mention of Olorun in the *Terreiros* or *Candomblés* of Bahia today.

Nor is there reference to Odudúa and her marriage to Obatalá, the wedding of Aganju and Yemanjá, and the Oedipus-type tragedy of the latter, or the birth of the Orishas resulting therefrom. All this has been forgotten in Brazil. Even Shango's fetich in Bahia has become " the stone of lightning," because popular belief has it that the fall of a meteorite is linked with thunder and lightning.

By far the most important change, however, related to the sex of the priest. As we have seen, with exception of Dahomey ceremonies attended by Vodunsi, male priests performed all religious rites save for those concerned with Orishakô in Africa. In Brazil, they were gradually superseded by priestesses.

The first step was the reduction of the several classes of priest in Africa to one: The Babalaô (the Babalawo of Yoruba cults, dedicated to Ifá and also called Babalorixá or " Father of Saints "). Then, as time passed, the male Negroes became more and more occupied in the slave labours of the fields and the females gained easier access, first to the masters, and later, when the number of white women in the cities increased and the masters began to marry the very young *sinhas*, to the mistresses of the Big Houses. With the special relationships this entailed, with the increased time at their disposal that they were thereby able to command, and with the tradition already established (as we have seen) of sorcery allied to concubinage, it was natural enough that the African woman should find herself more and more able to replace the male priest. Thus a new class of religious functionary was created : the Iyalorixá or " Mother of Saints." And the priestesses in Brazil existed in a territory admirably shaped to foster their influence.

As we have seen in the first chapter, the Portuguese colonists came to Brazil already imbued with a belief in spells. " As for that variety of witchcraft which was of direct African origin," writes Gilberto Freyre, " it was to develop here upon a European base of mediæval superstitions and beliefs."

" As was the case in Portugal, witchcraft or sorcery in Brazil, after it had come to be dominated by the Negro, continued to centre on the love-motive and in the interests of generation and fecundity. It was concerned with protecting the life of the pregnant woman and that of the child, threatened by so many things—by fevers, cramps, blood ailments, snake-bites, fallen sternum, the evil eye. The pregnant woman, for her part, was to be prophylactically safeguarded from these and other afflictions by a set of practices in which African influences, frequently shorn of their original character, were mingled with traces of the Catholic liturgy and survivals of native rituals " (that of concentrating the evil influences believed to cause illness in one part of the body, and then sucking them out, as practised by the Tenetehara Indians and described in Chapter One, is an example).

" Brought here from Portugal," Freyre continues, " the

61

various beliefs and forms of sexual magic proceeded to expand: the belief that the Mandrake root attracts fecundity and undoes evil spells against the home and the propagation of families; the custom of pregnant women of hanging a small bag of altar stones (holy stones from the centre of the altar) about their necks; the care taken by such women not to pass under ladders lest the child should fail to grow; their habit of donning St. Francis's Girdle as they feel the pangs of parturition coming on; the promises made to Our Lady of Childbirth, of The Blessed Event, of Expectation, of The Conception, of The Pangs, in order that the childbirth may be easier or the child a comely one. And when Our Lady hears the request, the promise is kept.

"This consists, sometimes, of the child's taking the name of Maria (if a girl); whence the many Marias in Brazil: Maria das Dores (of The Pangs), Maria dos Anjos (of the Angels), da Conceição (of The Conception), das Graças (of the Favours) and Maria de Lourdes. But the bulk of the beliefs and practices of sexual magic as developed in Brazil was coloured by the Negro's intense mysticism. Some of them were brought from Africa by him, while others, African in technique only, made use of native [Brazilian] herbs and animals. Nothing is more characteristic than the use made of the toad in hastening the consummation of delayed marriages. In Afro-Brazilian sexual magic the toad also becomes the protector of the faithless wife, who, in order to deceive her husband, has but to take a needle threaded with green silk, make with it a cross on the face of the individual to be affected, and afterwards sew up the eyes of the toad. On the other hand, in order to hold a lover, a woman must keep a toad constantly in a pot beneath her bed. In this case, the toad is a live one, fed on cow's milk. Other animals bound up with Afro-Brazilian sexual rites of this sort are the bat, the snake, the screech-owl, the hen, the dove, the rabbit and the tortoise.

"Nor should we overlook the important role that coffee came to play in Afro-Brazilian sexual magic. We even have an expression: 'Witches' Coffee' (*Café Mandigueiro*), coffee with a spell (*Mandinga,* derived from the Mandingo Negroes, so named by the British, who came to Brazil in sizeable numbers). It is taken with much sugar and 'a few clots of the menstrual fluid of the sorceress herself' (Basilio de Magalhães). This comes nearer to a love potion than to a witch's spell; but it is a potion such as could be conceived in no country but Brazil: very strong coffee, much sugar, and the blood of a mulatto woman. There is another technique which is employed, that consists in straining the coffee through the lower portions of the nightgown in which a woman has slept for two consecutive nights; the coffee is then to be drunk twice by the man, once at breakfast and again at dinner . . . A woman's soiled nightgown enters into many a love-spell, as do other nauseous things: hairs from the armpits or the genital parts; sweat, tears, saliva, blood; nail parings; 'the menstrual mucus excreted by Bartholin's Glands, and even stools' (Alfredo de Carvalho). Give him such ingredients as these, and the sorcerer (or sorceress) will tell you that he will 'soften the heart' of the most indifferent person.

"There are sorcerers who fashion dolls out of wax or cloth. Upon these *Calungas,* as they are called, the magicians inflict whatever punishment they wish the individual concerned to suffer; it is a matter of praying forcefully enough; the rest consists merely in doing various things to the figure—squeezing it, pounding it, stretching its arms, spreading its legs, all of which is reflected on the person of the distant victim."

Freyre relates here a common black magic practice which is found in different forms among practitioners the world over. It is one of the oldest forms of transference, more normally effected not just by "praying forcefully" but by a complex ritual of incantation. The word *Calunga* stems from the Bantu people of Angola, where it is the name of one of the more mysterious gods, whose fetich is a doll. I make no apology for quoting Gilberto Freyre so extensively. On such matters, he is the authority, and his writings demonstrate both the authenticity of these practices and the depth to which they go.

"It was not merely for amorous purposes," he says, "but for those having to do with the newborn as well, that the two mystic currents, the Portuguese on the one hand and the African or Amer-Indian on the other, were united in Brazil, the Portuguese represented by the white father, or father and mother, and on the other side, the Indian or Negro mother (mostly the latter), the wet-nurse, the foster-mother, the black mammy, the African female slave. The prophylactic concerns of mother and nurse here mingle in the one stream of maternal tenderness, whether it be a matter of bodily hygiene or of spiritual protection against witchery and the evil eye.

" With regard to the mystic protection of the newborn, however, it is the African influence that is stressed. A number of Portuguese traditions were brought here by the white colonists: that of dragging the umbilical cord through the fire or the river in order that rats might not eat it and the child grow up to be a thief; that of hanging a penny or a key about a child's neck to cure it of milk-curds; that of not putting out the light until the child has been baptised in order that no sorcerer, witch or werewolf may come and suck its blood in the dark; that of giving the names of saints to children, to frighten werewolves even further. But every one of these traditions has been modified here or enriched through the influence of the African slave woman, the old Negro woman who was the child's nurse.

" The Brazilian child of colonial times was surrounded by a greater number of ghostly forms, and more terrible ones, than any other children in the world." This was mainly the result of another kind of interpenetration: new fears brought over from Africa or assimilated from the Indians being added to the Portuguese obsessions imported from Europe. " On the beaches," Freyre says, " was the ' homen-marinho,' the ' man of the sea,' a terrifying creature that devoured people's fingers, noses and private parts " [a castration-threat present in other myths which seems to conform Freud's assertions].

" In the forest there are: the ' saci-pererê,' a small, one-legged Negro who pursues travellers; the ' caipora,' the man with his feet turned backwards, and the ' boi-tátá.' And everywhere there are the capering nanny-goat, the she-mule-

ABOVE: Orishas of Candomblé (Omulú, Ogun and Oxossi among them) in full regalia dancing to the sound of *combos*. BELOW, LEFT: The impressive incision ceremony in Candomblé. BELOW, RIGHT: After going through the many ceremonies necessary for full development in Candomblé, the daughter of saint—the Iaô—is ready for the ôrunkó, the ceremony during which she will officially receive her Orisha, in this case Oxossi, the god of hunting and of the forest.

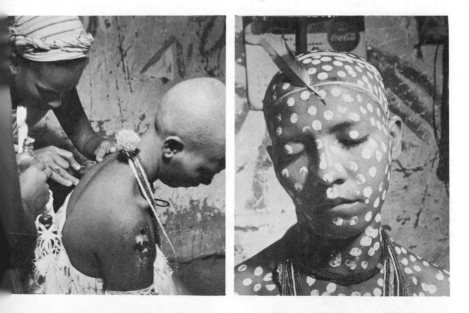

ABOVE, LEFT: Animal sacrifices appropriate to the Orisha of the Iaô are made and the blood is poured over the Iaô. ABOVE, RIGHT: After the sacrifices and the blood-bath the Iaôs sit inside the *pêji*, covered with feathers, surrounded by slain animals, images of Catholic saints and the Brazilian flag. BELOW, LEFT: The Iaôs sit inside the *camarinha* in contemplation, forbidden to speak, awaiting final preparations for the orunko. BELOW, RIGHT: A Iaô of Oxala (on the right of picture with face covered) at work helped by an *Ekédê*. The *Ekédê* is assisting a worshipper who has fallen under the control of an evil spirit.

without-a-head, the ' *tutú-marambá*,' the Negro with the pouch, the ' *tatú-gambeta*,' the ' *ximbaba*,' the ' *mãe-de-cabelo* ' and the goblin-with-hair-for-hands. In the creeks and lakes are the water-mother, the ' *mãe-d'agua*,' on the banks of the river the toad-goblin, the ' *sapo-carurú*,' and everywhere by night the ' *alamas-penadas*,' the souls-in-torment.

" These never failed to come and smear with ' ghost broth ' (' *mingau-das-almas* ') the faces of little children; and for this reason no child must neglect to wash his face or take a bath first thing in the morning. Another great danger for the young lay in being caught in the street ' out of hours,' when white-clad phantoms of the grow-and-shrink variety were likely to confront the daring. Or else their hammocks would be haunted by creatures with pock-marked faces . . ."

In such a climate, it was hardly surprising that sorcery flourished!

In time, the overt magic of the Africans, the covert and forbidden sorcery of the Portuguese, and the myths of the Indians interacted within the framework of slavery, itself less harsh than any in Portugal or her African colonies, to form a kind of religious common ground on which, like some kind of negative catalyst, each helped to soften the harder and more barbaric aspects of the other. The Negro was thus given the protecting figures of Jesus and the saints plus a whole new set of obligations, the obligations of the Catholic church, which were nevertheless far milder in their outlook than those they superseded. Catholic practices, on the other hand, already imbued with the Portuguese tendency towards magic, took on the influence of African fetishism in a far more direct and unhampered fashion than in Portugal.

The important point here is the false position of the Portuguese masters, both towards their own religion and towards the slaves'; relatively, they were hypocrites. The lack of spiritual integrity implicit in a system where every accent was placed on the appearance and none on the substance, where all the importance lay in style and none in content, gave the clue to the Negro which he was only too eager to follow.

There were many converted slaves replete with gentle, kind, sincere and genuinely love-filled Catholic feelings, especially among the *mucamas,* whose capacity for simple but true religious outlook was far superior in most cases than that of their masters and mistresses. But they were of course a minority. Those tribes or individuals whose "moment or degree of culture" was higher, whose religious concepts were thus more profound and crystallised, took full advantage of the facilities offered by so ambivalent a situation and devoted their considerable energies to maintaining alive their own religious practices and traditions.

CHAPTER FOUR

Candomblé

T H E introduction to *Jubiabá,* Jorge Amado's novel depicting the life of a famous *Macumbeiro,* the Babalorixá of a Candomblé in Bahia, contains in its current (11th) impression the words: " For this edition commemorating the 30th anniversary of Jorge Amado's first published work, Caribé, his brother-of-saint—they are both from Oxossi—specially designed the illustrations."

The author himself writes, on p. 111 of his work: " Jubiabá's house was small but beautiful. It was set in the middle of a plot of land on the Morro da Capa Negra (Black Robe Hill), a large ' terreiro ' in front of it and a back-yard behind. The spacious room occupied most of the house. There was a table with a bench on each side, and an easy chair, turned towards the room where the father-of-saint slept. On the benches at each side of the table, Negroes and Negresses talked. Two Spaniards and an Arab were also there . . . Jubiabá came out of the bedroom wearing a beautiful robe embroidered on the chest. The garment stretched to his feet and he wore no other clothes. A Negro rose from the table and helped the father-of-saint to sit down.

" The Negroes came over and kissed Jubiabá's hand. So did the Spaniards and the Arab. One of the Spaniards had a swolled chin, with a cloth fastened below it. He moved towards the father-of-saint and said: ' Father Jubiabá, I have a terrible tooth-ache: I cannot work or do anything. Caramba! I've spent a fortune with the dentist, and—

nothing! The tooth-ache is still there. There's nothing more
I can do . . .' He removed the cloth from his chin to reveal
an enormous swelling.

"Jubiabá looked at him and prescribed: 'Put some *malva*
tea upon the place and pray thus:

> *Saint Nicodemus, heal this tooth!*
> *Nicodemus, heal this tooth!*
> *Heal this tooth!*
> *This tooth!*
> *Tooth!*

"And he completed the prescription: 'You make this
prayer on the beach. You write it in the sand and each time
you erase one word, understand? Then you go home and put
on the tea. But without prayer, it is no good . . .'

"The Spaniard left [the equivalent of] five shillings and
went home to carry out his instructions. Next came a Negro
who wanted to cast a spell [*despacho*]. He spoke, in a low
voice, into Jubiabá's ear. The father-of-saint got up and,
helped by the Negro, returned to his own room. They returned a few minutes later, and, the next day, a strong spell
—manioc flour mixed with oil of dendê, several coins of silver
and copper, and a young, still-alive vulture—appeared at the
door of Henrique Padeiro, who caught a mysterious illness
and died a while afterwards. A Negro woman also wanted a
spell, but she did not go into the room, nor did she speak in
a low voice. She started to say: 'That shameless Martha!
She took my man! I want him to come back home '—she was
highly indignant—'I have children and she doesn't have
any—'

"'You get some of her hair and bring it over, and I shall
attend to everything,' Jubiabá interrupted.

"And all those Negroes who wished to cast spells paraded
in front of him. Some, he prayed over with a branch of bitter-
cress. And this is how next morning the city was filled with
spells, the results of which obstructed the streets so much
that passers-by, fearful, stayed away . . . Many times, rich
people came—Ph.D's, doctors, engineers, millionaires with
cars."

Thus Jorge Amado, internationally famous author of *Gabriela, Clove And Cinnamon,* and many other best-sellers. The writer himself is a son-of-Oxossi—i.e., his Orisha, the one designated as his protector and guide, is Oxossi. In other words, Amado, writer, sophisticate and man of letters, is quite openly a worshipper of the cult called Candomblé, a development of the religious rites of the Yoruba.

The largely undercover practices of rural Brazil of the 17th and 18th centuries travelled a tortuous route to attain so eminent a position in the middle of the 20th!

But, as we have seen, from African, from Indian and from colonist, the driving force was there. Nothing could stop it; no persecution, police or otherwise, could halt its continuous rise and growth.

The religious practices of the Negroes, encouraged by the ambivalent atmosphere obtaining, as outlined in Chapter Three, developed in two different directions in different regions—one in Rio de Janeiro, São Paulo and Minas, mainly the first-named, where the Negroes of Bantu origin from Angola were less influenced by Yoruba culture and consequently syncretism with Catholicism and spiritism was more marked; the other in Bahia, with extensions to the North and North-east, where Yoruba influence predominated and Catholic appearances as well as Catholic liturgical obligations were added, but where the influence of spiritism was until recently negligible or non-existent. The practices in Rio gave birth to the religious movement called Umbanda, with which we shall deal more fully later (see Chapters Nine and Ten). But for the moment, let us remain in Bahia.

One of the reasons why the cult is (if we may so term it) purer there, may be because of the demographic concentration of Negroes and mulattoes in that state—over ten million in 1950, the largest in the country—plus the double advantage of the city of Salvador. This town, Brazil's capital until 1763, offered the twin opportunities of a city that was yet an area not suffering the modernising influence of industrialisation (which is only now starting to a certain degree in Bahia state). It took time, of course, for an organised Negro cult to arise, operating autonomously and independently in its own quarters: religious ceremonies permitted on dates coinciding with Catholic feasts, held under supervision in the slave-quarters or the master's house on the farms was one thing; an independent place, whether building or plot of land, designed solely to accommodate religious practices carried out according to African traditions was quite another!

The only place where such a conception could flourish was in the city: it was physically impossible on the plantations, in the sugarmills or at the masters' houses. And only in a built-up area was there any opportunity of avoiding, or trying to avoid, police persecution. Financial means to promote the interests of the cult, too, could be found only in the city. Which is why the appearance of independent African cults is wholly an urban and suburban phenomenon.

The precise date of the first emergence of such an organised independent cult, independent of any outside influence whatever, totally directed, managed and run by Negroes, is not known. Most authors agree that it was around 1830, eight years after Brazil won independence from Portugal, that the first Candomblé appeared. A minority claim that this event dates back more than 200 years, but they are unable to produce any documentary evidence to support this.

Equally shrouded in mystery is the philology of the word Candomblé itself. It is supposed to derive from candombé, a dance once popular among Negroes on the coffee farms, the name being taken from the word used to describe their drums. The problem with the word as it stands today is that the two consonants " b " and " l," together, simply do not exist either in Sudanese or in Bantu languages. The name is more likely, therefore, to have been " imported " from outside, the theorists say—though how, and from where, nobody is able to tell. What is certain is that, some time ago, the yearly public festivities of the African sects began to be labelled with the word Candomblé . . .

This is now the generic name of a cult wherein contact is established with the Orishas and their spiritual Phalanxes through initiates, following a certain ritual in a place duly consecrated according to established formulae. The place where such cults are practised is called a Candomblé as well.

Early Candomblés started to appear in the woods, on the outskirts of the city, near a road, convenient to the tramways later on. The place should be " kept away from the lights of the city but not impossible to reach "—that was a favourite maxim of the founding mothers and fathers of the cult. The first Candomblé of all, *Engenho Velho* (The Old Mill), lay about 80 metres off a side road on the outskirts of Salvador, the capital of Bahia. It was in fact an abandoned mill-house. Others were less easy to reach. Some, like the famous Candomblés of Bernadino and Aninha, both vanished now, were really difficult of access: miles distant from any collective transportation, so that worshippers either had to walk or take a car.

The Candomblé is a closed community, a world by itself, fully organised, hierarchic, obeying no outside authority. Candomblés as a whole submit to no "government" or central authority in the fashion of a Pope, for instance: each is autonomous and individually independent.

Inside, absolute authority is wielded and exercised exclusively by the mother-of-saint or father-of-saint who is its head. This authority can be challenged by nobody: either you obey or you leave the Candomblé. In practice, due to the special circumstances outlined in the previous chapter, the majority of Candomblés are directed by women, by mothers-of-saint.

A mother-of-saint—Iyalorixá in Nagô, the main Yoruba language spoken in Bahia—is surrounded by daughters-of-saint. These votaries, initiates whom she herself has developed according to basic rituals, are called Iyauô (spelled Iaô for simplicity), a term truncated from the Yoruba Iyawô, younger wife. From among them, she chooses a few to help administer the Candomblé, each having specific religious functions. And, since seniority prevails among the Yoruba, the " oldest " Iaô, that is to say the one first initiated by the Iyalorixá and therefore the senior priestess, is with rare exceptions appointed Iyá(mother)-Kêkêrê(small), little mother, the second-in-

71

command. She in turn has an aide, called Iyá-Môrô. Two others, the Dagã and the Sidagã, are in charge of the *padê* of Exú (Eshu), the offering which must be made to the god before any religious ceremony at all can start. Another daughter-of-saint is in charge of cooking the food to be offered to the Orishas. She is called Iyá Bassê, the mother-that-cooks. Yet another, Iyá Têbêxê, leads the religious chants sung at the ceremonies. A special attendant (Ekedê) to each Iaô is without religious function, but as important to the Candomblé as the Ogadã, a patron appointed by the mother-of-saint whose function is to aid the establishment either by his prestige or with money. All these people must carry out their functions properly if the efficacious and smooth running of the ceremonies is to be achieved and the Orishas consequently to heed the requests made.

The Candomblé is usually held in a house or large *barrack* (tent in Brazil) specially built for the purpose or adapted to it. The exterior will resemble that of all poor houses in Bahia —a wooden framework, clay walls, sometimes whitewashed, and a roof on top. This last may be zinc or even tiled, but is frequently only straw. Originally all Candomblés had beaten mud floors because of an old saying that " daughters-of-saint should always dance barefoot on the earth, never on boards." Then some of the leaders began to floor their buildings with wood, and today the majority do.

The tent or barrack is a vital part of the Candomblé. It is the site of the famous feasts. It may either be a part of the house itself, as at Engenho Velho, or a separate structure, usually placed at the back.

If the house is to be used solely for Candomblé, then several of the inner rooms are set aside as " seats " for the Orishas. If the site is in the country, in the woods, then several " seats " will be outside, each surrounded by a small fence, especially that of Exú, which must be in the open air no matter where the Candomblé is situated. More fences surround sacred trees at which worshippers make promises and light candles to their favourite Orishas.

In contrast to Exú, there are also Orishas whose " seats "

must at all costs be indoors—Oshalá and Yemanjá, for example. That of Oshun, the water goddess, must be placed on the bank of a nearby stream (if one is available), while Oshossi should be seated in the middle of the woods. Such outside "seats" take the form of a miniature house, from three to five feet high.

In the construction of the Candomblé itself, special rules have to be closely followed, in particular the correct placing of the *axé*—a compound of sacred water, feathered creatures slaughtered for the occasion, newspapers of the day, and coins, all specially prepared by the mother-of-saint or father-of-saint and laid in the foundations during a special ceremony. About thirty years ago, when the Engenho Velho became too small to house all the worshippers who wished to attend and the visitors who wished to make a pilgrimage there, it was suggested that the building might be enlarged. The mother-of-saint of the time vetoed the idea because the *axé* is not transferable and must not be moved . . .

It is rare for the mother-(or father)-of-saint to live in the Candomblé itself. Customarily, they stay in the city with some of their assistants. Around the Candomblé, however, it is not unusual for the daughters-of-saint and "ogans" to build small houses where they can sleep after feasts which have lasted long into the night. At the main entrance, one may find a cross, a pair of oxen horns, or a fetich dedicated to the patron Orisha of the Candomblé.

In the past, as a means of avoiding police persecution and to make it easier for politicians to patronise them, Candomblés opened their doors to the civic authority and were used as places for the registration of voters for coming elections.

We have spoken several times of the Engenho Velho, the Old Mill, the first and most famous Candomblé. This, the father and mother of all other Candomblés genealogically speaking, was founded about 1830, several years before the final defeat of the Mohammedan dissidents, by three African women, Iyá Dêtá, Iyá Kalá and Iyá Nassô. It was probably the last who shouldered the main responsibility and it was undoubtedly she who " planted " the *axé,* for today the alternative name of the Candomblé is known to have been *Ilê Iyá Nassô,* the House of Mother Nassô. All three names are revered today, especially by those " traditionalist " mothers-of-saint who have through consecutive initiations descended, as it were, from one branch or another of the Old Mill Candomblé itself, This tradition, forming a kind of Candomblé elite in Bahia today, results both from the " inheritance " or passing on of the mantle of " mother " at the Engelho Velho, and also from a number of parallel streams originally stemming from those who had dissented and formed rival Candomblés.

The three African priestesses, the first mothers-of-saint, were succeeded by one Marcelina, who reigned happily and without challenge until her death. But the succession was not so easy. Her rightful successor was the " small-mother," Iyá Kêrêrê, whose name was Maria Júlia Figueiredo. Maria Júlia did in fact obtain the position, but she had a rival, another of Marcelina's " daughters " called Maria Júlia da Conceição, who refused to accept the will of the majority and left with her supporters to form the Candomblé of Gantois (named after the French owner of the building purchased for this purpose), destined to become another of Bahia's most famous Candomblés.

After the split, the original Engenho Velho changed its quarters from Barroquinha, situated on a ranch not far from Salvador, to another district on the outskirts of the city. Despite the objections of later mothers-of-saint, at that time there was obviously no proscription on the movement of an *axé,* and that of the Old Mill was duly removed to its new address and formally " planted " in the foundations with due pomp and ritual. After the move, the Iyalorixá, Maria Júlia Figueiredo, was succeeded by Ursulina, better known as Mother Sussu—but her successor's appointment once again threw the " House of Mother Nassô " into a turmoil; for again there were dissidents, again there was a rival: Eugênia Ana Santos, known as Aninha, bitterly contested the rights of the " legal " candidate, Maximiana Maria da Conceição (" Aunt

74

Massi "), who was elected instead of "*Sinhá*" Antonia, the "small-mother" unable to take over through ill-health. Aninha was not seeking the position for herself but advanced the claims of Uncle Joaquim, her brother-of-saint (they were consecrated to the same Orisha). She did not succeed in making him the heir to Engenho Velho, however, so they too left to form an independent Candomblé called Axé de Opô Afonjá. The leadership of this passed from Uncle Joaquim to Aninha herself, and in this position she became one of the most famous mothers-of-saint of all time in Bahia. At her funeral on January 4, 1938, when she had been over forty years a daughter-of-saint, of which more than twenty were spent as mother-of-saint, thousands flocked in to the city to accompany her coffin, tens of thousands lined the route of the procession to cry, scream, faint, weep or shout "She will be resurrected!'," and the whole of the city of Salvador was in mourning.

She left behind her many dozens, perhaps even many hundreds of daughters-of-saint, whom she had herself initiated and who would carry on the tradition.

At the Gantois Candomblé, meanwhile, the original breakaway organisation, Iyalorixá Maria Júlia da Conceição was succeeded by her daughter-of-saint Pulquéria, who became in her turn one of the most famous "mothers" of Bahia. Pulquéria was succeeded by a daughter-of-saint who was in fact her own niece, Escolástica Maria de Nazaré, better known as Menininha. And this priestess too was to develop into a landmark along the trail of the "great mothers."

We have been speaking freely of mothers-of-saint, fathers-of-saint, daughters-of-saint and so on. According to the beliefs of the Negro in Brazil, each person has a "guardian angel," but only those who "have a saint" can become a daughter-of-saint or a son-of-saint. In other words, translated into modern language, everybody has a spirit guide, but only those who are mediums can communicate with them . . .

In Yoruba-influenced Candomblés, there is a difference: the Iaôs (daughters-of-saint) only "receive" their own Orisha, their personal guide, and no other.

How does it all work? The first step is to determine whether you have a saint, and which one it is. Among the Yoruba, the Orisha was determined immediately after the birth of the child. In Brazil, this has altered: no longer does the Babalawo, with the help of Ifá, determine the Orisha; instead, this is done by the mother-of-saint, in most cases after the prospective initiate has grown up. Sometimes the Orisha is revealed to the mother of a child in a dream, in which case, it is said, the child will never be happy unless it is dedicated to that Orisha. Yemanjá is rumoured to have taken many down to the sea with her because they neglected to worship her properly after she had revealed herself in this way. Normally, though, the Orisha is undivined until the mother-of-saint determines it. She " sees " the Orisha through divination (even if the candidate, for want of a better word, has received manifestations of a particular Orisha before). Sometimes, when she is not one hundred per cent. certain, a mother-of-saint may consult a Babalawo. The priest then, in a manner reminiscent of his ancient function in Africa, puts the matter to Ifá through the medium of the sea shells, discovering the identity of the Orisha through divination.

Once the particular Orisha is established, the candidate must begin either to raise or to save the money for her initiation. Frequently, this represents a considerable sacrifice on the part of the candidate, who comes normally from the poorer levels of the population.

There are special expressions in Portuguese to define some of the actions involved in these matters, most of which are not susceptible to translation. Thus the head of the Candomblé, the mother- or father-of-saint, must " make " or " seat " the saint on the worshipper. The saint is " seated " on the worshipper through a series of ceremonies comprising the latter's initiation. These expressions are a trifle odd in Portuguese even, but they do make sense. They reveal also the humble, simple origins of the cult, emphasising that these derive from the " lower strata " of the populace.

Instead of saying the equivalent of, " It is necessary to develop your mediumship," they say, " You must make the saint." And instead of developing the mediumship through concentration, prayer and gradual identification with the spirit spheres (to use a modern spiritualistic terminology), they are ready to assume that the power, as it were, is "put there" through incantations and magic rituals. And because it is through the head that the Orisha dominates the worshippers, all attention is paid to it and many dub the initiation "making the head" rather than "making the saint." The initiation rituals are long and complicated, but before the initiate presents herself for them, right from the very first day that her Orisha was determined by the mother-of-saint, she has assumed certain obligations towards her Orisha and respected certain duties: the paying of a tribute on the Orisha's day of the week, the consumption of special foods and the abstention from sex on that day, and so on.

(For convenience, we speak always in the feminine gender, of mothers-of-saint and of daughters-of-saint, purely because in Candomblé the women predominate. With certain unimportant exceptions, precisely the same thing will apply to fathers-of-saint and sons-of-saint.)

Before the initiation, each candidate must make her own special robes, for each Orisha has his or her own particular colours and type of vestment. Then, the initiate is free to move to the Candomblé, where she will live until the "saint is made," i.e., until the end of the initiation ceremonies, the magic rituals.

Upon arrival, the first thing she does is to take a purifying bath, called *atín,* which has been prepared with special herbs that vary according to which Orisha is involved by the mother-of-saint. After this, she dons the robes, never before worn, for the body and whatever covers it must be clean, pure, new: everything has to be done to purify the initiate and all related to her in order to facilitate the coming of the Orisha, the contact with the divine.

The initiate begins her education into the secrets of Candomblé by learning how to sing for the Orishas, how to identify them by the chants and the drums, how to dance, how to pay homage to the mother-of-saint, and so on. After a certain number of days, they are not fixed and vary according to the progress of each particular candidate, there is a special meeting, with accompaniment by drums, singers, possibly even a few instrumentalists, who perform the chants of the initiate's Orisha seven, fourteen, or twenty one times, until the Orisha " takes hold of her." Usually, the Orisha " lowers," comes down, before the first seven chants are completed. Thus dispassionately may one describe the colourful spectacle, the compulsive rhythms and supercharged, dedicated atmosphere of a Candomblé at which an initiate first becomes possessed, becomes controlled by a spiritual entity that, in Yoruba, is believed to be a divinity termed an " Orisha."

For the candidate, however, this ceremony is but the beginning. After the " reception " of the Orishas, the initiates (there are usually a half dozen or so of them) progress to the most important parts of their initiations. First, they are confined in a room for a number of days, a minimum of seventeen, completely isolated from the rest of the world, not even permitted to speak, in complete seclusion, in spiritual retreat. Inside this *camarinha* (small chamber), communication with fellow inmates or supervisors is effected by means of hand-claps called *Paó;* the absolute minimum of words must be used. Before they can enter the *camarinha,* a strict depilation will have been carried out, removing all the hair from the skull, the armpits, and sometimes the pubes also.

The ritual depilation is followed by another piece of ceremonial in which the Iyalorixá washes and rubs the shaved head with sacred water containing traces of blood from all the creatures sacrificed at all times in that Candomblé. This is called " water from the *axés.*" A further rite practised in certain Candomblés permits the mother-of-saint to open a small hole in the centre of the initiate's head with the use of a razor blade, and also to make incisions in both arms (see illustrations). It is believed that secret herbs with anaesthetic qualities are used in this ceremony. A similar blade is used for depilatory purposes today, though this is not performed by the Iyalorixá herself but by her helpers.

In the *camarinha,* all the initiates sleep together on straw mats spread on the floor. To hide their bald heads, the Iaôs, the future daughters-of-saint, usually wind red or yellow cloths around their skulls. Early every morning, whether or not it is raining, each Iaô must go with her mother-of-saint and one or two aides to the nearest fountain or brook to wash herself in what is considered a purifying ceremony. Daughters-of-saint and other helpers in the Candomblé not directly concerned with the charge of the initiates must always ask permission to speak to them, saying three times the word *Karókê* (pronounced Kaaaaaaah-ro-quay, the " a " being given the greatest length possible).

When all this has been achieved with perseverance, resignation, respect and devotion, qualities, it must be admitted, found more easily among those of humble birth, the Iaô is ready for the big day: the day when her Orisha will " give his name." This ceremony, referred to as *ôrunkó* (and pronounced something like ohroonk-augh), is among the most popular of Candomblé, and among the best attended by " outside " people, by the public. On a night whose date has been set by the mother-of-saint, the Orisha for each initiate, the spiritual entity personal and peculiar to that Iaó, will publicly state his name; in " possession " of her earthly body, he will shout his name to an applauding public in the middle of the dancing and the drums. (We say an Orisha *personal* to each initiate: there is of course only one Ogun, one Xangô (Shango), one Oxossi and so forth. But the Iaôs at this ceremony do " receive," it seems, a " personal " Ogun, Xangô or Oxossi—spirit representatives, it appears, of the chiefs of the Phalanx bearing that name—and so there will thus be an Ogun of the Iaô Maria, the Xangô of Joana, an Oxossi of Conceição, etc.)

Sacrifices of goats, roosters, pigeons and other creatures, executed by the official sacrificer, the *axôngún*, begin the ôrunkó. He will be accompanied only by the mother-of-saint and some of the older daughters, her most intimate collaborators. The blood of the sacrifices is then used to bathe the sacred stones of the Orishas, the *itás,* in a secret, magic ceremony. This is carried out in a side room of the Candomblé,

79

the sanctuary, which is called the *pêji*. The mother-of-saint then disposes the initiates in a circle in the middle of the *barracão,* the tent. In the centre of this circle stand a bottle of dendê oil, a quantity of toasted manioc flour called *farofa,* and a glass of water or *cachaça* (a cheap Brazilian sugar-cane brandy).

Before the celebration can be carried any further, though, a most important task has to be undertaken: the appeasement of Eshu, spirit of the crossroads, the messenger and inter-mediary of the Orishas who can do both evil and good, and thus easily spoil the party. As has been mentioned before, two Iaôs, Dagã and Sidagã, are responsible for offering Eshu the *padê,* the water and *farofa* in the centre of the tent. This they do by picking up the offering and taking it 30 feet or more beyond the circle, throwing the liquid towards the trees and leaving the food to tempt the god if he so requires. (Besides setting up Eshu in his own seat outside the tent, the wor-shippers of Candomblé in Brazil have also created a singular figure, the " godfather " of Eshu, unknown to Africans, whose seat is within the house and whose mission, as a good god-father's should be, is to further the interests of those seeking to secure the god's goodwill.)

Once Eshu has been appeased, the main business of the evening can start. Chants are started up for each Orisha ex-pected, one at a time, asking him to state his name publicly. As the tempo of the singing and the rhythms of the drums intensify, the Iaô, each in her turn, begins to waver in her steps. She appears to lose her balance partially, wobbling along as though half drunk.

The *combos* continue to play, the chants ring ever more insistently in the ear, the atmosphere is charged with excite-ment, the climate, tense. Then, suddenly, as the air fills with the smoke of burned herbs, the initiate starts to shiver, quivering, trembling, shivering ever faster, shaking all over like a patient with a high fever.

Abruptly, she appears to lose consciousness, but without falling to the ground. Her eyes shut, but with neither pressure nor contraction. Her mouth flies open and a voice

cries out in a great shout the name of her Orisha:
"*Shangoooooooooo!*"

And all those present burst out into applause.

The formula is repeated for each Iaô, with minor variations in the manner of "descent" by each Orisha, since no two physical bodies are completely alike. Each initiate, after she has received her Orisha, is taken to an inner room where she is dressed in the full regalia pertaining to her particular Orisha: long skirts in silks and satins, all covered in trinkets, amulets from Africa to protect against the Evil Eye, strings of glass beads, sometimes trumpet-shell necklaces—all these may be used, all in colours relating to the respective Orishas. They are then reintroduced *en masse* into the tent, to the sound of frenzied and vociferous applause, each carrying the symbols of her own Orisha—an axe for a daughter of Xangô, a shepherd's stick on which the daughter of Oxalá, all in white, will support herself, a sword for the blue-clad daughter of Ogun, and so on.

At the entrance in this manner of the Orishas, no longer daughters-of-saint but merely female vehicles carrying the spirit of the divinity, the whole congregation rises, the mother-of-saint sings a special chant, and the air is filled with the joy and reverence of the public, all breathing a little faster, a little brighter of eye, but possessed of a subdued anxiety because the saints are there, the gods have come, and divinity is present.

Each Orisha (controlling, as it were, a daughter-of-saint) casts himself to the floor, face downwards, in the posture of a newly-ordained priest before his consecrating bishop; before the mother-of-saint, again he prostrates himself, afterwards embracing her three or four times. And the festivities continue . . . until, late in the evening, the mother-of-saint gives the order to end the ceremony. The Orishas return to the inner room, subsequently going back to the place whence they came, leaving in each case a very tired "daughter" behind. (In some Candomblés, the parting of the Orishas and the initiates takes place while they are still in the tent, the Iaô once more passing into a state of shivering and contortions from which she emerges with a galvanic jolt, as though shaken from a deep sleep, and the ôrunkó is over.)

After the " party," the regalia of the Iaôs is taken to the same stream used in the other rituals and washed very early the following morning, in a ceremony of purification.

Once the ôrunkó is over, the initiates themselves are free to enjoy a relative liberty. The mother-of-saint permits them even to leave the Candomblé for short strolls, for visiting other members of the Candomblé or for travelling to nearby Candomblés, and to be blessed (plus, as a side issue, to receive alms and handouts that may not only cover expenses but sometimes even exceed them!).

The first Sunday after the ôrunkó, a special ceremony is carried out, a gay and lively simulation of African customs called the " purchase " and " market " of the Iaôs. The " mother " lines all the initiates up and affects to " sell " them off, dwelling on the good qualities of each and proposing a " price " for them individually, while she explains that the buyer receives his purchase for life and that the Iaô, as would have been the case with a slave, must obey him forever. The " purchasers " are chosen beforehand, usually from among the family or close personal friends of the Iaô. In Africa, of course, the purchase would once have been " for keeps " and perfectly genuine: inter-tribal slavery has been going on for centuries and in certain regions still prevails today. In Brazil, once the deal has been approved by the " mother," the " purchaser " and the Iaô walk away together to the sound of the drums and applause of worshippers—the former's rôle being somewhat similar to that of an usher at a modern American graduation ball.

Next comes the market. Each Iaô spreads on the floor of the tent the best in Bahia cooking: pans of *Mungunzá* (grains of corn in broth sweetened with coconut milk), of *Vatapá* (manihot flour with dendê oil and pepper, slices of fish being interposed between), cans of *Aluá* (a drink made of rice flour or toasted corn with water, fermented with sugar in clay jars), plates of *Acarajé* (beans fried in dendê oil), of *Abará* (beans with pepper and dendê oil), of *Pipocas* (popcorn), bowls of *Acaçá* (a dish prepared in a special way from corn or rice flour), and a dozen other local delicacies. The initiates, still with their shaven heads and in full regalia, sit on small stools in front of their offerings, extolling the virtues of their wares to the worshippers and others present. It is in fact a true market, complete with all the shouting and banter and bargaining, but at exorbitant prices, since the financial takings are earmarked for the Candomblé and the Iaô herself! The noise and general brouhaha is tremendous.

At some Candomblés, during the market, one of the Iaôs, holding a liane in one hand, simulates a beating, a chastisement of the onlookers, who are supposed to " steal," not buy, the dainties.

At this point, it might be imagined, the end of the series of ceremonies constituting the consecration of a daughter-of-saint would have been reached: the Iaô's Orisha has been identified, she has gone through a period of initiation, she has " received " her Orisha, she has been segregated for a number of days, the Orisha has officially and publicly given her his name in the ôrunkó, and she has gone through the " purchase " and the " market "—surely she would be ready now?

In point of fact, she is not; she is not considered " made." A most important ceremony is missing, the final one that will definitely set the seal on her initiation. On the Friday following the " market," all the Iaôs, heads shaven, white spots painted all over, dressed in full regalia again, accompany either the mother-of-saint or the small-mother on a pilgrimage to hear mass at the famous Catholic church of Bonfim in Salvador. Only after this is a Iaô considered a fully consecrated daughter-of-saint. (In Candomblés centred on other cities, the pilgrimage is to the church nearest them.)

For the staggering fact is this: the consecration of initiates in what anthropologists and sociologists call a fetichistic and animistic cult of African origin reaches its crowning ceremony in the most improbable of all places—a Roman Catholic church!

Nothing could be more eloquent of the significance (and indeed uniqueness) of the religious syncretism occurring in

Brazil today. There is nothing comparable to it anywhere else in the world.

Candomblé has of course come a long way since its inception as an organised cult in 1830. At the beginning, very few whites took part in its rituals, and those that did acted secretly. Today, having triumphantly survived much criticism and intermittent police action, the movement has made its way from the hidden tents on the outskirts of Bahia to the world-famous Maracanazinho Stadium in Rio de Janeiro! On May 13, 1965, the anniversary of the freeing of slaves in Brazil, more than 500 associations of Umbanda (a far more evolved spiritual cult explained in Chapters Nine and Ten) met to honour the Iyalorixá of the famous Candomblé, *Axé de Opô Afonjá*. She had been elected " Mother-of-saint, 1965," a world title a little different and a trifle more profound than those sought after by the bikini-clad glamour girls of the western world!

The woman who heard the spiritual greeting of 500 *combos* on that day of mass adulation and frenzied excitement in the vast stadium had bestowed upon her the title of Princess of Iyá Nassô, in memory of one of the three Yoruba women who founded the Engenho Velho more than 135 years before. And she herself, her name is Maria do Espirito Santo, is said actually to be the great-great-great-grandchild of Iyá Nassô. Her Candomblé was founded some 80 years ago by the Iyalorixá Aninha, one of the most famous mothers-of-saint of all, as an offshoot from the Engenho Velho, the first known Candomblé.

Such an intensity of tradition, so close a weave of ties both physical and spiritual, probably goes a long way to explain how Candomblé has succeeded in progressing so far from its humble origin.

For, to leave for a moment the religious aspect of Candomblé, its influence on the general scene in Brazil has been manifold. Even the world-famous samba, to which dancers dip and sway in every continent, and which is responsible every year for one of the most extraordinary carnivals in the world, stems from girls who dance in the rituals of the Candomblé without "receiving" any Orishas. Voodoo, a word much used (and misused) in English to define Macumba, is but a derivation from the word Vodun—itself the Dahomey word for God, the equivalent to the Yoruba Orisha. But more than these examples of general usage, more perhaps than the May 13 rally at the Maracanazinho to honour the " Mother-of-saint, 1965," one current example is eloquent of the prestige in which Candomblé is held today.

The most popular samba at the Carnival in Rio in 1965, the song that won all the popularity contests, whose tune and lyrics are whistled more than any other, which literally ran away with the coveted first prize, was none other than the one called *Saravá Meu Pai*, an Umbanda greeting of the spirits of the old Negroes. The lyric begins:—

> *Saravá Meu Pai, vou me benzer,*
> *Vou pedir ao Pai de Santo,*
> *Para quebrar o teu encanto,*
> *Para me proteger.*

> *Hail, My Father, I shall bless myself,*
> *I'm going to ask the Father-of-saint*
> *To break your charm,*
> *And to protect me.*

CHAPTER FIVE

Spiritism Sets Foot in Brazil

W E have seen that Brazilian gentry practically sucked a knowledge of magic from the breasts of their Negro milk-mothers. This, allied to the widespread toleration and even encouragement of miscegenation, the hospitable climate with its ever-present sunshine and exuberant vegetation, an education emphasising the humanities and philosophical knowledge—all this contributed to the development of an innate spirit of tolerance which distinguishes the Brazilian character today, and to the mystic outlook of the Brazilian himself, with his lighthearted attitude towards strict rules and dogma.

The Catholic missionaries who were " in at the beginning " of Brazil's history were unable to enforce the rigid codes of their church in the lush and exotic country to which they had been sent, nor could the padres following them stop the land-lords, the white masters, from exploiting an easy access first to Indian, then to Negro women, with all the pleasures of easy and frequent intercourse that followed.

Thus the Brazilian became conditioned to a breaking away from the strict rules of Europe, and behaviour that would be socially unacceptable there, and intolerable to a European nobleman, came to be accepted as the norm in Brazil (Freyre, for example, relates several instances of landowners carefully selecting young Negro women from the household for the excellence of their breasts, and then having these wait at table during important dinner parties naked from the waist up).

All these factors, of course, would strongly influence the

mentality of the Brazilian intellectual, who in his turn developed a mind far more flexible and open than that of his European counterpart. He was thus that much more receptive to ideas, attitudes and suggestions which the Occident might normally dismiss as eccentric and unscientific.

Officially, of course, he would reject out of hand the " primitive rites " of African Negroes and their descendents. But he would be familiar enough with the magic world of fetichism in which they lived, and he would not be above secretly carrying an amulet, say, to ward off the Evil Eye: conscious or not, his allegiance to the supernatural was established; it was there.

Nor are things different today. As *Ramos says: " Brazil lives impregnated with magic. The medicine-man, the feticheer, has among our populations a prestige considerably greater than the directors of our destinies—it is necessary to have the courage to confess it." Padre Pascoal Lacroix, a Catholic priest and sociologist who made a profound study of the modern religious paradox of Brazil, concluded: " In our country, the general average of true Catholics does not exceed ten per cent. There is an extremely large number of neo-pagans and spiritualists in every locality, however small it may be, and a very high percentage also in the cities." Nina Ribeiro sums it up: " The number of whites, mulattoes and individuals of all colours and colour gradations who, in their afflictions, in their troubles, laugh at the powers of talismans and feticheers, but secretly consult them and heed them, is incalculable."

Such a link with primitive " animist " religious rites having been established, we see that the miscegenation of races not only has its counterpart in religious syncretism, but also serves as a bridge to the acceptance of a much higher, rational, intellectual, cultured philosophical approach to the consideration of man's relationship with the divine. So far, we have been talking mainly of worshippers and members of the public drawn from the humbler strata of society. Now the time has come to consider the better educated.

*Famous Brazilian anthropologist Arthur Ramos.

The first instance of such an approach being sought in Brazil resulted from the intellectual progress following the transference of the Portuguese reigning family to the country, where they found refuge from the Napoleonic armies who had invaded Portugal in 1807.

By 1818, there was already a group of neo-spiritualists at court, led by minister José Bonifácio de Andrada, later to become Brazil's " Patriarch of Independence." Theirs was not a religious approach; rather did they take their empiric cue from Hahnemann, the founder of homœopathy, with whom Bonifácio de Andrada maintained a correspondence. It was in fact through homœopathy that spiritualism penetrated Brazil: Hahnemann's approach to the cure of a body's ailment via the help of God, by making the soul react in search of a cure, appealed very much to the broadminded but mystically inclined Brazilians. It was not until 1840, nevertheless, that homœopathy itself was actively practised and spread abroad through two dedicated doctors: a Portuguese, João Vicente Martins, and a Frenchman, Dr. Mure, author of *Absolute Philosophy*. Both doctors were spiritualists in the sense that they were mystics believing in the power of a higher divinity as applied to everyday life, though since the movement proper was not to start until the days of Andrew Jackson Davies and the Fox Sisters in the United States some years later, it is probably more correct to refer to them still as neo-spiritualists.

The two doctors devoted almost all their time to treating the poor free of charge. Together with their " little phials of water with sugar " (as critics dubbed homœopathic medicines), and the small pills of which patients were directed to swallow one every hour, they succoured the sick and needy of Brazil. Their main aim was simply the cure of the body, but both of them supplemented the homœopathic medicines with " magnetic treatment," passing their outstretched hands over the patient without touching him, at a distance of three to four inches, as they prayed for God's help in the cure. Hahnemann also privately recommended this use of the *passe* as an auxiliary means to effect a cure, and later it became a main feature of spiritism, which was also to "borrow" from the two doctors the slogan under which they worked: *God, Christ and Charity*.

This motto was to become the cornerstone, the basis on which spiritism built its formidable edifice in Brazil. Instead of the table-rappings and other extra-ordinary, publicity-stimulating phenomena of spiritualism and the Fox Sisters, the Brazilian movement would find its roots in homœopathy, and its purpose in the practice of charity in the name of God and Christ and the cure of the body's ills.

In the meantime, the homœopathic, neo-spiritualist groups headed by the doctors and their friends in Brazil received with enthusiasm the publication in 1847 of Andrew Jackson Davies's *The Principles of Nature, Her Divine Revelation*. Davies was a poor cobbler who had had only a rudimentary education, and the book, which he said that he had written in half or in total trance, revealed a quantity of fantastic information which he could not possibly have had of his own knowledge, and proved a testament to his extraordinary powers of mediumship.

In 1848, Dr. Mure returned to France, leaving his associate to continue the good work and make more converts to the principles of homœopathy. Two of these, Doctors Melo Morais and Castro Lopes, later founded the first private spiritist group in Brazil. Documents register the group as having experimented in active communication with the "dead" as early as 1853, three years before Allan Kardec published his first book. The group, officially started by Morais, included Lopes, the Marquis of Olinda, the Viscount Uberaba, General Pinto and other notables of the day. Unlike the rituals of the African, spiritualism was introduced to Brazil by contacts in the very highest social strata.

The next development was the arrival in Brazil of a book. Brought into the country in 1858 in the luggage of a Portuguese nobleman, this was called *The Book of Spirits*. It had been published in Paris two years before, and it was one of the strangest, most intriguing, and certainly the most unlikely compendiums ever published! It contained one thousand and eighteen questions and answers about the problem that has tortured the human mind since the dawn of history, may be responsible for the " despair " of humanity mentioned in his first presidential campaign by Lyndon Johnson, and has by no means exhausted all speculation yet—Is there a life after death? And what is the purpose of our life here?

But in this case it was not the questions but the answers that were so (literally) out of this world! They derived from rapping tables, from pencils which wrote on pads without anyone holding them, from voices in dark rooms, from ignorant people who wrote in a trance on the most abstruse and metaphysical questions. And they were all collected together by a French professor, Denizard Hippolyte-Leon-Rivail, who wrote under the pseudonym of Allan Kardec.

Although it is dubious whether " spirits " were really responsible for the answers to the questions as Kardec claims, the fact remains that the completed questionnaire forms in effect a philosophical system of depth and the highest moral meaning. For the answers systematise the innumerable psychic experiments which were a characteristic feature of the period, striking a popular note even among the mighty, Napoleon III among others, and they also explain the mechanism obtaining at that time in " communications " with the dead, and in deriving the moral consequences of " their " teachings. In essence, the sum of the questions-and-answers affirms that man is a spirit materially enveloped by a body; that the spirit itself is non-material but that it has a " semi-material " cover individualising it and endowing it with " personality," which is referred to as a " peri-spirit "; and that the peri-spirit covering connects the spirit proper with the body. When the body no longer offers conditions suitable for functioning and " dies," the spirit continues to live, still enclosed by its semi-material peri-spirit. This state is normally invisible to us but can become visible, even tangible, under certain conditions. It is not an abstraction: it can be seen, heard, smelled or felt, which accounts for the many cases of psychic " apparitions " on record. And the spirit/peri-spirit state has the same " personality " as when it was enveloped by heavier material, i.e., the body.

Life in the world of matter (the book teaches) is a trial that the spirit has to go through many times, as many as may be necessary until moral perfection is attained. The spirit thus has to pass through many incarnations, in many different " bodies," and we each have many " lives." A spirit is superior, medium, inferior, or evil, according to his state of evolution. A good man is the incarnation of a good spirit, a bad man of a bad one. When they are enclosed only by a peri-spirit but have no body, spirits can communicate with man, *and the quality of the spirit answering man's call will be commensurate with the purpose and quality of the person, or group of persons, evoking the spirits.* The superior spirits will answer the call of the seriously inclined, those well-intentioned people who genuinely seek guidance with love in their hearts and a sincere desire to learn and improve. Those moved solely out of curiosity, a desire to experience different emotions and to have fun, on the other hand, will attract only those spirits with an affinity for that kind of attitude.

Like Swedenborg at the beginning of the 18th century, Kardec termed the person serving as intermediary between the physical world and the spiritual world a " medium."

The superior spirits, according to the book, teach that their *mores* are the same as Christ's: Do unto others as you would be done unto. In other words: do good, not evil. Egoism, pride, sensuality, the book shows, send us nearer to the animal level; loving our fellow men draws us nearer to the spiritual level. Each one of us should be as useful as is possible in accordance with the means God has put in our hands. In the world of the spirit, nothing remains occult: the hypocrite will be unmasked, our mental sins will be ranged out in the open, the offenders will constantly see the offended in their minds, this being one of the penalties and sufferings they will have incurred through their actions. Yet no evil is unpardonable, no sin too great for expiation through the many incarnations God offers, and all men will ultimately reach perfection according to their own desires for progress, in a longer or shorter period.

Such a doctrine of rational love, such a code of spirit world and spiritual life, the doctrine of reincarnation itself, these fell like rain into the intellectual desert where the Brazilian neo-spiritualists and followers of homœopathy stood parched, waiting for a sign. The French book was eagerly passed from hand to hand in the Imperial court. By 1860, Portuguese rivals began to appear in print—Professor Casimir Lieutand's *The Times Have Come*, and Professor Alexandre Canu's *Spiritism In Its Simpler Expression*, for instance. On September 23, 1863, the most prestigious of Brazilian dailies, *O Jornal do Comércio*, published a long article in praise of the new doctrine, an occurrence which would have been impossible had not spiritism had followers in very high places, for in the days of Dom Pedro II's Brazilian Empire the intelligentsia and the "notables" of the court were a very small percentage of the country's population.

The movement had enemies as well, of course. Four days later, the *Diário da Bahia* reprinted an article from the French *Gazette Medicale* poking fun at seances and ridiculing contact with the dead. One day later, four distinguished doctors of medicine in Brazil signed a rebuttal, which not only had a striking effect in Brazil but also called Allan Kardec's attention to his Latin American followers (according to a comment in his own *Revue Spirite*, vol. 8, p. 334).

The publicity was widely circulated and resulted in converts and adherents in several states in Brazil. A few months after the original article had appeared, many private spiritist circles had been formed, mostly in the homes of those sympathising with the new doctrines. These were intimate seances, started with a prayer and going on to an evocation of spirits. Messages were occasionally received from "the other world," but in general procedure was limited to study of the novel views and mediums were few and far between. The first spiritist magazine published in Brazil dates back to that time. First appearing in 1869, it was directed by Teles de Menezes, a member of the History Institute of Bahia, had 60 pages, and was called *The Echo From Beyond The Grave.*

In the same year, on March 31, Kardec died. His passing brought to an end the first period in Brazil and his native France of the movement to which he had contributed so much. For although there had been a spiritualist movement of a sort in Brazil before his time, it was only the seed of what was to come, and it took Kardec's own remarkable publication to bring that seed to flower. But the flowering was to be profuse beyond anyone's dreams, just because there was more to it *than* dreams: there was the understanding of the profound moral meaning of the principles involved, and there were the spirit messages. There were plenty of these in America too, of course. And in Europe. The difference in Brazil was that they were taken seriously; people followed their teachings; they were acted upon.

When Kardec died, no official bodies practising spiritism existed. The only groups there were, met in private houses, but the adherents of the movement were legion, mainly among professional people such as doctors, engineers, lawyers, university professors, artists and military men. Soon, the need for a society correlating the activities of all these individuals and acting as a spearhead for spiritism was felt. Such a body was incorporated in August, 1873, under the name " Group Confucius." This was no bow, however well deserved, in the direction of the great Chinese sage, but a form of homage to a particular spirit guide which had many times imparted messages in the home of one of the group's founders, Dr. Siqueira Dias, and had always signed them " Confucius." The group was predominantly of homœopathic doctors (its President, Vice-President and Secretary were all Hahnemann medics), and it functioned along the lines laid down by the movement's predecessors under the slogan *Without Charity there is no Salvation,* a sentence, coined by Kardec and his spirit communications, based on St. Paul (I Corinthians 8: 3-13).

Charity, indeed, was to become the driving force behind spiritism in Brazil. It took two main forms: spiritual healing and social assistance to the poor. Explaining the latter is no

93

problem: in the underdevelopeu regions of the earth, even today, happily it still exists. There are still selfless people, devoted and eager to serve, who are ready to sacrifice their own well-being in the interests of ameliorating the lot of others. About the former, however, a few words of explanation are necessary.

The spiritual healing practised in Brazil took on an entirely different form to that known in England and the United States of America. In the first place, Brazilian mediums actually *receive* medical prescriptions which are dedicated to them through a spirit guide.

The medium is known as a healing-medium and the prescriptions are mostly homœopathic. The Group Confucius was the first to establish an organisation dispensing a free service of homœopathic prescriptions given through healing-mediums on certain days of the week.

Secondly, and perhaps more importantly, mediumship was exercised under the evangelical motto *Give freely what you have received freely* (Matthew 10: 8, " Heal the sick, cleanse the lepers, raise the dead, cast out devils: freely ye have received, freely give " or, in the modern English version by J. B. Philips, " Give as you have received, without any charge whatever ").

Here were no entrance fees, subscriptions, " silver collections " or requests for financial " help to defray costs." The majority of the practitioners were well-to-do professional people and the prescriptions really were filled " without any charge whatever."

These two factors, total and genuine lack of cost to the healed and treatment by specific medicaments " prescribed " by spirits rather than generalised healing through their aid, are the main differences between Brazilian and other branches of the movement. The fact that they exist is the main reason why Brazilians adopted the term spiritism to distinguish their particular form from the more widely known spiritualism practised elsewhere.

There is one other thing underlining the difference: the identity of the spirit guides who make themselves known to

94

the mediums. For who were the chief "spirit doctors" actually "signing" these prescriptions? None other than Doctors Bento Mure and João Vicente Martins, the very pair who had in this life first introduced homœopathy to Brazil and treated the poor without charging under the banner *God, Christ and Charity*!

Such "continuance" of loyalty to the group especially distinguishes spiritism, many of whose sincerest followers that in "earthly" life excelled as presidents of spiritist societies, as outstanding mediums, as doctors to the poor, as writers or in other relevant activities, have "come back" from the "other world" and continued their work through modern mediums, thus lending the movement an unusual sense of coherence and a feeling of unending continuity.

To return to the Group Confucius, this body undertook to publish the first Portuguese versions of Allan Kardec's main works: *The Book Of Spirits, The Book of Mediums* and *The Gospels According To Spiritism*. Public reaction to the works, translated by the Group's Secretary-General, Joaquim Carlos Travassos, was enthusiastic and, like a chain reaction, readership has snowballed until, today, when all the books are selling faster than ever, sales exceed a million and a half copies!

The movement itself has blossomed from that first small group in 1873 into no less than 3,214 officially registered societies (as recorded by the 1960 census); the original free homœopathic service into 1,695 social assistance establishments now spread all over Brazil. And it must be noted, also, that the real number of spiritist groups, usually called Centres now, is far greater than the officially registered figure. This is simply because, to quote the President of the Brazilian Spiritist Federation, "the great majority in the interior of Brazil don't bother about legal formalities: only those in the big cities take the trouble of going through the red tape." An informed, moderate estimate of the true number of spiritist *Centres* in Brazil today puts the figure as high as 100,000.

A similar situation obtains in the case of the true number of spiritists themselves. More than a million were registered at the 1960 census. But the number of those calling them-selves Catholic, "because my family is Catholic and I was raised a Catholic," but who follow the morning Mass by attending a spiritist session at night, is at least three times as big, according to one eminent priest. A conservative assess-ment places the number of spiritists practising Kardec's system as over four million.

The original Group Confucius embraced the teaching embodied in *The Book Of Spirits* and *The Book Of Mediums,* but conspicuously ignored Kardec's *Gospels.* The latter work interprets the Gospels in the light of teaching by certain spirit guides, making, among other provocative assertions, the points that Jesus is not God, that miracles do not occur, that reincarnation is a fact but that neither Hell nor Heaven, as specific, isolate "regions," exist. Both resurrection and the Virgin Birth are myths, the book teaches, Natural Law being so perfect that God would never break it merely to prove His own existence: rather would he prove just how wonder-ful His Laws are by sending someone who would teach us how to live them.

Such views, although entirely commensurate with the data and acceptable by a logician as a theory respectable enough to fit the facts, were considered far too controversial to promul-gate in a country like Brazil in the nineteenth century. The people had strong religious sentiments and only if spiritism was allied to *orthodox* Christianity, free of any taint of the heretical, would it have a chance in the country, the group felt, besides which, a too-rigid adherence to Kardec's third work would destroy the main characteristics of the movement derived from the other two. It was only later that the book was accorded equal recognition with them.

Support for this line of thought was to come from high up, straight from the spirit world, in fact! A message from " Con-fucius " said: " Our mission, as well as yours, is to meet those with goodwill. Christ said: ' When you get together in My Name, I will be among you.' To us, and we are not the Master, has been given the task to assist you, to give you courage, and to say to you: Men of goodwill, may Faith,

ABOVE: Jerônimo Candido Gomide and his wife, Dona Chiquinha, founders of the city of Palmelo, seen in the background. This is the only spiritist city in the world. BELOW, LEFT: The 1964 stamp marking the centenary of *The Gospels According to Spiritism*. BELOW, RIGHT: A scene at the Spiritist Centre of Light and Truth in the middle of Palmelo. At the command of Candido Gomide several mediums extend their hands over bottles of water, thus endowing the water with healing powers.

ABOVE: Chico Xavier receiving a spiritual message at a session in Uberaba. At a kardecist session no uniforms or incense are used, but, as can be seen from the photograph, glasses of water are always present. BELOW, LEFT: Francisco Candido Xavier in typical 'receiving' position. BELOW, RIGHT: Jerônimo Candido Gomide preaches the 'Gospel According to Spiritism' at the Spiritist Centre in Palmelo.

Charity and Union cheer your hearts and permit the good spirits to be with you! With these sentiments, you will see your strength increases and your means to do good increase tenfold. And if you are humble and recognise that these things are gifts from our Father and not the effects of your own personality, then blessings will cover you and you will have the glory of having participated in the work of regeneration, applying the law of progress. Have Courage, Faith, Perseverence, and we shall always be with you."

Subsequently Kardec himself took the trance-medium under his control to underwrite the prevailing view and tell the group: " To work in the Lord's vineyard is to take to your incarnate brothers courage, consolation, abnegation and, above all, hope—and to take those at variance with you the path to happiness which they have lost. Work ceaselessly, and you shall be aided, enlightened and blessed."

A rare message from a spiritual entity considered to be of a higher status than either of these was rather more to the point. This Being, to whom even Kardec (from above or wherever he was) paid special homage, explaining that this guide had a very special mission towards Brazil, " transmitted " the following message:

" Brazil has the mission of Christianising. It is the promised land. The land of all. The land of fraternity. The land of Jesus. The land of the Gospel. It was not by chance that it took the name of the Holy Cross [as the country was originally known, soon after its discovery]. It was not by accident that it has received from the cradle the milk of Christian religion. It was not without reason that the first navigators saw it under the light of the Southern Cross. In the New Era, which is near, it will be the home of a people different from others through their Christian habits. It is up to those now hearing the heralds from space [the spiritual world] to summon all men of goodwill to prepare the New Era, to *recognise in Jesus the Spiritual Leader. With the Gospels explained in the light of Spiritism, Jesus's moral, sown by the Jesuits and fed by the Catholics, will accomplish its purpose, which is to rejuvenate the old men, the people born here or that will*

97

come here from all parts of the globe, tired of fratricidal fights and thirsty for brotherhood. The Spiritists' mission in Brazil is to divulge the Gospels in spirit and in truth.

" Those that wish to do their duty well, to which they have obligated themselves before being born, must thus assemble under this trinitarian canopy: ' God, Christ and Charity.' Where this banner is, there shall I be also."

The message, so specific and to the point, was signed " Ismael."

Later messages explained to the group that " Ismael " was in fact the spirit guide of Brazil itself, entrusted with the mission of guiding the nation towards its high spiritual destiny. All of which may sound a trifle melodramatic, or even " corny " by modern standards, but the important thing, and the sociological and historical fact, is that those receiving this message believed in it. And today " Ismael " is still recognised as the spiritual guide of Brazil—not just by a small group but by the country's many million Kardecists (as those strictly adhering to the principles embodied in Kardec's works are termed).

The activities of the Group Confucius led to the formation of other societies in other places and, on Christmas Night, 1883, a group of spiritists led by Augusto Elias da Silva decided to form a federation to unite all the existing " centres " and " groups." Da Silva had already taken the initiative by founding, at the beginning of the same year, the first spiritist journal. It was called *O Reformador* (The Reformer), was subtitled " an evolutionist organ designed to reform moral and philosophical habits," and was destined to become the official gazette of the Federation. Today it shares with thirty three other spiritist magazines a combined readership of 300,000, and its own circulation is in excess of 37,000.

However, even with allies as strong as those " from above," even with the help of teachings from these so-called spirit guides, all of an undeniably high moral and spiritual calibre, it is difficult on this earth to achieve agreement, to keep together a number of people in complete harmony! And spiritists are no less subject to internecine strife than other mortals. Theirs, however, was mainly of an interpretative nature: they agreed on the facts; it was how they were to be used that was at issue. Thus, one group would see in spiritism a fascinating opportunity to probe some of nature's most closely guarded secrets. "It is a scientific exploration of the metapsychical in man's nature," a member of such a group wrote. Mediums were guinea-pigs for the "scientists" to experiment with, seances were designed to obtain physical evidence of whatever there is that our eyes cannot customarily see, meetings became academic discussions of the use of scientific terms for mediumistic phenomena. Another group, taking their cue from the works of the French writer J. B. Roustaing, defended his interpretation of the nature of Jesus in the light of spiritist beliefs—this was that Christ's body was "fluidic," formed by a magnetic concentration which fully impressed the eye and deceived the beholder into thinking it was "real" . . . only it wasn't.

Such dissensions, all of which turned attention away from the basic humanities and simple nature of the creed, might well have provoked the disintegration of the movement.

That this did not occur was due to the fact that Kardecist spiritism, which accentuated more than any other branch the *Christian* character of the movement, providentially found its own Paul in a most unlikely leader, a famous doctor, politician, businessman and writer. Adolpho Bezerra de Menezes was born on August 29, 1831, and graduated as an M.D. in 1856 when he was twenty five. Four years later he had already made a name for himself, not only as a good doctor but also as a charitable one, a man who would treat all who knocked upon his door, whether they were able to pay or not. Those English general practitioners who complain of being "overworked" and threaten to resign from their National Health Service unless they are paid more money might do well to ponder one of his pronouncements.

A true doctor, said he, does not have the right to finish his meal, to choose the time, to ask whether the call comes from near or far, on the hill or in the suburbs. The one who does not answer because he has visitors, because it is late at night

99

or because the client cannot pay, is not a doctor but a dealer in medicine, someone who works to collect interest on the capital invested in his schooling . . . He is a rascal, who closes his door to charity . . .

With his renown among the poor, Bezerra de Menezes was a natural for politics and soon became, first a state deputy, and then a federal deputy. He was a brilliant orator and before long his fame had spread further still. He was a Member of the National Academy of Medicine and presented several papers before it, he founded a railroad, and he was president of several public utility companies. In 1880, he was elected President of the State Assembly. An impressive figure, resembling, with his long beard, the Brazilian Emperor Dom Pedro II, Bezerra de Menezes was always assured of a capacity audience whenever he spoke in public. A speech extolling the virtues of Kardecism, made before the cream of Rio society in 1886 by this nationally famous man, therefore received the maximum possible publicity as well as proving something of a bombshell! Sales of Kardec's books soared as the news spread quickly throughout several states, and many that had been too timid publicly to assert their allegiance to the spiritists now did so openly after a lead from a source so unimpeachable.

Nine years later, Bezerra was invited to become President of the Brazilian Spiritist Federation.

At first he hesitated. The hegemony of the movement was being disputed by several rival factions and the organisation itself was, as he himself expressed the situation, " in a mess, without a president and without orientation." That night, he went to the Group Ismael, the successor to Group Confucius, which continued to receive spirit messages from the spirit-guide of Brazil. These were " Ismael's " words to Dr. Bezerra that night:

" Accept the invitation: it is a call. We have told you more than once that the union of the spiritists and their orientation were entrusted to you. Do not doubt and do not worry about the difficulties. Do the work of the man; without his goodwill we can do nothing. Do your duty and we shall do ours. We shall be with you . . ."

" In that case," the doctor commented after the message had been read to him, " I shall accept. I pray for the help of Jesus and all his emissaries, as well as for all my companions in this gigantic task that lies before us."

Dr. Bezerra de Menezes was elected President and inaugurated on August 3, 1895. He immediately bent all his efforts towards calling public meetings at which the Gospels were to be studied according to the spiritist interpretation, towards implementing even further the idea of social assistance to the poor (" Which means putting the Gospels into action," as he used to say), towards increasing the sales of Kardec's books, and generally towards the more efficient propagation of Kardecism, or Christian Spiritism, as he called it, throughout the country.

The same path is followed today. The movement has grown, and continues to grow, enormously. Reincarnation is now a concept familiar enough to the average man to pass without comment in a context of general idiomatic usage. Newspaper columnists make use of the term to define types of political personality; for instance: " X thinks he is a reincarnation of Napoleon " or " Y speaks with the assurance of a returned Lincoln." And the degree of Kardecist penetration throughout the land may be judged by the Postmaster General's decision to make two special-issue stamps—one, bearing Kardec's picture, to commemorate the centennial of the publication of *The Book Of Spirits* in 1856; the other, later, to mark the centenary of *The Gospel According To Spiritism,* now on a " respectable " par with its mates. Kardecism is also responsible for a unique occurrence: the founding of Palmelo, the only spiritist city of the world.

Located at about 160 miles from the plush, ultra modern new capital of Brasília, it started as a hut in about 1925, where a tall, strong man called Jerônimo Candido Gomide cured lunatics, some so mad that they were brought to him tied down to a monkey.

" My only weapon is the Kardec's Gospel According to

Spiritism, and my faith in God and his emissaries, the spiritual guides. They do all. I am only an instrument " says Candido Gomide.

As his fame grew, more and more lunatics and other sick were brought to him. " We had to build other huts to house all the sick, and improvise ' prisons ' for the aggressive lunatics," tells Gomide.

The huts became houses, the " prisons " became a lunatic asylum, and in the centre of all, instead of the traditional Catholic church that can be found in most Brazilian cities, a Spiritist Centre was built and called " Spiritist Centre of Truth and Light."

The city today has a local population of about 2,000 people, while the itinerant sick that come and go increase this figure considerably.

Palmelo is also possibly the only city without a jail: " We have no use for it here. We all read Kardec's Gospels, and no one thinks of committing a crime . . ."

CHAPTER SIX

More About Allan Kardec

SCIENCE and religion, the professor and the theologist, the humanist and the priest, these have been presented as opposite poles since the time of Darwin and before. The materialist despises the man of religion for accepting on trust that which cannot be proven in clinical tests; the cleric fears the scientist for the scorching blast of his scepticism and the damage it may do to Faith. Yet none of these labels, these categories need be antonymous. " A religion that at no point would be in contradiction with the laws of nature would have nothing to fear from progress and would be invulnerable," Allan Kardec wrote in his *Genesis.* " Religions in general draw such a pretty picture of Divinity that they do not understand that, to absorb the laws of nature that science uncovers, is to glorify God in his works.

" Science and religion are the two levers of human intelligence; one reveals the laws of the material world and the other of the moral world. But, both having the same principle —God—they cannot contradict each other."

" The time has come," Kardec added, " for the teachings of Christ to be complemented and for science to unveil some of the meanings which He purposely left occult. For this, it was necessary that new ideas and new knowledge should bring us the required light, and such ideas could only come after the human mind had sufficiently matured. Science would have to contribute heavily to the birth and development of these ideas. It was thus necessary to concede time for science to progress ..."

In a later passage, with typical broadmindedness, Kardec sees clearly the materialist's point of view. Says he: "Each religion pretends to have exclusive ownership of truth; to profess blind faith in any part of the religious creed is to confess impotence in demonstrating that one is right."

"Unshakeable faith is simply the faith that can look reason in the face in all ages of humanity."

The man who wrote the above had been looking reason in the face all his life. A professor teaching mathematics, astronomy, physiology, French, physics, chemistry and comparative anatomy, an educationalist who had for several years been a disciple of Pestalozzi in Switzerland, Hippolyte Leon-Denizard-Rivail was anything but a mystic. "In the absence of facts," he wrote once, "doubts are plainly justified." Born in Lyons in 1804, he devoted the first part of his life to his chosen profession, publishing several works in the field of education, and giving religion and spiritual matters no more attention than any normal man of that age. It was not until he was in his early fifties that his attention was drawn to certain phenomena that had put all Europe under a spell.

In the middle of the nineteenth century "you could not go to any ' salon ' without seeing the whole of society anxiously pressed around a table at which were sitting several people with their hands outstretched on it, touching each other's fingers, everybody silent and concentrated, waiting with extreme curiosity to see the table start moving," wrote a journalist of the time. "From Montmartre to the Champs-Elysées, there was not a table that they did not move . . ."

"Table-rapping," the fashionable phenomenon which had begun in the United States after the Fox Sisters had astounded the world with the celebrated rappings of Hydesville, had conquered Europe!

The most famous salon was that of Madame de Girardin, *née* Delphine Gay, a famous writer and patroness of art, beautiful and full of wit, who was married to the Count Camile de Girardin, an eminent member of "high society" as well as being a politician. Honoré de Balzac, Alexandre Dumas *Fils,* Chateaubriand, and Théophile Gautier were among the notables who patronised her seances. Even Napoleon III, himself extremely interested, organised some sessions at Versailles before the whole court, and, according to witnessess, indulged in some lengthy conversations himself with the rapping tables!

The system used then was to recite the alphabet, the table " choosing " a letter at a time by rapping when it was reached in the recitation, the whole gradually building up into words and sentences.

Even though Jung might snort that it was mass hysteria; though a majority might dismiss it either as that or as an organised fraud (though, as Rivail himself wrote many years later, " it would be difficult to explain as a fraud how an enormous table weighing more than forty pounds, after answering questions for more than three hours, could be lifted six feet from the ground and then smashed into several pieces without anyone touching it ")—even so, let us, just for the sake of history, tell the story as it actually happened, whether or not we are willing to accept its premises.

The fact is that table-rappings were going on all over the place and all manner of questions were being put to whoever or whatever supplied the answers. Curiosity was greater than scientific interest, the desire for novel experiences greater than the thirst for knowledge. Although the query, *Who is there?*, was inevitably answered, via the raps, as *Spirits of those you call dead,* nobody really troubled to follow up the implications of this reply. Despite the presence of the highly cultured and the learned, no one bothered to go beyond establishing the mere presence of " the dead " and wondering at their extraordinary knowledge of personal trivia relating to the spectators. The ladies were in transports over the recovery of some lost object, the discovery of some secret concerning a lover; the men were eager, half defensive and half impressed, part scornful and part in awe, to know about their past and future. Nobody concerned themselves with the consequences except Professor Rivail.

At first absolutely incredulous about the mere possibility of a table " rapping," he was genuinely aghast at what he saw when finally he witnessed it for himself, and decided to probe fully into the phenomena and their implications. "It took me a whole year of constant work," he wrote, "before I was convinced of the reality of the phenomena at all . . ."

And when he was convinced . . . spiritism had been born! Strange though it may seem, this new interpretation, this doctrine or system known throughout a Latin American country of eight million square kilometres by most of its eighty million population, and followed by more than fifteen per cent. of the adults among these, was born through a session of table rapping a hundred years ago.

Originally, the method of "communicating" with the dead was to take a movable object such as a board, a box, or a basket even, to which was attached a pencil with its point resting on a piece of paper. The medium would then put his hand over the object and the pencil would start to move under the influence of the "communicating" spirit, thus writing out its message. Later it was recognised that this method was unnecessarily clumsy: the "object" was merely complicating the mechanics of communication and the medium could perfectly well hold the pencil himself and allow it to write under the spirit's influence when in trance. The former system did have the advantage of "demonstrating the independence of the medium from the communicating spirit," as Professor Rivail pointed out. But since the majority of seances at that time were not for the purpose of convincing a sceptical public but for the purpose of further informing those who already accepted on trust the fact that the medium was not "faking," the latter method was generally adopted as far more convenient.

Rivail was told during one of these sessions that among his former incarnations was one spent among the Druids under the name of Allan Kardec. The name pleased him, and he therefore decided that in future all his writings on the occult, the descriptions of his experiments in the super-natural, and the findings of his investigations into spirit communication would be published under this name.

This was the age of reason: the nineteenth century saw the

birth of Auguste Comte's Positivism, of Marx's Communism. The academies of science ardently professed their dissociation from the concept of God. Darwin was to administer the *coup de grâce* to the idea of man's origin as described in the Bible. Scepticism and materialism were the order of the day and religion was ineluctably associated with ritual, dogma and blind faith. On to this rationalist stage, then, Kardec dragged table-rapping, the sentient control of psychic phenomena and the other furniture of spiritualism at that time. Ironically, the reaction against materialism was to be started by matter itself—matter moving about, giving signs of " life," controlled by an intelligence, all in a manner completely at variance with all known physical laws!

Most people's approach to these phenomena was undeniably frivolous, yet there were many messages received that possessed a high moral, spiritual, philosophical and even religious meaning. By collecting these painstakingly and imposing an order, a sequence upon them rationally and methodically, Kardec synthesised a distillate of their teachings, and created thus the foundation of spiritism.

At the outset, of course, he had no such intention: he was merely systematising a great wealth of amorphous material, with no idea of what patterns it might reveal. Still less could he have realised at first that the table-rappings were produced by spirits, among them those whose teachings were of such a highly evolved significance that they could justifiably term themselves Messengers of God, nor that these might identify themselves variously as the " Comforter," the " Spirit of Truth " and so on, that Christ had promised to send (John XIV: 16-17), explaining all the mysteries shrouding the Gospels, such as the miracles and the personality of the Saviour Himself. He had no idea that from these communications a mystic religious idea was to evolve which could satisfy both reason and heart. For unlike all previous religious movements, which originated in a mystical leader whose acts, if not claimed as miraculous by himself, were later by his followers, and whose " special relationship " to God was invariably stressed, spiritism began simply with a phenomenon, something which could be witnessed as easily in New York, in Rome or in Paris. Nobody made any claims: the sole subject even to claim attention was that of the phenomena themselves.

At first it was simply table-rapping. Then it was rapping divided into categories (one rap for yes, two for no, and so on). Then it was words and sentences formed by selective rapping actuated during a recited alphabet. Then writing with a pencil attached to a board and, finally, direct writing by a medium in trance.

Kardec studied systematically for more than a year, " collecting " messages received at several different groups, among them those of his friends the Plainemaisons and the Baudins, in rue Grange-Bateliere and rue Rochechouart respectively. He made a point of obtaining data from more than one source and then checking the answers collected through one medium with those from another. " If the phenomena were *restricted* to the movement of physical objects," he wrote, " then they would have remained in the realm of the physical sciences. It was discovered, however, that the movements of objects were directed by an intelligence. If this mysterious power existed, what was its nature, what was its origin?

" A spirit; a genie, the mysterious Being answered, giving his name (which might vary from occasion to occasion) and further information about himself . . . An important fact to note is that none of the onlookers had ever suggested or anticipated that 'spirits' would be the answer to the phenomena: it was the phenomena themselves that revealed this and first used the word. It was quite unlike the story with the exact sciences, when frequently a hypothesis is formulated as a basis for reasoning, and later the facts are found to fit it.

" The change from table-rapping to the board with the attached pencil also resulted from advice, given simultaneously in the United States and several countries in Europe, from the spirits themselves . . ."

Kardec himself describes his researches as follows:

" I was confronted with a fact that was contrary to the laws of nature as we knew them, and repugnant to my reason.

But one night in May, 1855, at the home of Madame Plaine-maison, I myself witnessed the phenomenon of tables circling around, jumping and even running, as it were, in such conditions that any doubts were dispelled. That was a fact: there must be a cause, I thought. Something very serious is behind all this stuff that serves merely to entertain the spectators . . .

" Later, I met the Baudin family, who carried out weekly sessions that I began to visit. There, the Baudin sisters served as mediums, using a basket through which answers were given on subjects about which they knew nothing, including even questions that I had mentally made . . . the inference of an external intelligence was proven beyond doubt.

". . . I applied the experimental method, accepting no preconceived idea, and soon I fully understood the seriousness of my task, and I thought that in these obscure and controversial phenomena could be the key to the problem of the past and future of humanity. It was a complete revolution in the ideas and beliefs of the world.

" One of the first results of my observations was to realise that, as souls of men, the spirits did not have complete wisdom or science, that their knowledge was limited to their degree of advancement and that their opinions had the value of personal opinions only. This fact, which I recognised from the beginning, preserved me from the danger of believing in their infallibility, and also from formulating premature theories on the messages received from one or the other spirits.

" The mere fact of the communication with the spirits, quite independently from anything they might have to say, proved the existence of the invisible world: a capital point, an immense field open to our exploring . . . I soon realised that each spirit gave me an account of a *phase* of this world according to his position and knowledge. It was as one gets to know a strange country, questioning its inhabitants from every walk of life, each being able to teach something, but none being able to teach everything.

" It was up to the observer to form a complex whole, coordinating and co-relating one document with another as they were obtained. I proceeded with the spirits as I would with men, considering each one, from the smallest to the greatest, as elements of instruction and not as predestined revealers. To observe, compare and judge: that was my unchangeable rule.

"The sessions at the Baudins' never had a predetermined objective: at them, I tried to solve problems that interested me, on philosophy, psychology and the nature of the invisible world. In each session, I presented a series of questions methodically arranged, and I always obtained precise, profound and logical answers. The meetings were thus changed in their character: among the assistants now were serious persons who took great interest in my studies; the frivolous questions had lost their attraction to the majority. At first, I envisaged nothing more than my own learning; later, when I realised that the fruits of my studies were beginning to assume the proportions of a doctrine, I thought of making public the knowledge for all. It was these questions, developed and completed, that formed the basis for *The Book Of Spirits*.

"Next year, in 1856, I also attended meetings at rue Tiquetone, at the home of Monsieur Roustan and Mademoiselle Japhet, a somnambulist. My work was almost finished, but I wanted to review what I had in the light of answers from other spirits through other mediums . . . However the spirits asked for private and special sessions for this purpose, to avoid indiscretions and premature comment. But I was not satisfied with this revision that the spirits had themselves proposed. I got to know other mediums and whenever I had the opportunity, I formulated several questions, the ones whose answers seemed the most difficult, to put to them. In this way more than ten mediums assisted in the work and it was from the comparison, the fusion of all these answers, co-ordinated, classified, that I compiled the first edition of *The Book Of Spirits,* published in 1857."

The book, with its 1,018 questions and answers, is divided into three parts. The first deals with " primary causes "— God, the general elements of the universe, the Creation and the vital principle, etc. Part Two occupies itself with "the spiritual world of the spirits"—their origins and nature, the peri-spirit, the different orders of spirits, the progression of spirits, and the meaning of angels and devils. Subsequent chapters deal with the objective of the incarnation of the spirit, the return of the spirit after the body dies, reincarnation, the plurality of existences [and—in 1857!—contains an affirmation of the plurality of inhabited worlds], progressive transmigration [to more advanced planets], the destiny of children after death, sex in spirits, love, hatred and suffering experienced by spirits in the spirit world, and the spirit's return to earthly life. The section also answers questions on why we do not remember our past incarnations, clairvoyance, somnambulism and dreams. And it "zeroes in" on metempsychosis which, according to the answers given, is beyond the bounds of possibility.

The third part is the most important. It deals with moral laws, and there are twelve chapters of questions and answers on natural and divine law (which the book equates), survival, destruction, progress, equality, justice, love, charity and moral perfection, among other abstracts. Part Four occupies itself with hope and consolation, penalties, suffering, expiation and repentance, happiness and unhappiness now and in the future, heaven, purgatory and hell.

Kardec of course knew nothing of the answers he would get to his carefully prepared questions, and of course naturally he knew nothing of the subject. A full appreciation of the deep insight he came to have, and thus of the meaning of spiritism itself, can only be conveyed through a complete reading of his works on the subject, chiefly the one above, *The Book Of Mediums,* which reveals the fundamental mechanics of communication with the spirits, and *The Gospels As Interpreted By Spiritism.* The latter is the most complete work, presenting a full understanding of our past, present and future lives, with reasons, that can be accepted by any logical mind. It really does "speak to the heart and satisfy the mind," which is no doubt why it is now the most popular of Kardec's works in Brazil.

He himself defines spiritism very neatly as " at the same time a science of observation and a philosophical doctrine. As a practical science, it consists of the relations that are established between ourselves and the spirits; as a philosophy, it comprises all the moral consequences emanating from these relations." As a science, he wrote elsewhere, it dealt with the nature, origin and destiny of spirits, as well as with their relationship to the physical world.

Alfred Russell Wallace, the famous naturalist, put it: " Spiritism demonstrates the existence of other states of matter, and other means of being, that are unacceptable when analysed from the point of view of strict physical science. It demonstrates that the spirit can exist without brain (as we know it), independent of any weighable material substance; it destroys our preconceived ideas of the annihilation of our existence after the disorganisation and destruction of the physical body; it demonstrates through direct proofs, as conclusive as permissible under the circumstances, that the supposed dead are still alive, that these friends of ours are many times among us, although invisible. They themselves give us the certainty of a future life."

Spiritism, says Dr. Gustave Geley, " differs from the religions because of the complete absence of mysticism, evoking no revelations, much less the supernatural. It admits only the experimental facts, with the deductions that those facts will bear . . ."

In the final chapter, we shall evaluate spiritism and other concepts in the light of modern science. For the moment, it may be convenient to summarise the precepts arising from Kardec's work in accordance with scientific knowledge a century ago when he wrote it. It is of course impossible to communicate in a few words that which took several books to establish, but some synoptic idea of Kardec's teaching can be given by stating the Divine Laws, the Laws of Nature, that, according to spiritism, rule the universe, expanding these where necessary with explanatory material summarised from Kardec's writings.

—God is the Creator of the universe, the Supreme Intelligence, Supreme Love, the Cause of Everything.

—Spirits are the individualisation of the Intelligent Principle of the Universe. They were created by God simple, ignorant and with their own free will. Exercising this free will, they progress through multiple incarnations and evolve to ever higher stages of intelligence and love.

The spirit, Kardec learned, is as we have seen enveloped in a semi-material body called a peri-spirit. This, which is of a fluid nature, personifies the spirit and gives it its exterior individuality, just as the normal body as we know it, in the material world we inhabit, becomes the expression of the spirit while living in that material world. The spirit is connected to the body via the peri-spirit. When the body can no longer function, then the spirit, still enveloped in the peri-spirit, will leave it, much as a fruit will lose its seeds. This phenomenon is what we call death.

The act of taking a human body, of being born in a human body, is termed incarnation; that of leaving it, of dying, is called disincarnation. Similarly the spirit with an earthly body is an incarnate spirit and one without is a disincarnate spirit.

The peri-spirit is at the same time composed of electricity, of the " magnetic fluid " and, to a certain degree, of matter. As the spirit is the principle of intelligence, so it is the principle of organic life, of exterior perceptions. When it resides within the body, the organs serve as conduits to impress the peri-spirit with sensations. When freed from the material body, the spirit experiences sensations via the peri-spirit in the same manner: its impressions when disincarnate will depend upon advancement of the mind, morally and intellectually.

—Each spirit is responsible for his own actions. For each action there is a reaction—the Law of Karma—which is exercised through the Law of Reincarnation.

Spirits evolve and progress through the exercise of their own free will, by incarnating and disincarnating successively, until perfection is reached and further incarnations are no longer necessary. Experience is acquired in each incarnation, in different ages, environments, circumstances, countries and planets. What is learned in one is not forgotten in another although, except in rare cases, the physical body, the physical brain is given no recollection by the spirit of experiences in previous incarnations. (See final chapter, on higher degrees of evolvement and perception.)

This fact has frequently been used as one of the main arguments against the law of reincarnation. Apart from the rare exceptions e.g., those children remembering their last incarnation and giving names to their previous parents, details of where they themselves had lived, died and been buried, all checked, documented and found proved, Kardec himself advanced an argument cogent enough to still criticism. "What would be the position," he asked, "of a man knowing that he had been hanged for crimes in his past incarnation? Could he face the problems of this one? Would he not be haunted by a guilt complex? How many people actually do cast a veil over their past when they reach a certain stage in society? How many say, 'If only I could start again, I'd not make all the mistakes I have made'? That is exactly what God does for us: he gives us a second chance, a new body, a new environment. Nobody knows what we have done in the past; and neither do we. But all our qualities, those we have acquired in numerous incarnations, are there in the form we term talents, and our inclinations to evil, too. It is up to us to resist the inclinations, the temptations we feel. Our conscience is the voice of the spirit and will always point to the right way. In the eyes of the world we are a new man; in the eyes of God a spirit with a new opportunity."

But although isolated in this way from his own previous lives, man is not alone: since there are always multitudes sharing the same tastes, with parallel affinities, a spirit is always surrounded by a cluster of those with a like mind, and he himself always finds those spheres least likely to be inimical to his persona, good or bad.

Thus derives the picture of hell so well painted by Dante, for example, not as a place created by God for man's eternal punishment, but as a series of inferior spheres created by the mental pictures bred by evil minds. A Torquemada continues to be a Torquemada when disincarnate, for all sentiments absorbed by the peri-spirit in life, love, hatred, learning or ignorance, gaiety or sadness, friendship or indifference, are imprinted on the spirit and persist when the body dies. And he will therefore gravitate towards a sphere where there are many other Torquemadas. But the difference in the spirit world is that, as soon as he *realises* what he is doing, then the spirit is on his way back to the path of morality. Through sufferings both disincarnate and incarnate, which will be proportional to his deviation from the divine laws of morality and love, he will be able to expiate and repent the evil he has spread around him and change it within himself to the desire for love towards his fellow men. In other words, the spirit evolves and progresses through the law of reincarnation.

Although Kardec did not himself use the word, in Brazil this syndrome is known as the Law of Karma, from the Hindu word for " action " (or sometimes " fate "). Thus the law postulates, as in physics, that for each action there is a relevant reaction: if the action is good, the reaction is good; if bad, then so is the reaction. The spirit, being free to act as he chooses, will reap reactions from the actions he has sown, both materially and spiritually.

The question asked through the ages at this point is: If God created everything, did he also create evil? If so, why? If not, then why does he permit its continued existence? There is an answer. The spirits themselves (as quoted in Kardec's book) say: " The laws of God are perfect and unchangeable. He did not create evil spirits, but ignorant and simple spirits, giving them the free-will to choose and, through choice and experience, walk along the path of progress. Some chose well; others not. If it were not like this, where would be the merit? But all will realise one day that the law of God is the path to perfection: evil is only a temporary stage; light is eternal."

—Disincarnate spirits can communicate with incarnate spirits: the spiritual world is in constant contact with the material world, each reacting constantly upon the other.

Spirits communicate through mediums, using the magnetic fluid of the peri-spirit in combination with the existing fluid of the atmosphere and of the sitters to control either objects or the medium himself. When objects are moved about with no purpose other than to show a presence, noises are made, and so on (as at the majority of Western " seances "), then these phenomena are called Manifestations of Physical Effect. If, however, they are designed to exchange *thoughts*, through signals, rappings, writings, etc., then they are termed Intelligent Communications. The essence of the latter, of course, depends upon the degree of evolution of the communicating spirit, the more evolved of which are called Superior Spirits.

How are we to know which is which? By accepting the advice of the Gospel (John, I Epistle—4; 1): " Believe not every spirit but try the spirits whether they are of God." The more superior the spirit, the humbler he will be and the higher the morality of his teachings, the wisdom of his concepts and the love he proclaims.

If the " state of mind " of a spirit is such that he is still strongly connected and even attached to earthly life, he may on rare occasions sense feelings as though spirit and peri-spirit were still in fact enveloped within the body that has died. For in the spirit world you are what your mind is—the peri-spirit has now become your " body." The spirit of a suicide once said to Kardec at a seance: " No, I am not dead. Yet I feel the worms eating me up . . ." Of course, the worms were only gnawing the disused physical envelope that was dead, finished with. But this was still " connected " to the spirit via the peri-spirit, because of the state of his mind at " death." He had thought everything would be ended by his act, only to find that he, as a personality, as a spirit, as an entity, with all its sensations, was still in existence. And because he was still mentally connected, he still " felt " the sensations of his old body.

Normally, a disincarnate spirit in the spirit world is not subject to earthly sensations. Our variations of temperature, material obstacles such as walls, doors, stairways and so on, have no influence on spirits. The more advanced they are, the faster they can move about, some even as fast as thought itself. For the more advanced, the past and, to a certain extent, the future hold no secrets. The future presents itself to them as though it were in fact the present, though this is a faculty available only to those most advanced in love and wisdom, permission to reveal which to men is very seldom granted. (A spirit, asked when and how spirits were created, replied, in an answer quoted by Kardec's *Book Of Spirits*, " It is still too early for men to try to understand and for us to explain.")

—*There are innumerable inhabited worlds throughout the universe, in different stages of evolution, development and progress. The peri-spirit and physical body take on the form which is most adequate for whatever world the spirit is inhabiting.*

Before each reincarnation, the spirit is connected to the body while still in the mother's womb through the peri-spirit. Until birth, or rebirth, all the spirit's faculties atrophy in a sort of deep sleep, gradually to reawaken in the body in correspondence with its organs' ability to express the spirit's intellectual, moral and sentimental qualities through its own development and growth.

Spirits are neither phantoms nor strange beings with strange forms: they are very much living creatures, normally invisible but showing themselves to the human eye occasionally under special conditions. When rendered visible, they usually take on the form that corresponds to the body last inhabited in their evolution.

—*To progress along the path of spiritual evolution, there are two main requirements. The first is to love one another. The second is to acquire knowledge.*

According to Kardec, science proper uncovers the laws governing the material world, and spiritism is the science uncovering those governing the spiritual world. Miracles, for example, originally conceived as an " annulment " of the laws of nature by a direct intervention of God, do not exist as such. For the laws of God are the divine laws of nature and studying them will provide an answer to *all* phenomena: facts that appeared supernatural yesterday are natural today; the "miraculous appearances of angels" in the Bible are now known to have been spirit communications. The concept of Adam and Eve is a myth, the law is that of evolution and of progress.

God has sent superior spirits to incarnate on earth among the various peoples from time to time and teach them the laws of God. They have been called messiahs, religious leaders, prophets, and each has performed his task according to the circumstances under which he lived and the greater or lesser exercise of his own strength, his own will power. The so-called "miracles" surrounding the lives of almost all were invariably due to lack of knowledge on the part of men of the laws of nature.

When the spirits themselves were asked who was the highest spirit ever to incarnate in this way, their answer was a terse: "Jesus." And they went on to explain that the term "Son of God" in this context means simply that no other spirit, through his evolution, had yet translated the qualities of a true son of God better than Jesus. In that sense, he is the Master.

*　　*　　*

This then, briefly, summarises the beliefs of the spiritist. To quote Kardec: *This is what the spirits themselves have dictated. If your reason says NO, then reject it.* The reason this book was written and published is that there are millions in Brazil who think it does make sense and who have incorporated these laws into their lives. That is what matters . . .

But the laws pertaining to these communications are the laws of affinity: a meeting designed only to entertain will attract those spirits imbued with a similar purpose; one dedicated to a higher purpose, a more serious objective, will attract superior spirits. It is in fact much as happens in ordinary life, a religious preacher will not seek a circus in which to spread his doctrine; a clown will hardly find a church adequate for his performance (though cynics sometimes say that it looks as though that is exactly what has happened!).

No miracles, then; no special pardons for anyone; no privileges whatsoever. We, and only we, are responsible for our actions. Our life of today is the result of our past, and our future will be the result of today.

This, say the spiritists, is the law that embraces all spirits throughout the universe.

CHAPTER SEVEN

The Remarkable World of Chico Xavier

NINETEEN thirty two was the year when the state of São Paulo, chafing under the dictatorial inclinations of ruling president Getulio Vargas, staged the ill-fated revolution designed to overthrow him. Dictator Vargas stayed in office until 1945.

Ninteen thirty two was also the year of an extremely odd event, the publication of a book of new poetry by fifty six different writers, all of them dead these many years.

The anthology—it is unique in the world—displayed works by the best and most respected poets of Portugal and Brazil, each in his own distinctive style testifying to the non-existence of " death." Naturally, it caused a sensation in Brazil, especially in literary circles, to the point that the great writer, critic and columnist, Humberto de Campos, thought it his duty to comment. In the *Diário Carioca* of July 10, 1932, he wrote:

" Francisco Candido Xavier is the name of a young man of humble origin, born in Pedro Leopoldo, Minas Gerais state, in 1910. After passing through primary school in his hometown, he joined a textile factory as a labourer. Later he worked in a commercial establishment, a grocery store, and as this world was not too friendly, he started to think of the next, by joining the spiritists with the high functions and responsibilities of a ' medium.' Having to occupy himself with the mediocre spirits that in this life frequented the shop he worked in, Francisco Candido Xavier decided to be more selective in the world of shadows, choosing for conversations superior intelligences, writers, and especially poets, who had already passed to the other world. Through these conversations, in which the mouth took no part, his new friends transmitted some poems they had elaborated after discarnating, and these the young counter-clerk wrote down mechanically, without any effort either of his arm or his imagination. These spirits were ordinarily Guerra Junqueiro, Antero de Quental, Augusto dos Anjos, Castro Alves and so forth [the Keats and Byrons of the Portuguese language].

" Called *Parnassus Beyond The Grave,* the book of Mr Francisco Candido Xavier is very interesting for live poets, although it is a terrible menace for those who dislike poetry. *Lasciate ogni speranza, voi ch'entrate!* —there inside, in the kingdom of death, there are poets. And they sing! They sing the same way they sang here, without omitting even the precious language they used on earth. I would fail the duty imposed upon me by my conscience if I did not confess that, making verses through the pen of Mr Francisco Candido Xavier, the poets of whom he is the interpreter present the same characteristics of inspiration and expression that identified them on this planet. The themes broached are the same that preoccupied them when alive. The taste is the same. And the verse answers, as a rule, to the same musical rhythms . . ."

Humberto de Campos, one of the giants of Brazilian literature, a sharp tongued critic by no means easy to please, could not, in all honesty, deny the authenticity of style of any of the poets. And there are fifty six of them.

The medium—he had not even finished primary school and was only half literate—became famous throughout Brazil. Since then he has had published no less than 79 books, the total sales of which are 1,800,680 copies. At the time of the publication of *Parnassus,* he was just twenty one.

Monteiro Lobato, another great Brazilian writer, said of some poetry purporting to be by the famed Augusto dos Anjos and received through Xavier's mediumcy: " These verses are everything that can exist of Augusto dos Anjos . . . If the man had really produced all that is published in the

Parnassus himself, then he (Xavier) could be in any academy, occupying as many chairs as he wants . . ."

Francisco Candido Xavier, or Chico Xavier, as he is better known through use of the diminutive for Francisco, lives nevertheless a life very unlike what one would expect of so famous a man. He has always refused to accept a penny either from the sales of " his " books or from any other aspects of his work as a medium. First as shop assistant, then later as a typist in a department of the Ministry of Agriculture, he has always lived very modestly in his hometown. A few years ago he retired due to a serious eye illness and now resides in the city of Uberaba, Minas Gerais, still working as a medium at the local Spiritist Centre as often as he can, though at a reduced pace now that he is in his mid fifties and his sight is failing. People come to see him from all over Brazil, often forming long queues which wait many hours outside the Centre. He has appeared on TV in several cities, is loved by the spiritists and respected by everyone else, and draws huge crowds wherever he goes, receiving applause and adulation in excess of that accorded any film star in Brazil.

Once a week he spends several hours answering, as a medium, requests for medicines for those who have lost faith in the ability of doctors to cure their ills. And who is the physician of the spirit world who " fills out the prescriptions " that Chico Xavier transmits in trance? None other than Dr. Adolpho Bezerra de Menezes, doctor of the poor, famous president of the Spiritist Society, the " Paul " of the movement in the nineteenth century!

All the sick have to do is to give their names. Chico Xavier writes a name down on a piece of paper and then, almost immediately afterwards, continues with a prescription, writing nonstop at enormous speed. Sometimes the medicines prescribed are so new that they are still unknown to the majority of doctors; sometimes it has happened that a product has been suggested which is only about to be launched on the market and is not yet in the shops at all.

On one occasion back in 1935, the afternoon paper *O Globo,* today the largest in the country with a circulation of almost a million and a solid Catholic readership, ran a series of features on the medium. In one meeting sponsored by the journal, witnessed by reporters and several hundred spectators, Chico Xavier " relayed " a message written in English (a language he does not speak), written backwards and from right to left in a fashion that could only be read in a mirror!

But the year of the breakthrough, if one may so call it, for him was 1937. In that year he decided to give his publisher, the Brazilian Spiritist Federation itself, as usual without any payment, several messages from the great and beloved Humberto de Campos, the first critic to draw attention to *Parnassus,* who had died some years previously. Afterwards, Xavier " received " more messages, and eventually there were enough to form a book. This, the Federation published—as " by " Campos and " received through " Chico Xavier. It had an enormous impact and caused a storm of controversy . . . exactly the same kind of sensation as though an ignoramus from the Middle West had produced a completely new novel, precisely in the author's style and language, by the late Ernest Hemingway; or a bus conductor from Liverpool had produced an extra episode in *The Forsyte Saga* in the manner of Galsworthy. Newspapers, critics and public took sides in the debate; was it or was it not Humberto? Was it a fraud? Was it a miracle? If it was a fraud, how could the illiterate medium counterfeit the writings of one of Brazil's greatest stylists?

Thus the discussion raged, to be spurred into fresh activity a year later with the publication of a second "after death " book from Humberto de Campos, *Brazil, Country Of The Gospels, Heart Of The World.* Once again the newspapers carried banner headlines about the great writer returned from the dead.

Then yet another literary " big gun " joined in the fray. In 1939, Agripino Grieco—Brazil's foremost literary critic, acid of expression and feared by writers both professional and putative, a man whose diatribes against those who failed to measure up to his own exacting standards had earned him the reputation of "cyclone of the literary scene"—Agripino Grieco was passing through Belo Horizonte.

The spiritists, always ready to submit their star medium's work to the scrutiny of any expert, discovered where he was and invited him to a meeting to witness Chico Xavier about his business. Grieco politely refused. What happened then is best told in his own words. Said he: "There being so many complications on the terrestrial plane, I wished to refrain from involving myself in further ones on the astral plane, so I did not go to the session. The result?—Chico Xavier decided to come to Belo Horizonte. On the night chosen for the meeting, instead of going to my usual restaurant, I went to dine quietly at another. I don't know how they caught up with me there, but the fact is they discovered me while I was engaged on chicken-and-peas and they took me to the Association where spiritists and onlookers had met together to receive me. The hall was packed: it was one of the big nights for local Kardecism.

"I lodged at the head table of the directors, near Chico Xavier, who did not give me, as I rapidly summed him up, the impression of an intelligence beyond the ordinary: a thin mulatto, middle sized, craggy, kinky hair, and a slight white speck in one of the eyes . . .

"The chairman of the meeting asked me to initial twenty sheets of paper on which the medium was to write, to avoid any suspicion of a possible replacement of the text. I did so, and Chico Xavier, with vertiginous speed, letting the pencil glide with a skill that a man with the most expertly fast handwriting would lack, filled up the sheets. I read them as he wrote in quite clear handwriting.

"First, a sonnet attributed to Augusto dos Anjos. Following this came what I realised, quite evidently, to be the language and play of ideas peculiar to Humberto de Campos. One can say of course that this was one of those ' à la manière de ' pieces, like the writings of Paul Reboux and Charles Muller, a perfectly respectable interpretation. But as for me, as a literary critic who has studied the mechanics of style for thirty years, I can only say that I had the instantaneous impression of reading a glorious manuscript that was pure Humberto. Here were the de Campos means of expression, his amiability, his desire to seem austere, his tone, in between the serious and the advisory. Here were allusions to Greece and Egypt, to Acropolis, to the veil of Isis, so much to the taste, all of them, of Humberto de Campos; here was a reference to Saint Beuve, a favourite critic of both of us, a master of taste and clarity whom Humberto, no less than myself, never tired of exalting. A well designed pattern, in all, an article that no person of medium education would hesitate, on reading it, to describe as ' pure Humberto.'

" I was naturally stunned . . . Many days have passed and I still do not know how to solve this case. A phenomenon of the nerves? Extra-human intervention? I lack the specialised knowledge to come to a conclusion. Besides, I received a Catholic education and admire the geniuses and heroes that have lent such prestige to the religion that produced a St. Anthony and a Bossuet. My book, *St. Francis of Assisi and Christian Poetry* is a testimony of how much I worship the ethics and aesthetics of the church. And yet, I repeat it with all loyalty, the message signed with the name of Humberto de Campos has profoundly impressed me . . ."

Thus the undisputed doyen of Brazilian literary critics— evidently at odds to reconcile his official status as a Roman Catholic with the phenomenon he had witnessed and of whose authenticity he was convinced, yet which is termed by his church " arts of the Devil."

Brazil's largest newspaper chain, with more than twenty dailies, syndicated Grieco's impressions of the meeting and the public interest in " the dead Humberto de Campos " continued to increase at an advanced rate. More communications were published in a new book in 1940, *New Messages,* and another, called *Good Tidings,* the year after. This last was about the teachings of Jesus. In 1943, still another book by the " dead reporter " Humberto de Campos was put on the market. This was titled *New Stories From Beyond the Grave.* In a country where an edition of 20,000 copies sold is considered exceptional, the sales of books by the " dead " writer reached a total of 150,000, far more than he had ever sold in his life on earth.

Not unexpectedly, with such success in the air, there was going to be trouble. Somebody wasn't going to like it. But the attack came from a strange quarter. Humberto de Campos's widow, and his publishers, Jacksons, together decided to sue Chico Xavier and his publishers, but first they had to decide on what grounds to sue: was it for royalties, if it really was Humberto de Campos himself, writing " from the dead "? Or was it for damages, if the writings were fraudulent, if they were not by Humberto? Had the latter been the case, criminal charges would automatically have been preferred against the medium.

Ultimately they filed a suit believed to be unique in the annals of the world's courts: they asked the court to establish whether or not it *was* Humberto de Campos who had written the disputed books!

It was an impossible task—to ask a terrestrial court to decide on the existence or otherwise, in fact, of the hereafter. Not unnaturally, after lengthy proceedings, the suit was dismissed on a technicality and " for lack of legal basis."

Although the case caused Chico Xavier much moral and personal pain, publicity-wise, it could not have done him more good. And, during the lawsuit, help came from an unexpected quarter—Humberto's mother, Ana de Campos Veras. Said she to *O Globo* on July 14, 1944: —

"I read with great emotion the ' Articles From Beyond The Grave ' and I verified that the style is my son's. I have no doubts in stating this, and there is no scientific explanation for the fact, especially if we consider that Francisco Candido Xavier is a citizen whose education is mediocre. Only a very cultivated, very intelligent man with a refined literary taste could have written this work, so identified with the style of my son . . .

" Where is the fraud? If the courts decide that it really is Humberto de Campos's work, then naturally the royalties should belong to the family; but if they decide the works are not his, then it would be an act of justice by our fellow-countrymen if the intellectuals accepted Francisco Candido Xavier into the Academy."

The attacks and counterattacks died down after a while, but the medium himself went from strength to strength. Indeed, had he not been a Kardecist and thus considered it highly immoral to accept money for any services rendered as a medium, he would have been a very rich man. For the Humberto de Campos works and the "other world" anthology of poetry, largely because both dealt with the spirits of those *known* to the public, could not but result in sensationalism and the fame that accompanies it. Yet the writings succeeding them, "signed" by Chico's own spirit guide, "Emmanuel" and by "Andre Luiz," far surpass the works which caused such a furore, in the essence of their content, the variety of their scientific range and the actual revelations they make.

"Emmanuel" identifies himself as having been a tribune in ancient Rome and a Catholic priest in his last incarnation. Whether he was or not, whether he exists (or ever existed) at all—sometimes the whole thing seems so utterly ridiculous viewed from our normal occidental world!—there is one physical, material, actual fact: through the mediumship of humble, ignorant Francisco Candido Xavier, "Emmanuel" has written *nineteen* books . . . The phenomenon of the "spirit" author can be doubted, denied, dismissed as a gigantic hoax—but the books, not in the wonderful land of Oz but in prosaic modern Brazil, the books can be bought in any bookstore.

Among them are six novels that could well have come from the pen of a Graves, an Irving Stone or the author of *The Egyptian*—fictionalised history with a difference: the small fact that the author claims to know what happened because he was there! The first of these, *Two Thousand Years Ago*, relates the story of the Emperor Tiberius's envoy to Palestine, who was sent to the Holy Land at the time of Jesus Christ. Apart from the detailed description of sex, it has all the ingredients of the great novel and the best-seller: love and hatred, politics and religion, humility and pride, passion and indifference, plus another ingredient lacking in the literary successes of the modern world: a true spiritual message gently interwoven among the threads of the story itself. Another novel purports to be the " true " story of St. Paul. The Apostle, the book says, was under the illusion that Jesus was constantly speaking to him after that first encounter on the road to Damascus. But in fact it was Stephen, the first Christian martyr, whom Paul himself had helped condemn to death, who was his constant spiritual companion and guide. " Jesus chose his deadly enemy and his martyred follower together to spread the Gospels throughout the world, united by his love," the book claims.

The books both sold more than 100,000 copies.

In another, " Emmanuel " examines history as seen from the spiritual plane. Titled *On The Path Of Light,* the book throws a new illumination on the Adam myth. This stems, it claims, from what it calls " the massive consecutive incarnations of spirits from a higher world, a more evolved planet than Earth (which was then still in the Stone Age)," all of whom had been sent to an inferior planet because " they rebelled against the higher moral laws." Incarnating here, these spirits gave birth to what were later to become the civilisations of the Egyptians, the Hindus, the Indo-Aryans and the Israelis. The Egyptians were those who conserved most of their inborn knowledge from the other planet, leaving us the Pyramids and their esoteric reasoning as a testimony of their achievements. Most of these spirits, the book postulates, have now returned to their higher planet after varying numbers of incarnations here, having worked out or expiated their Karmas, though the Hindus today still offer a vivid example of their high spiritual evolvement. (Israel, " Emmanuel " predicts, despite being " hampered by spiritual pride and presumptuousness," will accept Jesus as the Messiah by the end of this century!)

After a number of theses, contentious, disputable or sound, according to viewpoint, he touches on one of the cornerstones of spiritist belief, based on revelations which have persisted since the time of Kardec: the approaching end of the world.

ABOVE: "There is no spiritism without charity" said Kardec. Here at the Spiritist Centre in Uberaba are some of the poor queuing for the goods which are distributed several times a year. BELOW, LEFT: Chico Xavier and the man he chose to be his successor, Waldo Vieira. BELOW, RIGHT: José Pedro de Freitas, known to all as José Arigó, the 'surgeon with the rusty knife'.

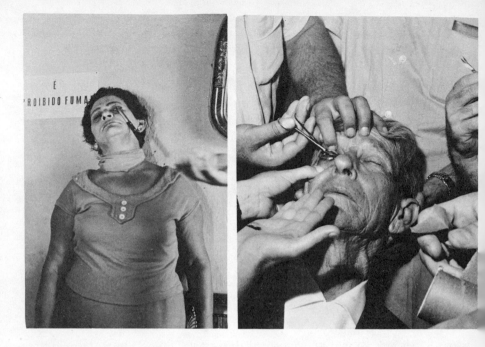

ABOVE, LEFT: José Arigó examines the eye of a patient. ABOVE, RIGHT: One of the thousands of operations performed by José Arigó without an anaesthetic. Using only nail scissors, he is cutting the tissue of a pterygium. BELOW: José Pedro de Freitas (José Arigó) is sentenced to sixteen months in jail for "illegal practice of medicine".

The cataclysm will occur at the end of the year AD 2000, these messages have always said, but it will not be the complete destruction of the entire planet so much as the end of an era, the obliteration of our materialistic age. (It does not seem clear whether this final catastrophe is an allegorical-spiritual one, the atomic holocaust we all fear, or a "natural" disaster.)

But construction will follow destruction; love will take the place of hatred. A new era will set in, in which this planet will be inhabited by a majority of spirits not only with Christian beliefs but also with Christian feelings, not in the form of a religion as such, but as a climate of the right kind of sentiments. The "good-hearted" will remain here, similar (or more evolved) spirits from elsewhere will join them and incarnate here, and thus a "better" world will be formed— the Kingdom of Heaven about which Jesus spoke.

Whether "Emmanuel" is right or not, the fact is that most spiritists do believe that we are living out the end of an era, that "the time has come . . ." The Earth now, he says, "is in a twilight which will be followed by a profound night, and the twenty-first century will witness the outcome of these dreadful events." And he adds elsewhere: "The night does not tarry and in its bowl of compact shadows let us not forget Jesus, whose infinite mercy, as always, will be the immortal clarity of that future dawn made of peace, fraternity and redemption."

Another book published in 1938 collects together innumerable messages displaying one colour or another from the spectrum of knowledge. Jesus has been the Master and Spiritual Director of this planet ever since it was born and has been guiding humanity since the time that men looked "very much like the anthropopithecus," the book says. "Fo-Hi, the compiler of the Vedas, Confucius, Hermes, Pythagoras, Gautama (Buddha) and others" were all his missionaries, each showing, in a manner suited to the civilisation in which he lived, an example of the precept Love Each Other.

After dealing with the successes and failures of Rome and

Christianity, the role of the subconscious in psychic phenomena, the existence of souls in animals, the vibrations which
permit communication with spirits, and civilisation in crisis
(isn't it always!), he turns to the relationship of science with
the spiritual. " We are at the end of a cycle of evolution," he
says, " and the more the scientists advance, the more will they
be aware of the subjective realities in universal phenomena."
The great mission of the spirit will then plainly be seen to
be as a creative element, organising and conserving all the
phenomena regulating the material life. Spiritual syntheses
of this kind are necessary to reveal the greater truths. " This
great task will be the luminous crown of science in the future;
this is our common goal for which we are working."

And to those who think that spirits, once they have been
contacted, can take over our destinies and solve our problems,
leaving us with no responsibilities, " Emmanuel " has this
to say: " The invisible guides of men cannot, in any way,
remove the material difficulties of their evolution on the face
of Earth."

" Emmanuel " continues: " If we speak of happy worlds,
it is for men to vibrate with us for the ideals of fraternity and
spiritual redemption; if we say that love fills all life in Infinite
Creation, it is for man also to learn to love life and his fellow-
men; if we mention the codes applied in other, more advanced
spheres, based on universal solidarity, it is because we want
them to merit here the attention and study they require. Men
should not stay in ecstasy, gazing at our descriptions: the
essential is to put yourselves to work. Each one individually
should improve his own heart first, harmonising it with
humility and love of the Gospels, then transform his home,
his cities and his countries so that everything on earth should
breathe the same happiness and the same beauty of the higher
planes, according to our narratives from the Infinite."

He also dictated to Chico Xavier literally thousands of
messages commenting on virtually every passage in the New
Testament. Any pastor lacking a text for his Sunday morning
sermon, in fact, has only to consult " Emmanuel " to find
inspiration (so long as he conceals the source!).

Before leaving this prolific guide, it must be mentioned that he has also adopted that other device of the best-seller, the sequel. As a complement to his novel *Two Thousand Years Ago,* " Emmanuel " wrote *Fifty Years After,* showing reincarnation in action, as it were, by following the subsequent lives of the characters described in the first book. An interesting demonstration of the law of reincarnation at work, and, as somebody said, if this fellow Xavier *isn't* a medium and writes all these things himself or with the help of friends, he should be given the Nobel Prize for skill and imagination (and something also for naivetée, for not taking a cent in royalties!).

Despite the attractions of all these books made available by Chico Xavier, to the scientific, practical mind, a more impressive series still is that authored by " Andre Luiz "—a spirit who claims to have been a famous doctor in his last incarnation on earth. In fact his first book begins with a description of what happened to him immediately after he died. All alone and in total darkness, he kept hearing shouts from somewhere accusing him of having committed suicide. " But I *haven't* committed suicide! " he kept shouting back. Yet the mental torture continued for ages of time, until . . . " I looked backwards into my own self and realised that, by drinking too much, eating too much, smoking too much, with the kidney trouble I knew I had, I must indeed have 'committed suicide ' in the sense that I had hastened my own end, shortened unnecessarily my own life. I looked back at my whole life, at my beginnings; I saw, thinking of my mother, how I gradually lost the purity of my good intentions, which gave way bit by bit to pride and vanity for having made a success of life. I felt alone, sorrowful. I wept. Then I prayed for help and suddenly, in front of me, was an immense, bright light, so bright that I could scarcely look at it. I thought it was an angel from Heaven . . ."

But it wasn't, Andre Luiz goes on to explain: it was a higher spiritual entity detailed to take him to a better sphere.

And from then on he gives a most vivid, lucid and detailed account of life within the spiritual sphere he was taken to . . .

Our Home, in fact, as the book is called. He describes how gradually he adapted himself to the new life. First, he felt hunger and was given some " food," a special type designed for the newly arrived (Don't laugh: it might happen to you; who knows?). Then he explains how later he learned to absorb energy by other means . . . He is constantly accompanied by a higher spirit guide who lectures, explains and interprets wherever he goes, rather in the manner of Virgil with Dante. And he himself describes to the medium with the dispassionate and knowledgeable eye and language of a doctor everything he experiences.

In a series comprising twelve books, starting in 1944 and finishing in 1960 with *The Mechanics Of Mediumship,* " Andre Luiz " deals with neurosis, obsessions, schizophrenia, the workings of the mind, the subconscious, conscious and superconscious—the Id, Ego and Superego of Freud—paying homage to the father of psychoanalysis but supplementing his teachings with " what really goes on," always showing the inter-relation between the spiritual and the material world. All this is done in the form of dialogues with the higher spirit guide mentioned above. The technique used is that the spiritual pair, invisible of course, visit the homes of earthly people to examine their problems. Then, much as a professor accompanied by students works in a teaching hospital, explaining each case to his pupils at the patient's bedside, the spirit guide answers the questions " Andre Luiz " puts about each family or person.

In his descriptions of *Our Home,* " Luiz " speaks of the departments into which the kingdom is divided, among them a " reincarnation department " which prepares the " moulds " of the physical body of spirits making up the members of the community of " Our Home " who are about to incarnate again on earth. Unlike the works of Kardec, in which everything is treated on the broad lines of generalisation, this book is specific to the smallest detail. At one of his visits to the " reincarnation department," for instance, " Andre Luiz " wonders about the significance of a dark spot he has noticed in one of the " moulds." The spirit guide " in charge " of the department explains that this organ will be subjected to an illness at a certain stage of development of the newly incarnated spirit, the result of excesses indulged in during the spirit's last incarnation . . .

Thus, it would follow, that if a man has been a glutton in one incarnation, he will have spoiled the " harmony " of his digestive organs, which fact is " registered " in the peri-spirit. Then, in his following incarnation, this disharmony will pass from the peri-spirit, magnetically transmitted to the genes through the complicated system of the DNA cell, the origin, the very stuff of life itself, any disturbance in whose harmony, we know, will be reflected in the body which it is going to form.

In *The Mechanics Of Mediumship,* rapping tables and baskets which make pencils write are left far behind. As a contrast to much of the wishy-washy generalisation that many people appear to think characterise any kind of spiritualist message, read the following passage from that work.

" When Einstein tried to imagine the indispensable qualities of the so-called *æther* which could allow it to transmit characteristic waves of billions of oscillations per second at a speed of over 300,000 kilometres per second, he did not succeed in accommodating the necessary mathematical values in a formula, because the qualities with which this matter should be endowed are not combinable, so he concluded that this matter did not exist, proposing to abolish the concept of æther and substitute for it that of a ' field.' A field is thus the space dominated by the influence of a particle of mass. Now, to establish in mind the idea of what has been propounded, imagine a flame in activity: the zone it illuminates is its particular field, and the intensity of its influence diminishes as the distance from its nucleus . . . without ever reaching zero, since in theory the field or region of influence, however faint, can reach the infinite.

" To return to Einstein's field, imagine the human mind in place of the flame. Just as the intensity of influence of the latter diminished as the distance of the nucleus of energies in combustion, being expressed in an ever-smaller fraction which yet never reaches zero, so the mental current extends itself according to the same principle, despite the difference of conditions . . . This current of mental particles manifests itself around each spirit in a manner of mental ' induction, and the greater the spirit's faculties of concentration and persistence in the direction of the desired objective, the ampler it becomes. As in the domain of physics and electrical energy, where induction stands for a process whereby one body with electromagnetic properties can transmit these to another without visible contact, so in the realm of mental powers induction expresses an analogous process. For a mental current is susceptible of reproducing its own peculiarities in another mental current which synchronises with it. And in mentalism as in electricity, the phenomenon obeys the conjugation of waves so long as the sustenance of the energetic flux is maintained . . ."

Many may dismiss such passages as pseudo-scientific rubbish. They may be. Kardec said that if spiritism is wrong, it will disappear; if it is right, it is science that will prove it so, and no criticism can stop it from progressing. So far, in Brazil at least, no one has been able to stop it progressing! Whether it is right or not, the future will show.

Certainly, though, a great number of people confidently expect it to be right. And after all they do have a reasonable amount to go on. Take the case of the book by " Andre Luiz " called *Evolution In Two Worlds*. This explains that the intelligent principle evolves throughout the ages both in the spiritual and in the material sphere, but not necessarily at the same rate—a phenomenon which lies behind some of the difficulties facing scientists trying, and failing, to establish a fully linked scale of evolution. The language used reads like a symposium of jargon from palæontology, biology, anthropology and related subjects. But the really interesting thing about it is that it derives from two mediums, Chico Xavier and a colleague whose aid he sought. In separate cities 200 miles apart, obeying instructions from the spirit " author," they each " received " a chapter alternately on Wednesday and Sunday evenings until the work was complete!

Another psycho-graphic medium, a medium whose speciality is the writing of messages received from the spirit world, is Hercilio Maes, a lawyer from the southern state of Paraná, recently in world headlines because of the disastrous fire which almost decimated the state. Maes is a world removed from Chico Xavier as a person, and there are many differences between them as mediums, too. More of a spiritualist than a spiritist, the university-trained Maes sells and publishes his books on a normal commercial basis. His method of " receiving " messages differs from Xavier's in the actual system of putting down what has been transmitted. Whereas Chico works through mechanic writing, his hand moving at incredible speed dominated by " an external, unidentified force," Maes mentally " sees " the thoughts or pictures transmitted by his spirit guide, " Ramatis," and then consciously writes them down in his own language in his own hand. Naturally this method is open to considerable interference, or allegations of interference, by the medium. Nevertheless, the work itself is most impressive and more than 100,000 copies of his books have been sold.

Maes, who is the next most famous medium in Brazil to Chico Xavier, is best known for a series of tracts about the end of the world. Like " Emmanuel," the guide " Ramatis " places this unwelcome event at the end of the present century. Unlike Chico's guide, however, he is specific rather than general, and he states firmly that of the three available alternatives, the disaster will be of the " natural " kind.

What will happen, the tracts explain in impressive detail, is that the earth's imaginary axes will change through ninety degrees due to the gravitational pull of an enormous new planet which will enter our system soon. With the globe thus revolving in a different sense, entire continents such as Europe will be completely destroyed and vanish forever beneath the new oceans which will form. North and South Poles will be totally de-iced and man will find unimaginable riches to help him form the new humanity of the Third Millenium. The process of de-icing, he adds sombrely, has already started.

(These tracts were published in book form in 1950. Coincidence or not, one of the findings of the International Geophysical Year in 1958 was that the earth as a whole had been heating for the previous five years at a higher rate than it had for centuries, and that both Poles were defrosting at a higher rate than ever before!)

And the chosen who survive the catastrophe to found the Third Millenium? Like Chico Xavier, who once said, "I am but a donkey that the spirits mount on," Hercilio Maes has no personal views on this question. But his guide, whose high moral tone, like those of his spiritist confrères, preaches salvation only through love and understanding, is explicit. He describes in frightening detail how the separation between good and evil will be made, how those due to sit at the right, and those at the left, of Christ will be chosen. Briefly, the idea is that Divine Law operates through electromagnetic force and its wavelengths. Those of us who, because our thoughts and actions operate on a wavelength in harmony with Christian teachings, can be said to qualify as good, will sit at the right. And those whose wavelengths automatically select them as bad will sit on the other side, and will be magnetically drawn via these same wavelengths to the new planet about to enter our system, where evolution is in a state comparable to our Stone Age.

Tickets, anybody?

CHAPTER EIGHT

The Surgeon of the Rusty Knife

I N Portuguese, the word *arigó* means a simple individual, a rustic, a crude but easy-going yokel, something of a boor even —but a good fellow. José Pedro de Freitas, a typical Brazilian from the mountainous state of Minas Gerais, was nicknamed José Arigó because he is just like an *arigó*: good natured, honest as the day is long, jovial and gullible. He loves his homeland and his hometown, his family, his children; he rarely wears a tie, wouldn't hurt a fly. He was raised on the fields, tended his father's land in his boyhood, said his prayers before every meal because of the stout Catholicism of his parents, and learned that spiritism is the art of the Devil.

Yet he is the subject of a pilgrimage drawing thousands from all parts of Brazil every month. The late Pope Pius XII sent him a silver casket inscribed with his personal thanks for services rendered, an eminent New York doctor travelled eight thousand miles to consult him, University professors from the Argentine have besought him to visit them in Buenos Aires.

For José Arigó operates tumours, carcinomas, lipomas, cataracts, pterygiums, and cysts among other growths, using no aseptic precautions, no anaesthesia whatever—and with only a common kitchen knife, nail scissors, a scalpel and nippers as instruments.

The operations are performed with incredible speed, taking from thirty seconds to a few minutes only, before many witnesses, in full daylight. And the patient is fully conscious throughout the operation, feels no pain whatever, and walks away afterwards with no more after-effects than a slight tiredness.

And the hæmorrhages, the sutures, transfusions, serums? the curious will naturally ask. José Arigó arrests the bleeding by passing a piece of cotton wool over the incision and the " sutures " are effected by a similar process.

José " Arigó " Pedro de Freitas is not a doctor, not a surgeon, not a witchdoctor, and certainly not a charlatan. He is in fact a medium.

Falling easily into trance, he is controlled by the spirit of " Dr. Fritz," self-identified as a German surgeon killed during the war of 1914-1918. During the time when he is controlled by this spirit, José Arigó, whose education was rudimentary and whose language is a basic Portuguese, speaks with a heavy German accent. Unless there are those present who speak German, when of course he converses in faultless German.

In various messages, " Dr. Fritz '" has explained that he does not do all the operations himself, but is linked with a French surgeon identified as " Gilbert Pierre," who is responsible for the ophthalmology, and a Japanese specialist named " Takahashi," who does the tumours. Other communications have stated that the spirit of Fabiano de Cristo, a well-known friar famous in his lifetime for his charitable activities, supplies through its own concentration and the medium's paranormal faculties a certain " green light " which in effect sterilises the environment, the instruments and the patient's wounds. There is on record an account, by a reputable journalist who attended a session of Arigó's, of a request from " Dr. Fritz " for " more green light, please." Immediately afterwards, the report states, several people in the audience near the medium lost consciousness exactly as though they had been anaesthetised.

We say " audience " advisedly, for thousands of people have witnessed these operations, among them dozens of doctors and many university professors, writers and journalists, during the seven years in which José Arigó has been performing them.

But the medium himself is totally unaware of what goes on while "Dr. Fritz" is "in control" and has no recollection of the operations after they have been completed. Indeed, when he was shown a ninety-minute film of his activities in trance—one of several which have been made—Arigó was unable to stand the shock and fainted clean away.

This is scarcely surprising if the visible methods of the operations are examined, many onlookers suffering the same phenomenon or at the very least covering their eyes in horror, not having the courage to continue watching. For the *modus operandi,* in all conscience, is bizarre enough.

You want to have your eyes examined for a suspected tumour? Then by all means go and see Arigó, but make sure you take somebody along with you either to photograph or film it, or both, or else those to whom you tell the tale will recommend you to have your head examined also.

For Arigó will take a kitchen knife, push the tip of the blade into the eye between the eyelid and the cornea, and then, not even looking at you, but gazing out at the audience, move the implement around in the socket with what has frequently been termed "incredible violence." Sometimes he will use the knife as a lever to procure a complete extrusion of the eyeball, or during an operation leave the fully-introduced knife hanging from the socket all by itself. Once he introduced a scalpel and a knife together, leaving both in that position for a space of time, an occurrence publicly confirmed since by several doctors who were present. But no matter how the onlookers gasp, no matter how many cover their own eyes or faint, Arigó just smiles, which is to say " Dr. Fritz " just smiles, and continues his explorations. Then, out comes the knife . . . and there may well be the tissue of a pterygium coming out with it! After which you smile and walk away, having felt no pain.

There is, of course, no charge. For like Chico Xavier, Arigó has never accepted a penny for his work as a medium and continues, when not in trance, to live the simple life of a *caboclo,* a *matuto* (which is to say, a backwoodsman, a hill-billy).

At present, however, Arigó is not operating.

No, he has not lost his remarkable faculties. But it seems that the local authorities have lost theirs. Due to persecution by envious priests with the mentality of Spanish Inquisitors, criminal charges have been laid against him by the State Medical Association for " illegal practice of medicine." In any other country, he would have been the subject of serious scientific enquiry promoted by universities and academies, but Brazil, as we have said, is the land of contrasts and para-doxes and the so-called " authorities," the government in general, have been conspicuously ignorant until now of the country's potential. There is some generalised hope that the serious and able revolutionary government installed by the insurrection of March 31, 1964, may bring about the necessary change of attitudes. In the meantime, Arigó is forbidden to operate. He has been invited by other countries to practise his mediumship there, and indeed offered the free use of hos-pitals with doctors and scientists in attendance to watch his operations. But he refuses to leave his hometown because " Dr. Fritz " has ordered him to stay there.

The hometown is in fact Congonhas do Campo, where José Pedro de Freitas was born on a farm on October 18, 1918. The city is world-famous through the works of sculptor Antonio Francisco Lisboa, better known by his nickname " Aleijadinho," which means " little cripple," who lived there at the beginning of the nineteenth century. Crippled in both hands and both feet, the artist was an epileptic who devised primitive instruments which were tied directly to his arms after he had been carried to the site of his work. Mainly this was the local churchyard, where his masterpiece, one of the world's great Baroque creations, was produced. This series of huge soapstone figures of the Twelve Apostles at eight-foot intervals has been hailed as a production of genius by critics all over the world because of the simple but immensely alive expressions of the faces and the majesty with which Aleijadinho endowed the figures.

Today, Congonhas do Campo has two stars: Aleijadinho and Arigó. Some come to see one; some the other. The smart ones go to see both. But those who go to see Arigó cannot fail also to experience Alcijadinho—not his work, not the Twelve Apostles created here on earth, but what he does on the spiritual plane. For the spirit of the sculptor is in fact " in charge " of all the work done through Arigó by " Dr. Fritz " and his astral colleagues; all the cures, all the operations are carried out under his spiritual " direction "!

Arigó's family have always lived in Congonhas do Campo and have always been staunch Catholics ("Even praying before meals!" their famous son exclaims). Antonio de Freitas Sobrinho, Arigó's father, better known as " Tonico," owned a certain amount of land and was for some years chairman of the town council on which he still sits as an alderman. Arigó's uncle, Lamartine de Freitas, was elected mayor in 1954, defeating his opponent by a mere 210 votes. The opponent ran the labour ticket defending the underdogs, while Arigó's uncle had the support of the church and the local conservatives, and there is a rumour that the votes were fraudulently altered during the night at the post office where the ballot boxes had been deposited instead of being transferred to a larger county as required by law. After being declared the victor, the new mayor called the defeated opponent into his new office and told him he must either leave town or discontinue his spiritist practices. This ceremony was witnessed by the local vicar.

And the opponent?—None other than the mayor's own nephew José Pedro de Freitas!

Arigó refused to obey the injunction and later the uncle, on his deathbed, asked forgiveness. " I was under pressure; I would not have consented for the threat to be carried out," were his last words to his nephew.

One of Arigó's eight brothers owns a restaurant in the state capital, Belo Horizonte, and the youngest is a law school graduate. An aunt, the only other spiritist in the family, is said to be quite wealthy, owning a ranch on the outskirts of town. Apart from her, the entire family is devotedly Catholic, having contributed heavily to the funds for building the local seminary and in many other ways supported the church. Even Arigó himself, for several years after "Dr. Fritz" had appeared, kept on attending mass and displayed on his door a sign reading *We are against low spiritism*—much to the delight of the vicar. It was only later, after he had realised the nature of the phenomenon which possessed him, that he changed to spiritism himself.

From such a solidly respectable bourgeois background, the boy had no reason to grow up a pauper, except that he was by nature an *arigó* and therefore lacked the talent to make money. Even today he remains a modest public servant like Chico Xavier, largely because he has always kept the company of others like himself, the underdogs. And of course, because in him they always find a sympathetic ear, a generous heart, his family regard him rather as the black sheep.

From the time when he first attended primary school at seven, dividing his labours between the classroom and his father's fields, he saw periodically a moving light, "a bright, round light, so brilliant that it nearly blinded me," and heard from time to time "a voice speaking in a strange language." But the explanation of these visitations was to be many years delayed. After only four years at school, the young *arigó* began to live the life of a bucolic adolescent, a simple, un-complicated life on the farm complemented by simple pleasures, billiards in the bar, endless small talk with friends, but no vices, not even any girls. He had no pre-marital experience at all, not because anyone had told him it was wrong but because he did not feel inclined to anything but the simple existence he had chosen. Then, a month before his twenty sixth birthday in 1944, he married Arlete Soares, the daughter of a conventional local family. They now have six children, all boys.

The early days of the marriage were anything but blissful, however. José Arigó went to work at an iron-ore mine, rising at three a.m. every day to walk the eight miles to the works and be there by six, wielding a pick-axe for eight hours, and then walking the eight miles home again. Struck by the misery and poor conditions of the badly paid miners, which were the same as his own, his wife having to sew all day to make both ends meet, he decided to stir his workmates to action. Says he today: "I told the miners that I had discovered that many among us bring empty pans from home for the lunch break because we are ashamed to show we have no food. Nobody can walk sixteen miles, work all day long and then return home, all without any food, and at such miserable salaries. You must do something about this."

The miners heeded his words. They elected him as president of their union, in which capacity he led a strike and was sacked, after the police had been called in and he had accepted personal responsibility for the stoppage, under suspicion of being a communist! A more radical man might indeed have become one after that, but Arigó merely looked for another job.

With his reputation as an agitator, of course, nobody would give him one and for some time the family had to live on his wife's earnings as a seamstress. The hardest part of all, he recollects, was having his children ask for money to buy bread in the morning, and having none to give. Eventually his father loaned him the equivalent of 100,000 dollars and José Arigó started a bar and restaurant that soon became the best in town. It was constantly filled with the tourists who came to see the famous local sculptures. Arigó even made money, acquired some land and bought a fine house in the city. That was in 1948.

In 1950, the national and state elections brought Lucio Bittencourt to town. Bittencourt was a candidate for the senate and also a campaign leader for Getulio Vargas, running for the presidency on a labour ticket. Naturally he dropped into "Arigó's Bar" to solicit the support of its owner. The two men immediately liked one another and became friends, Arigó pledging his miners' votes for Bittencourt and Vargas. But he also lent his support to a candidate for the local mayoralty—a man whose name meant "Beautiful Words," who opened a chalk factory in the town and gave work to many, who promised to open many more factories if he was elected, and to whom, with all his friends, " Arigó's Bar " offered unlimited credit.

Came the election. Vargas was elected. Bittencourt was elected. But " Beautiful Words " wasn't elected. He closed the factory, left the town with his friends, and was never seen again. Between them, they also left 200,000 dollars-worth of unpaid debts at " Arigó's Bar." Pedro de Freitas never could say No to a request for help, and they were not the only ones. So " Arigó's Bar " had to close down.

Some time before this, its too-good-hearted owner had found a small crucifix under some corn cobs in one of his father's barns. Since nobody confessed to its ownership, he kept it, to find an old man outside his house when he returned late that night, asking for food. Arigó brought the food, but the following evening the man was there again, and once more he demanded a meal. Again, Arigó complied. But when this had happened for several nights, Arigó's wife having had to get up from her bed to prepare the food on each occasion, he asked the beggar whether he could not come earlier, at a more convenient time.

" No," replied the old man, " I cannot. But if you like, you can bring me the food at the same time at the cemetery."

Not unnaturally, Arigó refused. Whereupon the old man said:

" All right. Take it every day at this hour to the front of the church, then. You have a good heart. It was I who left for you the crucifix you found. It is for you to use, for curing the sick, by holding it in your hand and making a prayer. Yours is a great mission . . ."

Arigó was profoundly impressed with this encounter, it is evident. For he at once went in search of the sick, and found that the absurd idea worked! The sick *were* cured . . . Among many others, a paralytic came to his house and Arigó said, greatly daring: " Throw away those crutches; you can walk." And the sufferer, astounded but confident, did just that—and walked his first hesitant steps. He really was cured.

Not long afterwards, José Arigó began to suffer himself from frequent and unexplained fainting fits, none of which the doctors could explain. Though he did not know it, his mediumship was beginning. Then one night he was awakened by the odd figure of a fat, bald man who told him in German-accented Portuguese: " You will cure many . . ."

" Dr. Fritz " had arrived.

At first, Arigó told his wife nothing of this. But the phenomenon was repeated, not once but many times. " He looks a monster," he told Arlete at last, " with his enormous belly and his heavy German face."

His wife refused to believe the story. " It is nonsense," she argued, and went to see Arigó's father.

" He is seeing phantoms, Tonico," she told him, much upset. " He says it comes every night and speaks to him. I think he is going crazy. We must take him to a doctor."

A priest was called to bless the house and exorcise " the devil." No result. The visitations continued, and now Arigó was fainting several times every day. And then it happened.

In the middle of 1950, Lucio Bittencourt invited Arigó to bring some of his miners to a political rally at Belo Horizonte. After it, he invited them all to a *churrasco*, a barbecue. With the exception of the always-frugal Arigó, they ate and drank heavily, returning to their hotel about two a.m. Then at five o'clock in the morning, the senator knocked at Arigó's door. " Wake up, Zé," he called, using the affectionate diminutive of José that Arigó's intimates employ. " Wake up and come with me to the drugstore. I need a razor blade, for I must shave and catch the first plane out."

Still half asleep, Arigó accompanied Bittencourt to the store. To his astonishment, the senator fainted when they were almost there. Arigó called a policeman and asked him to stand by while he went to fetch some coffee. When he returned, the unconscious man was stirring. " I apologise for troubling you," he told the policeman, " but I fainted from weakness: my companion here operated on my lungs earlier tonight."

Arigó looked at the senator, then at the constable, and said: " Pay no attention. I'm afraid he had a little too much to drink last night." But after he had recovered and been to the drugstore, Bittencourt insisted on this strange story. Arigó was irritated. " You take too much whisky and then you keep saying that I'm a spiritist," he said severely. " If my family find out about this, they will be very angry. We are strict Catholics and spiritism is the art of the Devil. I don't like such jokes."

The senator said no more but led him back to the hotel and insisted that his friend should examine his pyjama jacket. It was torn down the back as though slashed by a knife. Bittencourt turned to Arigó and said: " Surely that proves it! You came into my room and stood before me—then slowly you began to disappear, a fat, bald man appearing in your place, wearing a white apron. At his side were three others with equally foreign faces, all wearing white as well. The first one announced that he was going to operate on me . . . and then I blacked out and saw no more. And this was not a dream, I swear it! "

" You should have your head examined," was Arigó's sole comment.

But there was far more proof than the torn pyjamas. For in fact Senator Bittencourt had been suffering from a lung tumour, had indeed just returned from the United States, where several specialists had agreed that it was inoperable. Yet when, hurrying back to Rio and saying nothing of what had happened, he asked his own doctors to take some X-rays, they said after closely examining the plates:

" *The operation you must have had in the States was perfectly successful; the tumour has completely disappeared from your lung . . .*"

This case received the maximum of publicity, for Bittencourt talked of it to anyone who would listen, including the press. The phenomenon of Arigó was born.

His next recorded case was an operation on an old lady so ill that she had already received Extreme Unction and was lying on her deathbed surrounded by candles. Arigó had gone to pay his last respects and was in the room when suddenly he tensed, his expression changed, his eyes altered, and he dashed out into the kitchen. A moment later, he was back,

146

brandishing a large knife. " Stand back!" he growled at the mourners in a harsh, guttural accent. " Nobody is to come close!" And before a hand could be raised to stop him, he had plunged the knife into the dying woman's abdomen.

Moving at tremendous speed, as the terrified onlookers huddled in a corner, he opened the stomach wall, excised and removed a growth, and then closed the incision simply by pressing the edges together, flesh to flesh. A moment later, he came to and was astonished to see the knife by the old woman, a large, orange-sized growth by his own side, and the victim showing every sign of recovery. In fact in a few minutes, far from dying, the old lady was actually walking around.

The padres who had administered Extreme Unction could not believe their eyes—there was the " dying " woman in perfectly good health, there was the tumour for all to see, they had all watched the incision—yet there was not a trace of an incision there now! What had happened, they asked Arigó? What had he done?

He didn't know, of course. " I have no idea, father. None," he said in bewilderment. " I fainted, I think, I often do, I'm afraid, and when my consciousness returned, they told me the old lady had been operated on; that's all . . ."

But of course it was by no means all.

The story, added to the Bittencourt legend, spread and spread. And the number of sick people seeking his aid increased proportionately. He was working from midday to six p.m. now at a government agency. Before and after, working from dawn and far into the night, he ministered unto the sick. No sacrifice was too great, for he didn't know how to refuse a request for help. For nearly five years, as a medium for " Dr. Fritz " and the astral team directed by the spirit of Aleijadinho, he operated, diagnosed and prescribed—still attending mass and accepting the Holy Communion as a normal Catholic. Then, in 1955, he realised the implications of what he was doing, of whom he was the intermediary, and changed to spiritism, consenting to be associated with the building of a Spiritist Centre called Jesus Nazarene, where he still works today.

Unfortunately, he had already incurred the enmity of some members of the church. A year before, when he had unsuccessfully run for mayor against his uncle, he had aroused the hatred of the vicar, a supporter of the successful candidate. And since then a section of the Catholic clergy have waged an unremitting, no-holds-barred battle against Arigó. Anybody (it must appear to them) who arrogates to himself any suspension of the laws of physics must be a blasphemer and a heretic at the best; a charlatan at the worst. No doubt if Jesus Christ were to return again, He would meet a similarly jaundiced reception from His ministers. After all, it did happen before.

So far as José Arigó is concerned, it meant that his house was invaded several times by Marshals acting on information supplied by the priests, that he was attacked by a hired hoodlum, and that he was arraigned on a charge of illegally practising medicine. On this last, he was found guilty and actually condemned to two and a half years' imprisonment, a sentence which would have been carried out were it not for a pardon from ex-president Kubitschek (granted, it is whispered, because Arigó had secretly and successfully operated on one of Kubitschek's daughters). At the trial, the judge, a local dignitary, is reported to have shouted: " If you ' receive ' a so-called ' Dr. Fritz,' then make him appear now in front of me!" The convicting evidence was that of a doctor who had in all good faith testified *for* Arigó how he had himself been operated on by " Dr. Fritz " and had his life saved.

Later, Arigó was to be indicted again for the same offence, but we shall return to that at the end of this chapter. At the time of the second trial, however, *O Globo* published a photograph and a statement (on November 4, 1964) of a professional model named Maria de Fátima Marques Corrêa, who contacted the newspaper on her own initiative to tell how Zé Arigó cured her eye illness. " I suffered from an hereditary disease of the eye," said she, " and through the progressive loss of the crystalline of my left eye, I was slowly going blind. I had seen the best specialists in Rio and São Paulo without result . . . I suffered excruciating pains and the eyeball was constantly inflamed. That's when I decided to go and see Arigó as a last resort. He took one look at me, picked up a knife, pushed it into my eye, and scraped. Since then the pain and inflammation have disappeared. He said that an operation was required to restore my sight completely, but as he was already under an indictment, he could not do this. Instead of sending scientists to study him, they threw the book at him. I am ready to testify for him at any time . . ."

So are hundreds more. We shall restrict our own examples to testimonials given by those who are themselves members of the medical profession, and are thus least likely to exaggerate the claims of one whose activities in one sense run counter to their own. We add the examples without comment.

Said Dr. Ladeira Marques of Rio de Janeiro: " I witnessed an operation on the uterus of a patient, together with another doctor and several other persons. We went into the room where the operations take place. It is a small room of about fifteen square metres, with a wooden bed on the left, which however was not used for operations. Half an old door served as a board whereon patients were laid down for these. The daylight enters generously through the window and at night a strong lamp is used. No rituals of any kind. Scissors, scalpels, a kitchen knife, a pair of tweezers—these were the ' chirurgical instruments ' he used alternately. Instead of being sterilised, they were all kept in an old, rusty, empty can . . .

" For operations on the intimate organs, Arigó, or ' Dr. Fritz,' limits the number of witnesses: a natural precaution . . . Asking for the dress of the patient to be lifted, ' Dr. Fritz ' inquired of the husband whether he preferred an abdominal or a vaginal operation. The husband chose the latter. Without the help of a speculum [an instrument for dilating the cavities of the human body to facilitate inspection] he introduced three scissors and two scalpels into the vagina, brusquely—one can even say with violence. Each instrument was introduced with a single stroke, without hurting the lady, who felt absolutely nothing. He was holding one handle of the scissors when all of us saw the other start moving alone, as though another hand was gripping it and start-

149

ing to make the movements that correspond to the cutting of something, opening and closing the scissors.

"Although we could not see whether this was also the case with the other instruments, we could all clearly hear the noise of metals rattling and the characteristic sound of tissue being cut. After a few minutes, 'Dr. Fritz' removed a pair of scissors and, at the sight of blood, he stopped and said: 'Let there be no blood, Lord.' And the operation continued with no further hæmorrhage at all . . . Then he took a pair of tweezers, asked us all to pay attention, introduced it into the vagina and removed a piece of tissue about thirty one inches long and fifteen inches wide, which was shown to all present. I thought first that he had made an hysterectomy [surgical removal of the uterus] but as 'Dr. Fritz' later told the patient she could have children, I concluded that he had performed a neoplasty [removal of a neoplasm or tumour]. The patient was calm and relaxed throughout the whole operation, which lasted only a few minutes, and felt no pain whatsoever. No anæsthesia, sterilisation of instruments or aseptic measures were taken."

The name of the patient is Maria Emília Silveira, an inhabitant of Vitoria, capital of the state of Espirito Santo. Her husband, Ismênio Silveira, a public notary, stated that doctors had given her only a few months to live, cancer of the ovaries having been diagnosed after an unsuccessful operation. He took his wife to Arigó after hearing that he had cured a "hopeless" cancer in the wife of Virgílio Mendes Ferraz, a wealthy landowner. Ferraz had offered Arigó a cheque for 50,000 dollars after the cure, but this had been refused. The operation on Maria Emília Silveira was in October, 1957. Today she has a six-year-old son, born after the visit to Arigó.

Dr. Leite de Castro, of one of the main hospitals in Rio, said: "I have seen dozens of operations on pterygiums made with knives and scissors by 'Dr. Fritz' in Arigó, without any use of anæsthesia or anything else normally used in medicine. Any hæmorrhage was stopped immediately by Arigó. I saw him operate several cysts, open abscesses, take out strange bodies from patients, even a bullet that would normally have been inoperable . . . and he makes a point of doing incredible things aside, like wiping his scalpel on somebody's shirt in the middle of an operation. Once he even passed it over my hair. One woman from Bahia had a tumour about fifty inches long removed from her uterus, just like that. And I have never seen an accident occur: it is incredible—had I not seen it with my own eyes, I would say unbelievable."

Dr. Ary Lex, Surgical Clinic Lecturer at São Paulo University, member of the State Medical Academy and TV panellist, stated: "I had never seen a so-called mediumistic operation whose authenticity survived under test conditions. I went to Congonhas do Campo convinced that this would be just another case easily explained. What I saw is undeniably genuine. It was the first time I had ever seen such phenomena that were truly authentic. Arigó presents an extraordinary case of paranormal phenomena.

"In mediumistic trance [he] invited us to see him operate quite near him. I told him I was a doctor but he did not pay any special attention . . . In less than half an hour, in between many patients whom he told operations were unnecessary, I saw him perform four operations. For the others, he prescribed and told the patients to follow strictly the instructions.

"The first operation I saw was a drainage of a synovial cyst without any surgical preparation . . . The second was a lipoma [a fatty tumour] on a woman's arm. Arigó asked me to hold the arm, which permitted me to see the operation only a few inches away. He extracted the lipoma in only thirty seconds, but in the strangest way. He did not cut open the tissue; he sort of rubbed the skin with the back of his scalpel until it opened up. He then squeezed the lipoma with his fingers and it came out whole. The third operation was another lipoma . . . Then he operated on a pterygium. I myself held the patient's head. He did it with a nail scissors—absolutely impressive. He pushed the scissors in, cut the tissue inside and, when naturally it started to bleed profusely, he just passed a piece of ordinary cotton wool over it and produced immediate hæmostasis [stagnation of bleeding]. The only possible adjective I can find to define this is spectacular, astounding . . . At one point, Arigó ' cleaned ' the scalpel on the head of Professor Accorsi with incredible violence. Accorsi felt nothing and no infections were caused . . . Arigó should be scientifically studied. I have never seen or heard of anything like him."

Dr. José Hortência de Medeiros Sobrinho, a cardiologist and radioscopist (Roentgenologist) who had studied in Sweden said: " A Polish lady, twenty eight years old, was taken to a state hospital in a desperate state. She had a syndrome of intestinal obstruction [a syndrome is a concurrence of signs and symptoms of a disease]. She was immediately examined and operated on. A tumour, obstructing the transverse colon, was removed. A colostomy with the two openings was performed [colostomy is a surgical operation in which the colon is brought out to form a permanent opening in the wall of the abdomen. A colostomy bag is worn over the opening to receive bowel movements]. The tumour was examined and was established as malignant. The patient was suffering from cancer. During the operation, the existence of enlarged ganglia at the peritoneum and a nodule in the liver had been verified. Nothing could be done. Her case was hopeless.

" Nevertheless, she was transferred to the Central Hospital of Cancer and there her abdomen was opened again. In this new operation, it became evident that metastasis [the proliferation of cancer] had already set in, spreading throughout the whole abdomen and forming another growth the size of a chicken's egg in the left flank. The patient had meanwhile lost over forty lbs. weight, being at that time only sixty five lbs. in all. The medical report said again that the case was hopeless and beyond the possibilities of present therapeutics. Two pathologists, one the Director of the Department of Anatomic Pathology of the Hospital, independently examined the material of the patient and found that it was a case of mucous-cellular metastatic carcinoma. They thought she could live another two months, more or less.

" Her husband decided to take her to Congonhas do Campo to see Arigó. As a friend of the family, I decided to go along. The patient . . . was in a desperate state. Arigó attended her. Speaking with a German accent, he told her, ' You take this

152

and get well '—and he gave her a prescription. It specified several modern medicines in unusually high dosages; Kanamicine, Olobintine, Neurorobine and Dexteoxine. The first of these is a Japanese-discovered antibiotic whose usage has in my opinion been prematurely condemned because of certain violent reactions it can produce, but which I have observed to be of a temporary nature. Olobintine is an old German medicine not much used now, and Neurorobine is almost unknown, being made by a very small laboratory. I do not think any doctor would have prescribed these medicines, much less in the high dosage used by Arigó. Nevertheless, in spite of the abnormal dosage, the patient followed the instructions and, to our great surprise, after the first week, her improvement was of such a degree that she could get up and walk around. After two weeks of treatment, she had put on twenty five lbs., and a month and a half after that, she had gained a further forty five lbs., weighing a total of 132 lbs.— five more than before she had the first operation at the hospital. She seemed almost cured. The colostomy had not been removed, however, and she was taken back to see Arigó accompanied by her doctor, her husband and myself.

" ' Dr. Fritz ' said the patient was saved but would have to take another two prescriptions, one after the other. It is interesting to note that the second included Albamicine-GU, an antibiotic of the urinary system, which had also become inflamed as a consequence. He did not mention the colostomy and it was only after the prescriptions had been taken and the patient returned for the third time that Arigó said: ' You are cured; you can close the holes.'

" A new operation was performed and the openings were closed. It was performed by a well-known surgeon who reported that he found only a few fibroids in the abdomen but no tumour. The patient has been well ever since and her intestines work normally.

" The husband of the lady is Austrian and he spoke German with Arigó when the medium was in a trance. He said that he spoke normal German ' as any German would '."

*The above description is transcribed from a television inter-
view transmitted in São Paulo. During the interview, the
doctor described a number of other cases, including a cataract,
a synovial cyst which was removed and the incision closed by
pressing its edges together, and also the following*: " Arigó
pushed a scalpel in between the eyelid and the eyeball of a
blind boy; his eyes were clear but he could not see. The
patient did not react, did not scream, did not try to reach the
medium's hand, did not try to defend himself. Arigó pushed
the eye out to an extent that enabled me to see the back of the
eyeball. He turned the scalpel around inside and then repeated the process to the other eye. While he was operating
on one eye, the patient kept the other open. After the operation, Arigó said the boy was cured and sent him away
immediately, to start examining the next in the long line of
people waiting, just as if nothing had happened . . . And the
boy *was* cured. He could see, but he could not tell me the
names of most of the objects I showed him, which proved he
had in fact been blind from his childhood as his uncle had
claimed before the operation."

*Dr. Oswaldo Lidger Conrado, from a state-owned hospital
in São Paulo, reported*: " The father of a colleague of mine,
seventy two years old, had cancer of the larynx and the floor
of the mouth, with all the characteristic symptoms and
terrible pains. He had been given two months to live . . . We
took a plane to Belo Horizonte and had to leave the patient
there as he was too weak to continue the trip to Congonhas do
Campo. We went on alone to Congonhas and met Arigó . . .
he gave us a perfect diagnosis of the patient and then gave us
a prescription . . . My colleague's father recovered surprisingly: the chain of ganglia disappeared and the lesions of the
mouth and larynx healed. He got so much better that he went
himself to Congonhas three times. The pains also relented
and his general condition was much better. After the treatment, the doctors of the Cancer Hospital in his hometown of
Salvador, in Bahia, examined him again and gave him at least
another year. A cure could not be expected, but his recovery
at all under the circumstances was extraordinary, revealing a

capacity for distance-diagnosis beyond any explanation in accordance with our present knowledge."

Finally, from the viewpoint of a patient, Hamlet Marone, sixty eight, an employee of the Royal Bank of Canada in São Paulo, tells of a visit he made to Congonhas while on a sightseeing holiday in Minas Gerais: " I did not go to be operated on, nor to seek a prescription. There were a lot of people in great need, with a variety of illnesses. I was in the room just for curiosity, to see how Arigó worked. To my astonishment, ' Dr. Fritz ' asked me to come forward. ' You have to be operated on,' he said to me in his heavily-accented Portuguese. ' We'll take care of your pterygium.'

" I was amazed, because I really did need an operation, though I had never considered having it this way. ' Dr. Fritz ' had me sit in a small chair, took two pairs of simple nail scissors and, without any precautions, pushed them into my eye and started operating . . . I did not feel anything. My eye felt as though under anæsthesia. I myself was surprisingly calm. There wasn't excessive blood, and he stopped the bleeding by passing a bit of cotton wool over the eye. He had me blindfold my eyes for a couple of hours and then, after a second treatment, the veil was removed and I was ready to leave. A São Paulo specialist told me later that my operation had been perfectly successful, and so it has remained to this day."

There are many more cases, many testimonies from satisfied patients collected in letters, newspapers and books. A reporter, Moacyr Jorge, presented dozens in a series of stories syndicated through a newspaper chain. J. Herculano Pires published more in a book on Arigó. And the journalist, Jorge Rizzini, the first to write about Arigó at all, publicised more still. But more impressive than a hundred books are the films that were made of some of these operations. The first was made by Rizzini on eight mm. stock under precarious technical circumstances, but it does clearly show blood running down a patient's face and the immediate hæmostasis which follows Arigó's pass with the cotton wool. Another has been shown in São Paulo movie houses and a third was screened on a TV show boasting more than two million viewers.

* * *

These are the facts concerning José Pedro de Freitas, known as Arigó. For Brazil's spiritists, they constitute yet another proof, the most astounding and undeniable yet, of the correctness of spiritist interpretation of the natural laws governing the nature of man and his soul. As for the rest of us—well, there may be an explanation for the phenomena we have described. But nobody, so far, has come up with a good one. Nevertheless Arigó is not an hypothesis: he is a fact, not religious but material, just as his successes are facts, proven and witnessed, however inconvenient to the established order.

Must this be denied because it is repugnant to that order and its concepts?

Here in Brazil there are not lacking those answering that question in the affirmative. Moreover, they are willing to go to extraordinary lengths to destroy the facts so "inconvenient" to their positions—religious, political or professional. Those who have attempted to destroy spiritism from the start, for example, have astutely influenced the writers of the Penal Code to include an Article (No. 284) making spiritual healing a crime. That is why the judge had an easy task satisfying those interested in Arigó's condemnation by passing the sentence he did. Yet here is another contradiction: legally all spiritual mediums who are healers can be arrested as criminals. But they are not.

Why not? Because, with the exception of "special cases" like Arigó's, most judges are lenient in their interpretation of the law and the police in practice only persecute spiritist practices of African origin.

Again why? Because most of them secretly incline towards the movement anyway! Nevertheless, in spite of Article 141 of the Constitution, which guarantees to all the free practice of religion and assures the citizen that nobody shall be refused protection of the law because of religion, Judge Fernando

Celso Guimarães, a small, bespectacled fellow in the Rio court, was able to say to the father, a spiritualist, in a custody suit: " If you take your children to a spiritist session, I shall have you arrested."

On Friday, November 20, 1964, county judge Márcio Aristeu Monteiro de Barros, without advising José Arigó's lawyer as he had promised to do, giving a verdict on a charge laid in 1961, condemned the medium to sixteen months in prison for the crime of witch-doctery. " Witchcraft," declared the judgment in part, " is punished to safeguard the individual and the public well-being. The man who, without being a doctor, determines the nature of a sickness or illness by their symptoms; who, without being a doctor, makes operations; who, claiming to be in the ' control ' of a ' spirit,' in trance, prescribes or operates, or supplies herbs; who uses ' passes,' attitudes, postures, words, prayers, exorcisms or any other means to facilitate childbirths, cure a rebellious cough, snake bites, cancer, lower fever, tuberculosis, hæmorrhage, cataracts, deafness, etcetera—this citizen represents a tremendous danger to the health of an undetermined number of people whose custody unquestionably is entrusted upon the state."

A curious thing to say, especially in view of the statement a few days later by the Health Minister that Brazil had a deficit of 22,000 doctors, 66,000 nurses and 10,000 medical technicians. In the country, the Minister added, there are 40,000,000 sick, not counting the children. How, then, can the state take custody of the health of the people when there are already over forty million sick and a shortage of 22,000 doctors? Without their healers, millions in the interior, whose nearest doctor may be dozens, even hundreds of miles away, would be left to fend for themselves.

If the sentence passed on Arigó were to be carried out, Brazil's infant and adult mortality rate would increase. Surely the country's health problem would be better dealt with by trying to find *more* Arigós, while encouraging more of the younger people to train for a medical career?

The whole thing, one fears, is but a flagrant example of

another fact: the existence of two Brazils—one in reality, the other only on paper, devised by politicians and the judiciary to satisfy appearances. I love my country and my countrymen: there is no people with such a wealth of brotherly love and the right sentiments. Yet, as a Brazilian, I have to acknowledge that the reason why Brazil has so far only been the country of tomorrow, never the country of today, is largely because those that have taken the responsibility of governing its destiny have proved to be ill-prepared for the task.

But they are only the few. March 31, 1964, may change the course of events. In any case, the many will at the end prevail and religious liberty will be guaranteed once and for all in Brazil.

In the meantime, spiritism flourishes. Charity is its corner-stone—charity towards the poor, charity towards the sick. And one of the main aspects of that charity, one of the chief reasons for its success, is the free spiritual healing so generously dispensed . . . that and the fact that, all over Brazil, the total increases of those who had lost their hopes of finding a cure, yet finally discovered one at a Spiritist Centre.

Flourishing, too, is José Arigó. He cannot operate, of course, at the moment, not until the case is finally resolved. But this does not mean that his activities as a medium have ceased. He continues to see the multitudes who seek his aid in the cure of ills for which earthly medicine has proved inadequate. And " Dr. Fritz," dispensing " diagnosis and prescriptions only " for the time being, still works at his customary incredible speed.

What would happen, the good " Doctor " was asked recently, if the sentence on Arigó was carried out?

" Then we will materialise in public squares in full daylight and operate upon the needy for all to see, so long as Arigó remains in his cell," the spirit message replied unequivocally. " No-one can thwart God's will; no-one can stop the sun from shining . . ."

If that should happen, one may be pardoned the hope that one might be lucky enough to be around with a camera!

This was some time ago. Meanwhile the Minas Gerais state Court of Appeals confirmed the sentence passed in a lower court and José Arigó is lingering in jail, where he will have to stay for nearly another year, if he is not pardoned for good behaviour before.

Why? For what crime?

Maybe you, the reader, can explain.

I cannot.

A more sensible alternative might have been to build a hospital in Congonhas do Campo to house all the sick that wanted to see José Arigó, surrounding him with the same medical organisation that exists in Lourdes, with a research team to examine each case, before and after Arigó's treatment or operation.

People may be unwilling to spend two thousand dollars just to see the beauties of Rio but they will certainly be willing to spend that much or more to get well.

Brazil is in constant need of dollars. This could be quite a good source.

How about the Government giving it a thought?

CHAPTER NINE

Kardecism Meets the Sorcerers

*Umbanda tem mironga | Umbanda tem dendê | Quem quiza
conhecê Umbanda | Tem muito que aprendê . . .*
*Umbanda has secrets | Umbanda has unguents | Whoever
wants to know about Umbanda | Has too much to learn . . .*
so says one of the ritualistic chants associated with the cult
that, in a recent Congress held in Rio de Janeiro, claimed for
itself ten million followers all over the country.

Certainly there is much to learn about the movement,
which is strongest in Rio, São Paulo and Rio Grande do Sul,
the Brazilian pampas state, especially about its origins. For
although ardent followers dub it " the religion of the poor
that will conquer the world," and others acclaim it as " the
religion of Brazil " (a book with that name having been
widely bought), Umbanda's appearance on the South American scene is in fact comparatively recent. Gilberto Freyre's
monumental study in the development of Brazilian civilisation, *The Masters And The Slaves,* was published in 1933,
for example, and although he examines deeply every facet of
magic, witchcraft and Negro sorcery in Brazil, there is no
mention of Umbanda.

Many of Freyre's acute observations are nevertheless relevant to any study of the origins of Umbanda.

Says he: " The frequent occurrence of sorcery and sexual
magic among us is another trait that is looked upon as being
exclusively of African origin; but the first volume of documents relative to the Holy Office in Brazil records many cases

ABOVE: Umbanda mediums, clad in their white uniforms, do homage to the great sea goddess, to the sounds of *combos* and clapping hands. BELOW, LEFT: Mediums 'receive' spirits of old negroes and help to solve our problems. Here is one, smoking her pipe, and being consulted by a blonde girl, on Copacaban beach on the night of Yemanjá. BELOW, RIGHT: Black and white fraternize. The cabalistic sign is clearly shown on the left side of the white uniform of the 'head spirit' medium.

ABOVE: Statues of the Virgin Mary, Jesus and Joseph form the altar on the beach, together with bottles of champagne and coca-cola. BELOW, LEFT: Images of Catholic saints, statues of Indians and negroes, and African negro fetishes share the altar for spiritual practices. Umbanda is the result. BELOW, RIGHT: Pop corn, onions, red wine with cachaça, dendê oil and lighted candles are some of the offerings to Ogun, the Yoruba Orisha.

of Portuguese witches. Their practices may have undergone an African *influence* but in essence they were expressions of European Satanism (which to this day can be met with in our country) mingled with Negro or Indian rites. Antônia Fernandes, known as Nobrega, stated that she was allied with the Devil and at her consultations the responses were given to her by ' a certain thing that talked, kept in a glass.' This is mediæval magic of the purest European variety. Another Portuguese woman, Isabel Rodrigues, nicknamed ' wry-mouth,' furnished miraculous powders and taught powerful prayers. The most famous of all, Maria Gonçalves, whose sobriquet was ' Burn-tail,' took the greatest familiarities with Satan. With much burying and digging up of kegs, Burn-tail's witchcraft was almost wholly concerned with problems of impotence; for it would appear that these colonial sorcerers' clientele was very largely made up of the lovelorn, those who were unhappy, or those insatiable in their passions.

" In Portugal, for that matter, it is known that the most cultivated and illustrious personages were involved in witchcraft." And Freyre goes on to quote Júlio Danta's *Figures Of Yesterday And Today*—instancing Dom Nuno da Cunha, Grand Inquisitor at the time of John V, " swathed in his robes of Cardinal's purple like a kind of silkworm " and trembling in fear of sorcerers; " grave physicians like Curvo Semedo " who treated conjugal infidelity with " a certain witch's brew made of the shoe soles of the woman and her husband "; and " crafty apothecaries in black-spotted capes and with big silver buckles on their shoes " who made a fortune selling a herb known as *pombinha,* which was cast upon hot stones and made into an incense with the teeth of a dead man! This strange practice, Dantas reports, was designed " to awaken love in the decrepit organism of old men and to thaw the disdainful frigidity of youths."

Such a vogue for the occult and aphrodisiac spells was hardly to be wondered at, Freyre observes, " in a land that had been so drained of people that only by an extraordinary effort of virility was it able to colonise Brazil." And once on the South American mainland, he adds, this tradition of resorting to witchcraft to maintain that virility keyed in naturally enough with the religious beliefs of their African slaves, themselves imbued with sorcery and fetichism, to develop a climate of social progress intimately connected with magic influenced by the intense mysticism of the Negro.

It is important to note here the type of relationship which was established, apart from the subjective influence that magic had upon the psyche of the colonisers, between the Negroes and their masters. With the exception of the *mucama*, the Negro milk-mother who became the confidante of the mistress of the house and the darling of its children, the Africans were submitted to complete and total serfdom " in an aristocracy that was practically illiterate " (Freyre). Moreover, besides the indignities from master and overseer which the Negro had to suffer, his women, too, were subjected to a double tyranny, that of the masters who took them for concubines, and that of their jealous wives.

The ladies, and their daughters for that matter, the *sinhá-moças*, were often excessively cruel. Writes Frederico Burlamaqui in his memoir on *The Slave Trade And Domestic Slavery, 1837*: " The most common phrases, when her mistress is suspicious of husband or lover, are, ' I'll have her fried,' ' I'll roast her alive; I'll burn her,' or ' I'll cut out such and such a part.' And many times these threats are put into execution, often only because of a mere suspicion."

How right he was! The white ladies were willing to perform any act of cruelty on their female slaves, almost always motivated by jealousy of their husbands, according to Freyre. " There are tales of *sinhá-moças* who had the eyes of the pretty *mucamas* gouged out and then had them served to the husbands for dessert in a jelly-dish, floating in blood that was still fresh; tales of young baronesses of adult age who out of jealousy or spite had fifteen year old mulatto girls sold off to old libertines. There were others who kicked out the teeth of their women slaves with their boots, or who had their breasts cut off, their nails drawn, or their faces and ears burned ... a whole series of tortures."

The men were little better. " There is no slavery without

sexual depravity," it has been well said. And the original colonisers of Brazil, arriving in the strange country without women, picked first the Indian, later the Negro slave women, to assuage their lust as they chose. The sons of the *fazendas* (farms), too, were encouraged to indulge their vices from an early age though, as Father Lopes Gama pointed out " the Negro women and a large part of the mulatto women, for whom honour is a chimerical term signifying nothing, are ordinarily the first to bring about the early corruption of the young masters, giving them their first lessons in libertinism, in which, from childhood, they are engulfed. And from this there comes, for the future, a troop of young mulattoes and offspring whose influence in the families is to be a most pernicious one." Freyre comments here that the depravity and " pernicious influence " derive not from the Negro as such but from the slave, which is quite a different thing. The Negroes in Africa, he points out, require all kinds of aphrodisiacs to spur their sexual desires, far from being at their mercy. In Brazil, it was the white masters, with little to occupy their time but to give orders, who naturally enough developed a sexual excitation of the most recondite kind, who required (sated as they were) ever more bizarre *divertissements,* who became habituated thus to their own more sadistic tendencies. Sex, for them, became a hobby, an end in itself.

The much-vaunted " purity " of the white Portuguese women who later joined their menfolk in the new country was in fact "at the expense of the much-maligned mulatto women; it was at the cost of a promiscuity and laxness of morals stimulated by the white masters at the slave hut that the *Sinhazinhas* remained pure and chaste " (Freyre). And this laxity did not only work in the direction of the women: an anonymous chronicler of Pernambuco wrote in 1817 that the masters, " eager to augment their herds, stimulated the great lubricity of the plantation Negroes." Among the slaves the most popular with the masters were " those who were the womanchasers, the deflowerers of maidens, those who lost no time in taking Negro women, that they might increase the slave herd and thus the paternal capital."

No wonder the Brazilian lad is sexually precocious today and enjoys his reputation as a womanizer! (Though the actual deflowering of maidens is somewhat frowned upon, since the law provides that, if she is under age, then the lad must marry her!)

At the other extreme, the sentimental Brazilian character made much of the milk-mothers—the black mammies who suckled the children, taught them the little they knew, acted as confidante to both boys and girls, and encouraged them to pray. Even the *sinhá-moças,* when they were not jealous, sought the aid of the *mucamas* (as has been pointed out in an earlier chapter) to solve their love problems, chase away an unwanted marriage choice, snare a desired partner or cast other spells. The masters too were not above dabbling in the mysteries of the *mandingueiros*—an aphrodisiac potion here, a specific to hasten the consummation of a delayed marriage there . . . these were a commonplace of the times.

Such a duality of behaviour, coupled with the convention of beauty-standards deriving from the *mucama* and the slave mistress, was bound to have a profound effect upon Brazilian *mores* for all time.

And an equal ambivalence characterised the religious scene, as we have observed. Nominally Catholic, the slaves were in fact allowed to continue their African rites in secret, though had the Fathers realised that this *laissez-faire* policy would lead to a religious movement of such unprecedented vitality, it is dubious if they would have been so compliant! Nevertheless, the importance of these anomalies, of the relations between master and slave, white and black, Portuguese and Indian, to the upsurge of the spiritist movement cannot be over-emphasised.

Freud established in his analysis of the human psyche that a person can feel both love and hate for the same recipient. This is exampled on a national scale in Brazil.

The hatred felt by individual slaves for individual masters or mistresses, and vice-versa, was never generalised in Brazil. The masters used the Negroes according to their whims, abused them in every way, satisfied their lusts, treated them as inferior beings—but with disdain, not hatred. And the slaves, through miscegenation and an unusual sense of humility, found themselves too busy striving, first, to pass from the services of the *senzala* to the big house, later in climbing the social ladder, to indulge, in hatred or vengeful feelings. " By no manner of means is there in the Brazilian, as in the Anglo-American, two warring halves: the white and the black," Freyre has written. " We are two fraternising halves that are mutually enriched with diverse values and experiences."

As we have seen, innumerable " Catholics " today attend mass in the morning and a spiritist session in the evening of the same day. This is symptomatic of a society overflowing with the results of the many different shades of love and hatred that existed between masters and slaves, the many special prejudices born together with the innumerable mestizos, mulattoes and people of all shades and colours resulting therefrom. And it is just one more example of the imprint such a history leaves on the psychological and psychic pattern of Brazil, a pattern on which first Kardecism, then a syncretism of Negro, Indian, Catholic and Kardecist beliefs called Umbanda was to make its mark.

We have demonstrated how constant contact with the supernatural, even in its most primitive form, prepared the ground for a rapid acceptance of Kardecism in Brazil. This was further helped by a certain elasticity of mind, a liberality of outlook in the early spiritists. The Africans and their descendants have highly evolved spiritual entities, too? they asked. Spirits that come back to teach the truth of the Eternal? Why they are the same as ours—the Orixás* of the Yoruba, of the Nagô-JêJê cult . . . Good and bad spirits acting all around us at all times? Why the Bantu have them, too, a multitude of them; only they call them Ma-Bamba in Angola and Kilulu in the Congo . . .

But Kardec was an intellectual, a European with scientific training; not for him the magic, the rituals, the superstitions the African brought to Brazil. Kardecism provided a mental

*To use the Portuguese spelling of Orisha customarily adopted today.

experience open to those with minds, those exercising the intellect. Doubtless its message of love and charity was for all to understand, but first all had to read and understand the Gospel according to spiritism . . . and, as always, reading and thinking were minority pursuits. There were no chants, no drums, no rituals, nothing that met the eye: the message was for the soul and not the senses.

But it is by the senses that the majority live. What about them?

Indirectly, Kardecism *was* to be the answer. Before its appearance in Brazil, all Negro cults, however often Brazilians resorted to them in secret, were dismissed as animistic, fetichistic mumbo-jumbo. Kardecism brought new light to the whole question of spirit communication, however: its appeal to the intellect gave the subject a different standing, a new respectability. It was the bridge needed to span the gap between the white and black cults, and those on both sides too ignorant to take advantage of it, now saw the Negro rites from a new viewpoint. And what attracted them mainly was that they practised magic, which Kardec denied them (" Magic power exists only in the imagination of the superstitious; there is no sacramental word, no cabalistic sign, no talisman that has any action over the spirits," one message in Kardec's first book observes severely).

Since Kardec had made the acceptance of spirits as such respectable, however, the time was ripe for a religious movement embracing the generality of his principles but adding the mysticism, the ceremonial, the music and colour that he lacked. Thus Umbanda . . .

It is now claimed that " the law of Umbanda is the same religion as that practised by the Egyptians, the Yogis, the Lamas, whose origin is lost in time immemorial." While this may be true, its actual first appearance on the stage of history was at the beginning of this century, probably in Rio de Janeiro, as the result of Kardecist influence on the existing Negro cults there.

The majority of the latter were of course Bantu, not Yoruba, in origin. Their theogony and rituals were far less

166

complex than the Yoruba worship of Orixás, being concerned only with the reverence of the departed and the souls of ancestors. The cults practised in the Rio " Macumbas " [a generic term given to the place and the cult of the Negro worship] were therefore more open to relatively easy " infiltration " by Kardecist influence, as they had been before to Catholic influences. It is perhaps important to note, despite assurances to the contrary by followers, that the term " Umbanda " never appeared as a definition of a cult, a " law " or a religion before the early nineteen-hundreds. Ramos uses the word itself to describe the priest officiating, and still calls the cult Macumba. Stories about this cult written in 1904 by João do Rio also call it Macumba. Taking due note of the claim that the word derives from the Sanskrit *Aum-Bandha,* which seems to mean " the limit of the unlimited " or " the divine principle," made in 1941 at the first Umbanda Congress, it would seem that the explanation given by one of its earliest followers, José Pessóa, is simpler and fits in better with all the available data.

As with almost every movement of wide influence, Umbanda started through the iniative of one person, although he never made that claim, nor did he realise that he was pioneering something that was to grow and grow. It is of course possible, though not probable, that others took the same initiative independently at the same time. Be that as it may, according to this story the whole thing started through a medium named Zélio de Moraes.

The climate of opinion at the time was that of acceptance, the possibility of spirit communication had been established by Kardecism; the point now was to agree on what sort of spirits! Doctors, to operate and prescribe, yes; others to give lessons in love, charity, humility, wisdom, fine! But these were professional men, lecturers. Or had been on earth. They were splendid if you were suffering, or if you were of that minority used to discourse and intellectual discussion. But what about the daily life of ordinary people, the poor and humble? What about love and money problems? What about magic? And what about the other spirits? What about the spirits of the humble and poor who had departed, what about the spirits of Negroes and Indians (called *caboclos*), for instance? Were *they* not worth communicating with?

No, said the Kardecists. Yes, said others who had experienced the Macumbas of Rio and had contacted the spirits of Negroes and even *Caboclos* at them. And it was a group of the latter who orientated themselves around the medium Zélio de Moraes and started the practices later designated with the generic name Umbanda.

Why? Because as a medium his spirit guide was not a doctor, not a philosopher or message-giver, but an Indian calling himself " Caboclo das Sete Encruzilhadas " (" Spirit of the Seven Crossroads ").

(Lest the mention of an Indian spirit guide—almost a cliché in European spiritualist circles!—should raise a scornful smile, the writer may perhaps mention here that he has been to dozens of Umbanda sessions and "spoken" to innumerable Caboclos and Negro spirit-guides. He was at the time slowly gathering material for this book, which has taken years to compile, but did not as a rule reveal this fact. He would ask no question, but the spirit or whatever it was " incorporated " in the medium would often start saying, unprompted and on his own initiative, something like: " Nice work you are doing, talking about us, uh? White sons often make complicated what simple . . . Oxalá—Jesus, you say—give orders. We obey. You think about this . . . *Saravá ésse fiô.*" Negro and Caboclo spirits usually " speak " in broken Portuguese. What is undeniable is that very often they speak sense, at least to millions of people in Brazil. In Rio alone, according to Friar Boaventura Kloppenburg, a special envoy appointed by the Catholic church to fight any kind of spiritist manifestation, there are *a minimum of 30,000 centres* of Umbanda . . .)

Zélio de Moraes, then, was a blondish, six-foot simpleton with not more than a primary education, known to be modest and sincere and in the habit of experiencing visions. Since his childhood, these had frequently incorporated the figure of an Indian. " Some time in the nineteen-twenties, friends told me about Kardec," he said to the writer, " and added that I could put my mediumship to the service of many needing guidance there, without going to Macumbas, which I dislike." At the time of the interview, several years ago when he was already over sixty, he could not recall the precise date.

Anyway, since Macumbas were forbidden by the police in Rio, the group decided to cross Guanabara Bay and start sessions with Zélio in the town of São Gonçalo, where, since it was in the neighbouring state, the law was believed to be interpreted less rigidly.

The plans for the journey, the rituals and practices of the sessions on the other side of the bay, all the dogma, these were dictated by the " Caboclo of the Seven Crossroads." The mission, writes José Pessôa, was " to purify Umbanda from its essentially African rites which have been practised since the first wave of slaves was brought to Brazil by the Portuguese. And in this mission I accompanied Zélio from the beginning, since more or less 1920."

The Circle of the Caboclo of the Seven Crossroads, once established, kept increasing " because of the material and spiritual help he gave to those who took the trouble to visit him, because of the sick he cured through his herbs . . . because of the comfort he gave and the counsels he offered to those who knew not what to do the next day." And to those who ask what Indians have to do with an African cult, the spiritual explanation, offered by numerous Caboclos interviewed by the writer, is that, both being races of slaves, the Indians and Negroes united on the astral plane to bring the message of humility to the " sons of earth " and help them with their problems. José Pessôa, small, kind, white, retired, bald-headed and over seventy years old, explained that friends kept on asking to be taken to the sessions, and that what began in a rented backyard soon graduated to a house specially purchased for the purpose, called " Tenda Nossa Senhora da Piedade "—" The Hut of Our Lady of Piety."

And here was the essence of religious and racial syncretism : Negro and white worshippers together, practising a more evolved form of African ritual, under the influence of Europe's Kardecism, under the leadership of an Indian spirit guide, and under the name of Our Lady of Piety! Yet the spirit " appointed " by the Caboclo as the " great master," the spiritual leader of all, is none other than—Jesus Christ, whom he calls by the African equivalent, Oxalá . . .

Consistently enough, the pattern within the framework of Umbanda itself is equally kaleidoscopic. Each medium has his own group clustered around the spirit guide incorporated— in the Latin sense of *in-corporare,* to take within the body— in himself. And each guide makes his own rules. One might think that, if everything was done according to the orders of the spirits, each group would therefore be part of a more or less homogeneous whole. But it's not as simple as that. Very few mediums, for a start, are controlled by their spirit guides to the point of having no personal influence on the messages as transmitted to the public. Most add their own thoughts and beliefs to a greater or lesser degree though, in the main, this is confined to matters of ritual and ceremony. But it does mean that one Umbanda session may *appear* very unlike another a few blocks away!

Another factor to be borne in mind is whether or not the medium is among those, and they were, and still are, not few, who charge for their services. If so, they do it on their own account, because Umbanda, like Kardecism, makes a point of working for charity, and thus are in a position to alter the rules as they wish. Yet another element is the medium's own concept of how the spiritual work of the Caboclo and Negro guides should be carried out. One old " black father," an " Uncle Tom " as he would be termed by the Southern Americans, told the writer through his medium, " We do what we can with what we have got."

The foregoing, it must be emphasised, is a personal opinion. There are others who say that the diversity of rituals within Umbanda stems from the notion that the nationality of the leader of any group governs the type of ritual it will employ. This is true to a degree. There is certainly a Lower and a Higher Umbanda, as the *Umbandistas* style themselves, which varies as the distance from the original African customs. Thus there are those who smoke cigars, drink *Cachaça* (the native brandy made of sugar-cane juice), use drums, sing chants, dance at ritual meetings, kill animals, and use snakes (usually small pythons), while others when under the control of their Negro or Indian spirit guides just smoke cigars and do not even drink *Cachaça*, which is called *Marafo* or *Marafa* at Macumbas and in Umbanda.

To the police, unfortunately, until the end of the Vargas regime, such nuances were not apparent. It was all Macumba, black magic, sorcery and, with periods of increasing or decreasing severity, all those who practised it had to be arrested ... Prosecutions remained almost constant and the image of those prosecuted (and persecuted) was all bad: it was the province solely of those members of society at the lower, more ignorant end of the social scale.

Here is where we see the ambivalence of sentiment at work; here is where the master/slave relationship obtrudes upon the present-day scene. Instead of recognising in these practices something similar to those familiar from the milk-mother, the socialites rejected them as inferior, primitive rites to be scorned out of hand. And no help was to be expected from the mulattoes themselves: they were far too interested in climbing upwards in a society dominated by the values of a western civilisation to defend the beliefs and practices of their ancestors.

The master mistreated his slaves, yet he went to bed with them.

Society, dominated by a master complex, persecuted Macumba or Umbanda, but at night, when nobody was supposed to be looking, stole out to seek their representatives in far-away places with the idea of seeking " magic " help in the solution of its problems—now, as centuries ago, simply questions of love or money. Brazil, in fact, persecuted but feared, despised yet respected the evidence of religious fervour in its midst. Freud's concept of ambivalence was and still is at play.

In fact it is true to say that if the persecuting masters went to bed with their slaves, society went to bed in the same way with Umbanda.

" If Macumba was not, *in spite of all its prestige*, a ' thing '

171

forbidden by the laws of our country, we would see posters at railroad stations saying: 'Want to solve your problems of love? Want to win the lottery? Want to achieve your dreams? Then look for the 'Pai de Santo '," so read a front-page story in *O Globo* for July 7, 1937. And the story went on to describe, in the ironic, cynical tone expected of a journalist writing about anything serious or beyond him, what transpired in the Macumbas of those days. " But the law does not permit this kind of publicity in Brazil," the story added. " And to the Macumbeiros there happens what happens to bookmakers and to forbidden love: being persecuted, they develop to a degree that may be called a true miracle of multiplication . . ."

In Rio, the paper continues, " everybody knows where the Villa Maria is. Everyone knows that there lives the Pai de Santo, Francisco de Paula. And it is from that old house, from its large *terreiro*, that drums beat out rhythms, and prayers are said all night long. Inside is a long, white room, with an altar in one of its corners filled with sweets, cakes candles, money and images of the Saints who are patrons of the 'black magic'.

" The limousines that drive the high and mighty out there, with headlamps always on to find their way in the tortuous streets of the Irajá district, amaze the dwellers . . . Workers, washerwomen, men without profession—the people—mix with the rich who go there to consult a tall, black man who speaks with a soft voice and has slow movements . . . they ask him to solve problems that don't have easy solutions by the employment of common, earthly means. The ' Macumbeiro ' receives them with a happy countenance, a smiling and paternal attitude. They go inside the white room, make their prayers and return to the ' terreiro.' And then they go home with the hope that all they have wished will come true, leaving a few *mil reis* (shillings) as a token of appreciation for ' Pai Pedro ' (the spirit entity), and some sweets for the spiritual protectors. Thus they think they have bought happiness—not at a bad price . . .

" The majority of petitions relate either to love or to football. In the 'Macumbas' success is almost always sought in one or both. The husband who had a fight with his wife, who then walked out leaving no address, goes there to seek the aid of St. George [religious syncretism] to find the *jeito* (the Brazilian term for the 'artful fix,' the dodge that will put it all right, the correct gimmick). The football fan implores the 'saints' to help his team win. And all the requests are written on a piece of paper which is folded and fixed to the floor with a dagger. This is the 'magic fix.'

"The police precinct, having heard about this kind of work, probably through somebody whose pleas had remained unanswered at the Macumba, raided the house, arrested the 'Macumbeiro' and seized his instruments of magic . . . 'Pai Pedro' refused to explain anything and kept the names of his customers secret . . ."

The journalist who dreamed up this piece was obviously little versed in the intricacies of Umbanda or Macumba, but the article is interesting for two reasons: first that, as early as 1937, the movement was as popular and prestigious as that; and secondly that reference at the beginning of the feature. If "everyone knew" about the Villa Maria as the story says, why did the police only act after a tip-off? Obviously because the powerful people who frequented the place could normally keep them under control, but once an official complaint was registered, they were forced to act. The story does not say what happened to the Macumbeiro at the police station. But the writer knows what happened to a very famous Umbanda medium, the leader of a centre, named Mrs. Hilda Roxo. Now a stout and elegant lady in her fifties, Mrs. Roxo was at the time a renowned beauty. "When I was arrested," she said in an interview, "I was thrown into a common cell. Later several men came in and surrounded me. They said nothing but their intentions were obvious. My power was stronger than theirs, however. I concentrated on all the Phalanxes of my spirit guides and we produced such a vibration that the men were quite helpless and lost their virility . . ."

The news of this event travelled fast, even reaching the Catete Palace, from where at this time dictator Getulio Vargas ruled Brazil. When his friend, surgeon-professor Castro Araujo, told Vargas of the incident, the president expressed an interest in meeting the medium.

" I was received in his enormous office on the first floor," Mrs. Roxo said. " He got up from behind his jacaranda desk, greeted me with kindness, then looked at me sternly and said: ' If you " receive " spirits, you can tell me where I put a document I examined this morning, and what was in it.' I concentrated and then felt my spirit guide beginning to take over. I lost consciousness because I was under his control, in trance . . . I was told later that the guide had told Vargas where the document was, what was in it, and some other things. Professor Araujo said later that Vargas had been very impressed because the ' other things ' referred to intimate thoughts of his that nobody could possibly have known about, and because the contents of the document had been secret too . . ."

After this encounter, Mrs. Roxo was left strictly alone by the police.

Today, better known by the name of Reverend Mally Hilda, her title as priestess of the spiritualist school she founded, she is one of the small gallery of prominent Umbanda mediums who have been practising the cult for over twenty years. Her Fraternity, which has assets of more than £30,000, has built a temple in the middle of woods in the mountainous city of Terezopolis, an hour's drive from Rio. Besides the temple, there are apartments for the members of the Fraternity, the priests and priestesses, a school for poor children and a clinic where they receive free medical attention, set among the woods and beside the stream that flows through the 2,000-acre property. The rites practised at the temple, as often happens with Umbanda centres, are slightly different, more personalised, than those at the majority of places, perhaps because Mrs. Roxo was born of mixed white, Negro and Indian blood.

She and the Macumbeiro mentioned in the newspaper story were not, of course, alone in being arrested and persecuted by the police. Zélio de Moraes and many, many more have frequently spent the night inside the local jail. But none of this has been of any avail. The Brazilian character is not one to meet a problem head on, like a Spanish *torero* with a bull (the Brazilian would rather whisper into the animal's ear: " you just fake it that I killed you, then we'll both get out of this alive! "). Certain exceptions—the bestial tortures and depravity still exampled within the police, for instance—apart, the Brazilian normally displays a personality filled with kindness and warmth. As among the slave masters of old, there may be disdain, there may be social prejudice, but there is no hatred. Therefore as fast as the police persecuted the mediums, so the people, the poor on foot and the rich in their Cadillacs, would flock to the *terreiros* to see them. And no sooner was a famous Macumbeiro, the head medium of a *Tenda* or Centre of Umbanda, arrested than there was a discrete tinkle of the telephone, a mysterious call, and he would shortly be freed.

Thus Umbanda grew and grew, until, in 1941, the *Federação Espírita de Umbanda* (the Spiritist Federation of Umbanda) organised the first Congress of the movement (*Primeiro Congresso Brasileiro do Espiritismo de Umbanda*). Says the Organising Committee in its preface to the Annals of the Congress:

" Spiritism was introduced into Brazil by Kardec's work in the fourth quarter of the last century, the fundamentals on which the spiritists of Brazil still base their actions. Their greatest contribution has been in the field of religion, having through their Centres instilled faith in the hearts of the masses, awakening in them the feeling of fraternity and love for their neighbour. The reputation acquired among us ... in these last twenty years, has spurred the foundation in this capital [of Rio de Janeiro] of a great number of associations specially designed for the practice of this manner of spiritual work.

" Its practice varied according to the knowledge of each nucleus of practitioners. The necessary homogeneity in its practices is therefore non-existent, which has resulted in the confusion of other, inferior, spiritist practices with those of Umbanda [meaning Macumba]. This Congress was organised with the purpose of studying, debating and codifying this thrilling manner of spiritual work, once and for all to expel from our *milieu* what is practised in the name of spiritism of Umbanda, but that in our stage of civilisation has no longer a justification for its existence."

The preface goes on to make three important points:

1. That Kardec's works are recognised as the " fundamental basis " for spiritist practices in Brazil;

2. That Umbanda is a " different " fashion of working in this field; and that it appeared as such in the nineteen-twenties;

3. That primitive rites involving such barbaric things as hair shavings, blood baths and the like are " unjustified in our stage of civilisation " and have no part in Umbanda. And that an Umbanda " code " was needed, to define exactly what *was* Umbanda and homogenise the cult which, because of the individual freedom of all practitioners and their " lack of knowledge," had been infiltrated with all maner of different rites, many of them not Umbanda at all; and, most important of all, that Umbanda itself is not just a collection of Negro fetichist practices inherited from the Africans along with witchcraft and sorcery . . .

The basic fact of the existence of spirits, in the Kardecist sense, is accepted. Reincarnation is accepted. But the spirit guides in Umbanda do not, as we have seen, transmit beautifully phrased and written messages of high intellectual content: being Indian and Negro, the manner of their spiritual work is different; the mechanics of mediumship in which they are involved follows a different dynamic. The ritual of Negro custom is present, along with its chants, its drums, the cigars and the *Cachaça*. Magic, rejected by Kardec, is ever present in Umbanda.

Nevertheless, just like the highly intellectual spirit guides that communicated with Kardec, the Negro entities and Caboclos also consider Jesus the Great Master. Says *Resolution*

176

Seven of the First Brazilian Congress of Umbanda Spiritism:
" We recognise Jesus, whom we call Oxalá, as the Supreme
Master of Spiritism of Umbanda."

With the methods and rites employed to do His will by
the *Umbandistas,* we shall deal in the next chapter.

CHAPTER TEN

Saravá Umbanda!

Saravá Umbanda!, shouted the man on the rostrum. *Saravá Umbanda!*—Hail Umbanda!—more than seven thousand Umbandistas roared back enthusiastically. Fireworks crackled into life and exploded high in the air above the delegates from ten states who stood rigidly to attention in the vast arena. A light breeze stirred the white suits and dresses, fluttered the colourful congress ribbons pinned on corsage and lapel, as massed bands crashed into the opening chords of the Brazilian National Anthem. The second Umbanda Congress, held in the Maracanazinho Stadium in Rio de Janeiro in July, 1961, was under way.

The choice of site alone symbolised the difference, the progress that had occurred since the first congress exactly twenty years earlier. Then, it was a matter of scrambling secret meetings in the *Tendas* and *Centros* of Umbanda after the Negro and Indian guides had been asked for specific instructions on every facet of the ceremony. Now, press and public fought for seats in the Maracanazinho, the "small Maracana" [the world's largest stadium], and the attending dignitaries were seated at a vast table placed in the centre of the cement basket-ball court where the last championship games had been held. Among them was a representative of the Governor and two State Deputies.

There was something special about the last two: they had both been elected on an Umbandista ticket by Umbandistas.

One of them, Moab Caldas, forty one years old, a small, stocky, brown-eyed, quick-speaking, "tanned" state employee, was elected in 1960 to represent the pampas state of Rio Grande do Sul, with a majority of 10,200. In spite of announcing his candidacy only a month before polling day, Moab Caldas was among the three most-voted-for Deputies in the State. His big election slogan, splashed across the front pages of several of the best *gaucho* [native of the Rio Grande do Sul] newspapers, declared: " If elected, I will take my oath dressed in my white Umbanda uniform and I will ' receive ' my Coboclo in the State Assembly."

He did not keep his election promise, although he was elected, but then, of course, as he himself said later, this was not " because I didn't want to, but because the House rules do not permit the wearing of uniform by representatives . . ."

The second Umbandista Deputy, he was called Attila Nunes, was elected by Rio Umbandistas and obtained much of his following by running a two-hour radio programme consisting of nothing but Umbanda chants and combos, intermixed with news of what goes on in the world of Umbanda, both here and in " Aruanda " [the spiritual dwelling of the Indian and Negro spirit guides]. Advertisements were also transmitted calling attention to the " magic soap " of Ogun or Oxossi (Yoruba divinities that now stand for St. George and St. Sebastian), the " best magic bath to cleanse you from all evil," and so on. He opened and closed the programme with his own *ponto cantado,* a sung magic spell that corresponded to his spirit guide, a beautiful Indian girl called Janaína [pronounced Jah-nah-ee-nah]: *Suarêee, Suará, Suarêee.*

Said forty six year old Deputy Nunes, " according to people that call me, and to others who have given me the information personally, there are more than a thousand families in Copacabana [the plush district on the world-famous beachside] alone who tune in to my programme in order to hold their own private sessions of Umbanda in their homes. People whose names will make tomorrow's headlines are among them . . ."

He also circularised a card bearing his picture and a number of cabalistic signs to all Umbanda associations in Rio, saying; " Have a representative in the Assembly who really is all yours!"

They did . . . And Nunes not only became a Deputy but was made vice-president of the Assembly, also filling the role of president *pro-tempore* when the president himself was away, thus becoming the second authority in the state.

The newly acquired prestige and the enhanced status that this brought showed in the bearing of the Umbandistas. The men and women in the Maracanazinho Stadium at the second Congress were bursting with self-assurance, happy and proud in their faith and its " respectability." Their leaders, unfortunately, permitted this feeling of exultation to swell a little too far and spill over into a tide of plain boasting.

The official speaker, a white man, a lawyer with fierce grey hair and blue eyes, claimed that " Pharaoh Akhnaton, who reigned thousands of years before Christ, was the first Umbandista." Moses was also an Umbandista, he added—and, of course, Jesus. [Akhnaton was in fact the adopted religious name of the Egyptian Pharaoh and theologian, Amenhotep IV, who reigned from 1375-1358 B.C., and founded a monotheistic cult adopting the sun as the central symbol of the Almighty. Versed as he was in the occult sciences practised in Egypt at that time, it is nevertheless as absurd to dub him the " first Umbandista " as it is to arrogate to the cult the names of Moses and Jesus Christ.]

Deputy Moab Caldas pursued the same slightly inflated course. Said he: " Umbanda is the natural religion of Brazil: we do not have to lower our heads to anybody. In Rio Grande do Sul alone we have more than twelve thousand registered Umbanda associations, besides hospitals, radio programmes and innumerable publications. The party succeeded in electing several Aldermen and I, with only one month in which to make propaganda and do my electioneering, received the third highest vote of any Deputy in the state. And nobody but Umbandistas would have voted for me. Umbanda is going to revolutionise Brazil! *Saravá Umbanda!*"

" *Saravá Umbanda!*" seven thousand voices hailed back obligingly.

Deputy Attila Nunes was more optimistic still. " Umbandistas! " cried he. " If only you all unite, then we can elect several Federal Deputies and even State Governors! "

With the statistical number of supporters the movement can command, this is theoretically possible; what has so far proved impossible is for the Umbandistas in fact to unite. For their leaders, when not overtly ignorant, are all so radically individualistic that they can agree on nothing—save that Umbanda is the greatest thing that ever happened to religion! Everybody wants to command, everybody wants to be the leader, so that the movement in a broad perspective resembles nothing so much as that celebrated Haitian army which boasted twenty nine generals and only five privates . . .

Henrique Landi, a white, fifty seven year old production engineer who was on the organising board of the second Congress, agreed that " if we unite around a common goal, independently of the individuals involved, we can become the strongest religion in the country." But he added warningly : " Umbanda is the most contradictory religion in the world. We are disunited because each one wants to go his own way and expects all the others to follow . . ."

Maybe it is just as well that the Umbandistas cannot unite, for they do not at the moment appear to have the kind of leadership necessary to turn their newly acquired power into a religious, social and political movement of the type they envisage; they seem to lack figureheads of the authority, sophistication and responsibility that their numbers demand. And meanwhile Umbanda has no code, no ground rules, no homogeneity of ritual, and no defined aims other than to practice charity by doing spiritual and social works.

Perhaps in this simplicity lies its greatness, and nobody realises it!

The sequel to the meeting at Maracanazinho Stadium provides an illustration of the disunity, irresponsibility and, it must be admitted, ignorance, prevailing. Forty eight delegates called a meeting in the Council Room of the eight-storey headquarters of the Brazilian Press Association to explain and discuss Umbanda rituals and define its goals. The first item on the agenda was a condemnation of an obscure association and its medium because their hut had been burned down (and, presumably, by implication, a condemnation of the spirit guide, since the medium had been under his control at the material time!). Another resolution concerned Umbanda's Enemy Number One: Friar Boaventura Kloppenburg, who had by that time written several books against the movement and appeared on television with Black Magic instruments to demonstrate that they had no power and that there was no reason to fear them. The motion was debated and a vote taken to ignore the Friar rather than to urge spiritual action against him. (Although, as one of the leaders explained, " we could easily invoke his guardian-angel, who, being a higher spirit, would therefore agree with us, when we explained the situation to him, that his protégé was not doing right. We would not thereafter ask the guardian-angel to do him any harm, exactly—perhaps just to relax his watch every now and then . . . when Padre Boaventura was crossing a busy street, for instance . . .")

Padre Boaventura is still around. He has relaxed his crusade against Umbanda, however. Perhaps the church has realised that, by attacking the Umbandistas, it brings about the only thing they cannot themselves achieve: unity within the movement!

Today, according to Henrique Landi, there are more than thirty major sects within Umbanda, all claiming to be the genuine article. " At the first Congress," says he, " a basic ritual was approved and all Umbanda associations were called upon to observe it. For the Umbanda mediums or priests, general rules that could easily be followed were laid down, and in both cases things were so arranged that the framework was sufficiently elastic to take in all existing practices; any individual differences of rites or procedure could easily have been conserved within these rules. Yet hardly any attention has been paid to them . . . Now we are trying to do the same again, but I have very little hope that anything more will come of it, or that the rules will be followed any more than before."

There is a saying in Umbanda, Landi reflects sadly, which means " In your own home you are the king." The prevalence of this line of thought, he adds, " has so far over-ruled any efforts of unifying or trying to correlate our rituals or our aims."

The reason for this, in the opinion of the writer, is simply that, whereas the Umbandistas themselves claim for their movement the status of a *religion,* it is in fact—lacking founder, system, code, a unified ritual or even a unified philosophy—no more than a *religious cult.* A certain amount of codification may however be attempted among the existing schisms, provided an impartial objectivity is maintained. First, though, it is necessary to define loosely what is, and what is not, Umbanda in the general sense, which in practice means defining the difference between Umbanda, Quimbanda and Macumba.

All three of these relate to practices which stem from the original Negro cults brought to Brazil by the African slaves.

Umbanda stands for those Negro-derived practices now performed to a greater or less degree under the influence of Kardecism, its purpose being to help man overcome the difficulties of this life. Its instrument is White Magic and its banner is for Jesus and Charity.

Quimbanda is in many ways its exact opposite. Having its origin in the Bantu term *Ki-Mbanda* (the high-priest who is at the same time doctor, prophet and sorcerer), the word today has been twisted to stand for the generic name for Brazilian cults of African origin where only *Black* Magic is practised. The spirits (Exús) " used " by the worshippers are to do evil only and are considered to be at the foot of the astral ladder. (The Exús themselves, many are careful to point out, can do evil *or* good. It depends upon what they are asked.)

Macumba was the generic name for *all* these practices, now separated into Umbanda and Quimbanda, in use at the turn of the century. The word is still used today for two purposes: (a) as a synonym for Quimbanda; and (b), usually by those not too well versed in the matter, as a general term to describe all practices of any kind where *any* kind of magic is employed.

And how is the man in the street to tell from the outside which witch is which? There is one unfailing pointer: the true, genuine associations of Umbanda *never* charge for their spiritual work. You might be asked if you would care to make a (non-obligatory) contribution to their social assistance fund, which is devoted to the betterment of the poor; you might be required to buy certain substances or objects for use in some particular rite. But, like their counterparts in Kardec's spiritism, the Babalaôs or Iyalorixás* of Umbanda provide their spiritual help free of any financial charge whatsoever. So, having thus identified Umbanda in relation to Quimbanda and Macumba, the student is now free to classify and codify, insofar as this is possible.

Within the broad confines of each separate sect, every Umbanda association, whether it is called Centro, Tenda, Cabana or Terreiro, literally meaning respectively Centre, Tent, Hut or Plot of land, obeys only its own head spirit-guide, whose medium is usually the president of the association. The guide may be a Caboclo (Indian), a Negro (called " Pai " Something, as " Pai Tomás " would correspond to Uncle Tom), or any of the African Orixás and their derivatives. (A female guide, particularly if Negro, would be called " Vovó " Something—Vovó Cambinda, for instance, Grandmother Cambinda). The situation, in fact, is analogous to that obtaining with the Candomblés of Bahia.

An association, of course, may have affiliated associations obeying the spirit-guide of the parent body—it's not entirely an every-man-for-himself affair. The most eloquent example of this, an exception, it must be admitted, is the Tenda Espírita Mirim, headed by the Caboclo Mirim and his medium, the septuagenarian Benjamin Figueiredo, which boasts more than thirty affiliated associations spread over the states of Guanabara, Rio de Janeiro and Minas Gerais, with a consolidated membership of 25,000 worshippers and no less than 3,200 mediums! This must be some kind of record.

*Babá, Babalaô. Babálorixâ, all mean male priest; Iyalorixá means priestess.

Customarily, though, one finds a different ritual in each association. Landi too speaks of a " High " and a " Low " Umbanda, between which the whole spectrum of possible practices is stretched, from the " Low " imported, primitive Negro rituals such as those described in the chapters on Candomblé up to the point where Umbanda most nearly approaches Kardecism at the other end of the scale. In these " High " practices, the ritual may be restricted to the smoking of cigars " to clear the air of bad vibrations," the use of combos to beat out the rhythms, and the singing of chants " to call the spirit-guides of the Indians and the Negroes, and to keep up the concentration." Not even the fiery *Marafo* is used.

A basic line, a common denominator may nevertheless be established—a community of belief, if not of ritual, that runs through the great majority of the associations. Variations that can be, and are, played upon this *leit-motif* are legion. But in the main the Yoruba theogony inherited from the slaves has been retained. The Supreme God is Olorun, though a distinction is made between this deity and the figurehead of the trigony, represented by Obatalá (Father), Oxalá (Son) and Ifá (Holy Ghost). In practice this is simplified to Oxalá (Jesus Christ), who remains alone as the great chief and leader.

Umbanda divides its theogony into seven " Lines," each line corresponding to " a great collectivity of spirits that have astral affinities and certain determined missions on earth." In other words, a Line is a legion of spirits which, like doctors, artists, musicians, architects and engineers on earth, share certain aptitudes and are specialised in certain types of activity besides having the necessary mental, cultural, sentimental and intellectual affinity. Each Line is directed by one of the major Orixás of the Yorubas.

The seven basic Lines of Umbanda, together with their respective Catholic counterparts and, lastly, the corresponding God in Greek mythology, are listed as : —

1. Oxalá—Jesus Christ—Apollo.
2. Yemanjá—Mary, Mother of Christ—Diana.
3. Ogun—St. George—Mars.
4. Oxóssi (also spelled Oxôce)—St. Sebastian.

5. Xangô—St. James (not Jeronymo, as some have it)—Jupiter.
6. Oxun—St. Catherine, goddess of fresh water—Venus.
7. Omulu—St. Lazarus—Saturn.

There is, of course, disagreement in detail here too! The *Tatá* (an Angolan word for high-priest), Tancredo da Silva, who is schooled in the African tradition and seasoned in its innumerable ritualistic procedures, avers that the above are the Seven Lines of Umbanda. So does Oliveira Magno, who has written many tracts on the subject. " Not so," say many others, including Aluizio Fontenelle and Benjamin Figuei-redo, head of the mammoth Tenda Espírito Mirim. Omulu, these respected " deviationists " claim, works with all Lines, because it is he who has the last word over who is to discarnate (die). Others say that he works also with Black Magic and therefore commands the Exús, those lower-grade spirits who are the " employees " of the Orixás but who may, when on their own, work either for good or evil. To replace Omulu, these authorities say, there should be included an " African Line," comprising the spirits of all the Negroes, from all the African races, under the command of St. Cyprian, A sub-division of this faction also quarrel with the Sixth Line. Instead of Oxun, the goddess of freshwater lakes, rivers, fountains, and of love and marriage, they say, this should right-fully be the " Line of the Orient "—the legion of all masters of occult sciences such as the Hindus, the Incas, the Chinese, the Egyptians and so on, under the command of John the Baptist. (The inclusion of this Line is quite obviously the result of Kardecist influence.)

The Lines are each divided again into several Phalanxes, each with its chief. It may be easier to visualise this complicated hierarchy if the Lines are regarded as armies, each under the command of a four-star general. Each " army " then subdivides into its Phalanxes or " divisions," each with a three-star general at its head. And some Phalanxes are again split into two or more subdivisions (" battalions "), each with a two-star general in command. Each four-star general, each Orixá, has of course his or her favourite colour, food, number, type of beads, day of the week, invocation chant, magic symbol, fetich, insignia, favourite herb, perfume and style of greeting. Here is a run-down of the Lines and their Phalanxes:

The First Line: *Oxalá/Jesus Christ*
Oxalá-Alufan is the " three-star general " who is second-in-command. He only " comes down " to take a medium under control every seven-times-seven years. Next in the Line is Oxalá-Guian, who " comes down " every seven years. Oxalá-Dacun and the remainder of this rank " come down " each year. Saint Anthony, St. Cosme and St. Damion, known as Ibejis, St. Catherine and St. Francis of Assisi, are among these leaders of Phalanxes in the First Line. The colour used by the *Filhos* or *Filhas de Santo*, the children of this saint, those mediums whose Orixá or spirit-guide belongs to the Oxalá-Line, wear white in religious ceremonies, sport white beads with three red ones among them, make their offerings of white bread, vegetables and light wines. Oxalá's favourite food, however, is *canjica*, made of corn. His day is Sunday, though special incantations have to be made on a Friday. The fetich is a golden ring; the metal, gold.

The Second Line: *Yemanjá/Our Lady of Glory*
The goddess of the sea and salt waters commands seven Phalanxes: (a) that of the Mermaids, whose head is Mother Oxun; (b) the Undines, commanded by Nanãburucu (corresponding to St. Mary Magdalene); (c) the Caboclas of the Sea—feminine Indians whose spirits " work " with the sea under the orders of Indaiá; (d) the Caboclas of the Rivers, commanded by Yara; (e) the Phalanx of Sailors, led by Tarimá; (f) the Calungas, commanded by Calunga, the personification of the sea in the Bantu tradition; and (g) the Phalanx of the Guiding Cross, commanded by Our Lady of Seafarers. Sea shells and stars are Yemanjá's fetich, watery white her colour, a fan her symbol and insignia, Saturday her day, and green corn her favourite food. Her beads are watery-white, though some say they should have three

green, three golden and one blue among them. Her fete is August 15, but the great event each year in Rio is on the last night of the old year, towards midnight, on the beaches. When any of her representatives "come down" in a Terreiro, she is to be greeted with the shout *Odoia!*

The Third Line: *Ogun/St. George (in Rio) or St. Anthony (in Bahia).*
Crossed swords are his fetich, the horse and the rooster his favourite creatures, red his colour. Red and green must his beads be, and Thursday his day of worship. Seven are his Phalanxes: (a) that of Ogun Beira-Mar (Ogun Seashore), whose members work with the people of the sea; (b) Ogun Rompe-Mato (Ogun Break-through-Forest), allied to the Line of Oxóssi, king of the woods; (c) Ogun-Yara, allied to the Caboclas of the rivers commanded by Yara (above); (d) Ogun-Megê, allied to the African people called Megê; (e) the Phalanx commanded by Ogun-Naruê, allied to the ex-African slaves from that tribe; (f) Ogun-Malei; and (g) Ogun-Nagô—both allied to the African peoples of those names. (Tancredo da Silva lists also Ogun-Dilê, Ogun-Dinae, Ogun-Delodê and Ogun-Timbiri. There are probably many more Ogun—some spell it Ogum, but the "n" is the correct form—spread around the many associations practising this cult, but those listed above as head of the Seven Phalanxes of Ogun seem the most important.)

The Fourth Line: *Oxóssi/St. Sebastian (in Rio) or St. George (in Bahia)*
The king of hunting, as we have seen in Yoruba mythology, has the bow and arrow both as fetich and as insignia. Corn, peanuts and coconuts are his favourite foods and green his colour. The beads are white and green (some say all green with three red ones). Thursday is the special day of worship. Oxóssi, too, has seven main Phalanxes, commanded by Caboclo Urubatão, Caboclo Araribóia, Caboclo das Sete Encruzilhadas (the Seven Crossroads—the spirit credited with his medium, Zélio de Moraes, as having founded

188

Umbanda), White-Eagle (commanding the Phalanx of North American "Red" Indians who work in Brazil), Grajaúna—who commands the Phalanx of the Guaraní Indians—and Cabocla Jurema, who leads a Phalanx of female Indian spirits specialising in spiritual work performed in the forests. Among other spirit-guides belonging to this line, the most famous is Caboclo Cobra-Coral, a powerful entity employing a coral snake to dispel Black Magic.

The Fifth Line: Xangô/St. James

Xangô, in his capacity of Thor, is the Orixá ruling the thunder and lightning, the rain and the rocks. Under his direct command work Xangô-Agajú, whose Catholic equivalent is St. Peter, and under whose orders, claims *Tatá* Tancredo da Silva, was founded one of the most important Umbanda federations, the Confederação Espírita Umbandista, and also Xangô-Caô or Xangô-Menino (Boy Xangô), whose equivalent is St. John the Baptist. His fetich is a meteorite, his insignia a lance and a hatchet, his favourite dishes rooster, tortoise and billygoat. Xangô's colour is purple, his beads red and white (others insist they should be brown with three white-striped ones). His day of worship is Wednesday. The Xangô Phalanxes are seven—as indeed are all the others, seven and its multiples being a number highly valued in all occult sciences, whether Egyptian, Caldean, Israeli, Hindu, Persian or from any other source. They are: (a) the Phalanx of Yansan, a female Indian guide said to be St. Barbara; (b) Phalanx of the Caboclo of the Sun and of the Moon; (c) Caboclo White Stone; (d) Caboclo of the Wind; (e) Caboclo of the Waterfalls; (f) Caboclo Earth-Tremble; and (g) a Phalanx of old Negroes of the Quenguelê tribe.

The Sixth Line: Oxun/St. Catherine

This feminine Orixá, corresponding to Venus in the Greek mythology, is the complement to Yemanjá, goddess of the sea. Oxun is the Orixá of freshwater lakes, rivers, fountains,

189

etc. Some have it that the most "popular" of this Line is Mamãe Oxun, Mother Oxun, whose Catholic equivalent is Our Lady of the Conception, while others place this entity under Yemanjá. Oxun's fetich is small coloured stones. Fish from the rivers make her favourite food, and Friday is the day to worship her (as might be expected). Her beads are blue and yellow. (Another Orixá, Oxunmarê, is the bi-sexual spirit of the Rainbow. Edison Carneiro, one of the world's foremost scholars in Negro tradition and custom, points out that the hyphenated spelling Oxun-Marê, which would seem to place the entity in this Line, is quite incorrect, though frequently used. In fact, he says, Oxunmarê has nothing whatever to do with Oxun, the fresh-water goddess.) Any division of this Line into seven Phalanxes is far less pronounced than in the cases of the other Lines.

The Seventh Line: Omulu/St. Lazarus
Much controversy adheres to this powerful Line, as we have already pointed out. Since Omulu is credited with the power of life and death and thus rules over the cemeteries, he therefore has charge over the inferior entities that "work" there, the notorious Exús. Because the Exús can work for evil as well as good, there are those who exclude this Line from Umbanda, saying that it properly belongs with the cults using Black Magic. Exú is agreed by all to be a servant of the Orixás, their messenger to men, the one who performs the more menial tasks—or, as one author oddly put it, the spirit which "does the Orixás' dirty work"! Be that as it may, each Orixá is credited with having one particular Exú as his personal aide. Others point to Omulu as heading the "Line of Souls." This, they say, is composed of inferior spirits of those who, having been Babalaôs on earth, failed to complete their mission here and are continuing it from space. Omulu's day is Saturday, though the day for special worship is Monday. Favourite colours: black and yellow. Favourite dish: popcorn. The fetich is a sickle and the insignia a spear. There are at least fifty Exús, each one with a special function. (And to make

things even more complicated, some authorities say that, while some Exús work under Omulu, there are others owing allegiance to the King of Exús, Exú-Rei, classified as an equivalent to the Catholic Lucifer.)

Da Silva says that Exú-Lalu is the head of the Exús and a servant of Oxalá-Alufan. (Alufan means priest in the Megê language.) Oxalá-Alufan therefore implies either Jesus himself or a very near " general," and his Exú, his " batman " as it were, naturally enjoys a corresponding status in the celestial hierarchy. Exú Barabô belongs to Xangô-Agaju (St. Peter); Exú Tiriri belongs to Ogun-Megê; Exú Tranca-Rua (road blocker) to Oxóssi; Exú Mirim (Mirim = small) to Ibeji (Cosme and Damion, the twin Orixás, Castor and Pollux); and Exú Dakê is a servant to Omulu himself.

There is, it must be noted, also a female Exú, head of all the representatives of Eve among this Phalanx. Her name is Exú Pomba-Cira, and it is said that she prefers to work with men.

Here are a few other Exús and the special talents by which they are customarily known: Exú Caveira (Skull), assistant to Omulu, dominates the cemeteries and all Black Magic worked there; Exú Marabô speaks slowly, uses words delicately, likes fine drinks and expensive cigars, and proves very difficult to get rid of, or to handle, once he takes hold in a " terreiro "; Exú Curadô (The Healer) knows the value of herbs, and can cure as well as kill; Exú Arranca-Toco facilitates the finding of hidden treasure; Exú Pagão (The Pagan) enjoys engineering hatred, fights, the break-up of couples, etc.; and the Exús -Pemba and -Brasa (burning coal) favour the continuance of illicit loves.

Man through the ages has shown that he respects and is far more in awe of the powers that do evil than he is willing to honour those speaking of and spreading love only. It is therefore only a natural consequence of this psychological attitude that, of the pantheon of higher and lower " gods," Exú should be perhaps the most deeply respected and feared!

His territory is the cross-roads—especially at midnight, particularly on Monday and Friday. Not only in the country, but in all parts of Rio, from the Copacabana to the remote Madureira district, lit candles, open bottles of *Cachaça*, red wine or beer can be seen at this time standing there along with unlit cigars and open boxes of matches. This is a form of the famous *Despacho*, through which supplicants give the entities whose help they need the various ingredients necessary to keep them happy. In the case of the Exús, this is supposed to result from their quaffing the beverages and smoking the cigars (which they themselves light from the matches left conveniently nearby). Roosters and some live animals are sometimes offered also.

There can hardly be a Brazilian alive who does not know that the cross-roads is a place to be feared, especially at midnight. Not all admit to sharing this fear, of course. But many of the " brave " ones secretly tremble and those genuinely unaffected are a minority. The general attitude was neatly summed up in a famous two-frame cartoon which appeared in the slick magazine *O Cruzeiro*, which has a circulation of almost half a million. The first frame showed a sophisticated young man approaching a cross-roads in his expensive sports car. He was turning to his equally sophisticated girlfriend and saying: ". . . of course *I* don't believe a word of this nonsense about cross-roads "—and in the second frame, he is shown to have made an elaborate manoeuvre to avoid passing over a *Despacho* left in the middle of the intersection!

As an example, here is a recipe given by Oliveira Magno to aid those seeking the favours of Exú Pomba-Gira (the female spirit, you will recall): " On a Friday night, under a crescent moon, go to a female cross-road (one of the four routes must be closed, making what in Britain would be termed a T-junction), taking with you yellow *Farofa* in a pot of clay; a bottle of *Cachaça;* a cigar; and a box of matches. You must ask for permission, and then sing the following magical chant:

Que bela noite,	What a beautiful night,
Que lindo luar;	What gorgeous moonlight;
Exú Pomba-Gira,	Exú Pomba-Gira,
Vem trabalhar (bis).	Come here and work (repeated).

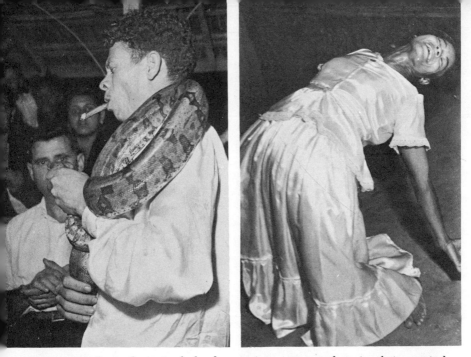

ABOVE, LEFT: Some 'horses' of the lower rites use a python in their magical practices, like this one, who seems to be under the control of an Indian spiritual entity. ABOVE, RIGHT: Here is a manifestation of the powerful and feared Eshú controlling a medium or 'horse'. BELOW, LEFT: Sometimes Umbanda or Macumba mediums take on rather odd expressions when under the control of some spiritual entity of a lower grade, as in this case. BELOW, RIGHT: An Indian spirit guide utters his characteristic cry. They smoke cigars whilst old negro guides smoke pipes.

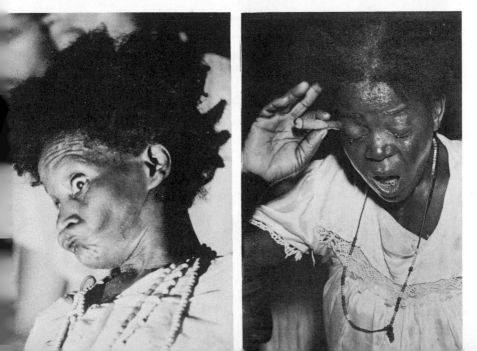

ABOVE, LEFT: A special 'despacho' (a magical spell) to appease a police inspector who was persecuting Umbanda and Macumba centres. This was successful after a time. ABOVE, RIGHT: An Umbanda priestess reads the future by looking into a glass of water containing pebbles. This Umbanda altar provides another example of religious syncretism. BELOW: Umbanda practices include 'obligations' to saints and the Orishas to be made at rocks.

"Then you must place the *Farofa,* open the bottle, and leave them together with the cigar and matches at the centre of the cross-roads, saying: 'This I offer you so that my path shall be opened and untied and my wishes fulfilled.' Immediately after this, sing this other magic chant:

Salve tá tá Pomba-Gira!	Hail tá tá Pomba-Gira!
Salve Exú mulher!	Hail Exú woman!
Ela é na encruzilhada,	She is on the cross-roads,
A que faz tudo o que quer (bis).	She who does what she wants ...*

"Then finish your *Despacho* by saying: 'Just as, at the cross-roads, you do everything you want, so let all I desire be accomplished. I am confident '."

Side by side with the cross-roads tabu, which has become ingested as a part of the Brazilian *persona,* there are related magical concepts which have become nationally accepted as belonging to the country's vocabulary. The *Encosto,* the *Coisa Feita,* the *Caminhos Fechados* and *Caminhos Abertos,* the *Corpo Fechado* and *Corpo Aberto,* the "Evil Eye" and the *Olho Grande,* these are all terms prominent in modern usage, and all stemming from the practices of Umbanda/Macumba and of spiritism, though more from the former, of course. (People in general, despite their beliefs in these things, are uncertain in their own minds about the differences between Candomblé, Umbanda, Macumba, but aware of the opposition of Umbanda and Quimbanda, knowing that the former is to do with White Magic, the latter with Black; the former works good, the latter evil " miracles ".)

Encosto is a noun incorrectly derived from the verb *encostar,* to lean against. It is used to express a situation wherein an inferior spirit has " leaned against " a person, causing him to become unbalanced through its negative influence. Thus a deceased father, disliking the fiancé of his daughter, may be-

The rhyme (not necessarily always to the same scheme) and the repeated final line of the quatrain are typical of these chants.

193

come an *Encosto* and so perturb her mind that the nuptials are called off. Or he may do this because his spirit does not yet realise it has " died." It is a commonplace to hear a friend say something like: " I'm so depressed and nervous, I don't know what I'm doing. I can't control myself. I must have an *Encosto.*"

Coisa Feita, literally, means " thing done." In practice, it is used to stand for an evil thing, deliberately done, by Black Magic. " *Até parece Coisa Feita*—this looks like a Thing Done " is a phrase often heard to express awe at some domestic disaster or some concatenation of unfavourable circumstances that looks like a direct slight by providence.

Desmanchar, a verb meaning " to undo," is an immediate consequence *of* the *Coisa Feita.* It is used in the sense of undoing the harm wrought by Black Magic through the use of White Magic. If things go badly, if every aspiration is defeated by the course of events, as happens from time to time with all of us, a friend may say: " This smells like *Coisa Feita.* You ought to look for a Centre and *Desmanchar* this . . ."

Caminhos Abertos (or *Fechados*) means " open paths " (or " closed paths "). If things go wrong, as outlined above, this may not be due to a *Coisa Feita*: it may be because "your paths are closed," i.e. your way to success is blocked. To open them, you have to go to a Centre or Macumba, the ritual used depending upon which you choose and the Line they work with. The Orixá, if you consult one, might tell you: " We have to open your paths. To do this, Exú Tiriri must receive a *Despacho* in order that he will lead away a Phalanx which is hindering your steps and blocking your way. So at midnight on Friday, you must go . . . etc., etc." Another might tell you that you need the help of the Caboclo Canchoeira, the Indian of the Waterfalls, and that you must take some specific food, or perhaps just candles, to a particular waterfall and make your request. There are as many variations as there are sand grains on a beach.

Corpo Fechado means that your body is closed—to all evil. No *Coisa Feita* can get hold of you. This term is customarily

194

reserved for the state of grace enjoyed by initiates and worshippers of these diverse cults.

Corpo Aberto is the contrary—your body is open; you are in a state where you are an easy prey to Black Magic, the *Coisa Feita,* and you must do something about it quickly! You must see that it is closed. (Some Filhas de Santo, daughters of the divinities or mediums, use this expression alternately with *Corpo Sujo,* i.e., when they are menstruating and therefore cannot work spiritually. It is a widespread notion common to spiritualist cults the world over that a woman is unable to work in that sense when she is in this state, the body then being " open " or " unclean.")

Amarrar is a final category, another type of *Coista Feita.* The word means " to tie up," and is applied figuratively not to a thing but a person. It's a variation, in fact, of the old girl-gets-boy game, because while men doubtless resort to extra-terrestrial forces to " tie up " the choices of their hearts (or interests!), it is in fact more usually the girls wishing to snare a particular lover or marry a particular man who make most ample use of them. Oddly enough, proportionately this is not as might be expected confined to lower or middle classes but seems actually to be commoner in the upper reaches of society! Perhaps because, as in the days of old, the rich find it easier and more discreet to make contact: the coloured maid or cook, today's equivalent to the *mucama* of the *senzala,* can act as messenger and general intermediary between the " client " and the Macumbeiro.

The important point to make though, whether one is dealing with a *Coisa Feita,* an *Encosto* or someone desiring to *Amarrar* a partner, is that all these words are part of the normal vocabulary of the normal Brazilian. The concepts for which they stand, though they may not be discussed at smart cocktail parties or Itamaraty Palace receptions, are not limited to a small group of worshippers, a particular cult: they are as inbred part of the Brazilian personality as miscegenation, as the River Amazon, as the Negro, as the choice of the *mulata,* the crossbred girl, as national pin-up. The Brazilian may not like it, he may not approve of it, but there it is (and even the society cocktail party can provide snatches of gossip overheard in corners such as: "*Ele está conz Encosto*—he has got an Encosto—poor fellow!" or "Look at her. She made a Macumba to ' Amarrar ' So-and-so . . .")

So far as those suffering from an *Encosto* are concerned, the more modern, a small minority with the means to pay for a psychiatrist, may seek the help of one, but the majority will naturally seek the aid of a spiritist association. And since the Umbanda-type organisations are the more numerous, that is where such a person will usually end up. What happens then depends on where they go.

If they are fortunate enough to possess friends qualified to impart knowledgeable advice, they will probably find themselves at one of the better Umbanda centres. If not, they may go to one of the Macumba centres, on the outskirts of Rio, perhaps, or up on one of the hills surrounding the city, and fall into the hands of less scrupulous operators. Here, the Macumbeiro or Macumbeira, the head priest or priestess, may say that an enemy has done something bad, to right which " they " are demanding that you should do a number of things. " For this," the Macumbeiro might say, " we need to buy the necessary things to *Desmanchar* the *Coisa Feita*." An especially bad Exú, he might add, is out to ruin the client. Perhaps Exú-Ganga [who is no worse than other Exús, in fact, though the client will be told he is]. And this Exú, with a great Phlanx behind him, will assuredly ruin the client's whole life, unless a certain sum is paid to obtain the necessary materials.

A person who might normally dismiss all this as arrant rubbish might well be inclined, psychologically, to accept such " nonsense " if he was at the time sufficiently depressed and worried; he might even be a little scared inside himself, though unwilling to admit this. And to make assurance doubly sure, the Babá may call a medium, who will fall to the ground and writhe about in tremendous contortions while crying out in a " spirit " voice some confirmation of what the client has been told.

Regrettably, this kind of thing goes on all the time, for

the sad fact is that a great number of people make a living from Macumba, a fact frowned upon and condemned by the Umbandistas, whose motto, like that of Kardec's, is to give freely what is given to you. Charity is the *raison d'être*.

But because of a twin ignorance, that of the people seeking aid from Macumba and that of its practitioners, such a profession can flourish and expand. The writer has heard personally of hundreds of cases, each one different in its details but essentially the same. And strangely enough it is among public servants and people with a medium college type of education, especially women, that Black Magic is rampant. With the natural rivalries, jealousies and petty enmities that persist in the multifarious sections of Brazil's mammoth ministries (the bulk of which remain in Rio, despite the creation of Brasilia), the *Coisa Feita* is a Godsend to those nursing grievances. The " wallflower " envious of a colleague's success with men, the wronged wife, the embittered secretary passed over in the promotion race, the present and the cast-off lover—all these make a " work " (work of magic, i.e. *Coisa Feita*) against the objects of their displeasure, and sometimes vice versa. Which means in turn that hundreds of Macumba or Quimbanda associations are kept financially well-fed.

Side by side with this prosperity for the lower Macumba and Quimbanda associations, a parallel success attends the charitable efforts of Umbanda. Thus while the Catholic Church struggles to right what is officially called " a chronic shortage of priests "—between 9,000 and 11,500 for a populalation of 75 million which is 93 per cent. Catholic, as against 50,000 priests for a Catholic population of 40 million in the U.S.—there is no shortage of mediums. And this is true of all cults as well as for Kardecism. The Tenda Espírita Mirim has over 3,000 mediums alone, a third of the total of priests for the whole country! In Rio, the Umbandistas are building a hospital that will have more than 300 beds, and all associations, from those working in the shabbiest hut to those housed in their own four-storey buildings, are expanding rapidly with no help save that given voluntarily by their own followers (and that of the Orixás and spirits, of course).

197

Nevertheless, ignorance is not the preserve of the Macumba and Quimbanda people. In Umbanda too, middle class people accept the most outrageous assertions by Babalaôs " because, who knows, anything is possible in magic, and I don't understand much about this anyway!" Among the poorer classes, this is less surprising, since ignorance prevails there, as it were, by right.

Take the case of the mother who ran sobbing into the Social Assistance Department of a spiritualist association, bewailing the fact that her children were to die.

" But why?" asked the nurse calmly. " Why are they going to die? What's wrong?"

" Oh, my God, my God, I don't want them to die," moaned the distraught mother. " Near my home there is a Macumba, and they told me I had to give a large plate of sweets and food to St. Cosme and St. Damion—the Ibejis, you know— and that if I don't, both the children will die . . . And the truth is, they have both been so ill that I don't have enough money to buy what they want. In fact, I have no money at all. What am I going to *do*?"

" Calm down. For Heaven's sake calm down and think a bit," the nurse soothed. " Would you yourself put your children to death because they were unable to give you something *you* wanted?"

" Of course not," the woman wept. " What a question!"

" Then," said the nurse severely, " how dare you imagine that Our Father is worse than you are? Do you really think he would kill your innocent children just because you don't have the money to buy presents for one of his messengers?"

The woman stopped crying, thought, and realised at once the sense of what she had been told. She rose to her feet as one who had been given a first glimpse of the fields of paradise, thanked the nurse emotionally and hurried home. And, of course, the children got better and are alive and well today.

Not everyone is so understanding. Take the case of L. F., a Negro maid 48 years old who hardly makes enough to live in a shack an hour and a half's journey by shuttle-train from her employment. She saves the little money she has to keep up her obligations to her " gods " as defined by the Babá, the intermediary of the Orixás. Recently she spent several months without buying anything at all for herself, walking around shabbily because the Babá had told her she must *fazer a cabeça* ("do her head")—undergo the initiation ceremony in the *camarinha* by which a *filha de santo* has her Orixá confirmed (as in the Candomblé described in an earlier chapter). The cost: the equivalent of five months' salary.

To do this, she had to spend a whole month isolated in the *camarinha* in a Rio suburb, and then had to have her daughter undergo the same ceremony, at the same cost.

She is but one among hundreds, if not thousands.

Accidents, too, occur. Near the Itanhanga golf course, set in the gorgeous scenery of the Rio littoral about an hour's drive from the Copacabana beach, there is a fifty-foot water-fall popular with the *filhos de fé* (sons of faith, i.e. worshippers) as a place to make obligation to the saints and to the powerful Caboclo da Cachoeira. Every now and then their exuberance proves too much, and the next day's papers carry a front page picture of the worshipper under a heading reading: *Killed while paying homay to Orixá.*

Other recent stories have included that of a young girl, M. L., murdered by her own mother because the latter had received the " revelation " at a Macumba seance that the girl was pregnant by her own father. The autopsy showed that in fact she was a virgin.

Another: " M. J. R., a *Pai-de-Santo* (Babalaô) knifed his enemy, P. R., to death but declared that he was totally innocent because at the time of the crime he was under the control of Exú Seven Crossroads, who was therefore responsible . . ."

And another: " L. A. M., 'a war veteran suffering from neurosis, changed his medical treatment for a Spiritist centre of Umbanda. During one of the sessions, he suffered a violent crisis, pulled out a gun and shot the Babálorixá dead and wounded several others, shouting: ' Caboclo Arruda is with me! Nobody is stronger than I . . .' "

Here, obviously, we are dealing with a mental case. But

what the Babá or person responsible should have seen, once the divinities had been contacted, was that he should have been confined to a hospital.

These cases are the exception rather than the rule, of course. Such events, as well as the exploitation of the sufferings of many to make a living for the few, are the result of individual ignorance and individual amorality rather than of any lack in the principles of the cults themselves. Must the Catholic Church be blamed for Torquemada's excesses in the name of Jesus? Should Jesus Himself be blamed? It is important to distinguish between the higher and the lower practices, between the good and bad, between the sincere and the dishonest.

The true associations of Umbanda *never* charge to *desmanchar* the *Costa Feita,* to " open the paths ", and so on. The most you will be asked is to buy what may be needed for the *Despacho* you have to place on the beach, at a crossroads, or by a waterfall (Careful: don't fall down!). But you buy them yourself: you will never be asked for *money* on behalf of an Orixá, money without which the spiritual work cannot be done. This is basic.

It may be a humble hut or an enormous building such as the Centro Espírita Caminheiros da Verdade ("Walkers of Truth "): if the people there are sincere and with honest intentions, they will not charge. But sincerity and honest intentions, however charitable, rule out neither ignorance nor vanity, unfortunately.

There was, for instance, the case of the vivacious and stout " gaucha ", Irene Soares, from the Pampas state of Rio Grande do Sul, who called a press conference to announce a statement that would " shatter the destiny of Brazil ". She had been told by Mamãe Oxum that she was to take over the presidency of the country to save it from chaos, it seemed. She had told President " Jango " Goulart of this order, she said, and she had already selected the ceremonial robes she would wear. It only remained for Goulart to set the date. She was interviewed, and repeated the statement, on Rio and

São Paulo TV stations. But President Goulart remained un-impressed.

Apparently he shouldn't have been. Mamãe Oxun was most offended at this rebuff to the latterday Joan of Arc and extracted her vengeance two years later, when she sent the whole Brazilian army after Goulart. Indeed, had he not hared over the border to Montevideo, he would probably now be in some remote island jail, presumably reflecting on how much better it would have been to have turned his job over to the chosen daughter of Mamãe Oxun! Or so they say . . .

The vanity of head priests or priestesses also leads them to express their social importance, gained through their mediumship, in a way sadly at variance with the charity and humility which ought to characterise the movement. Some of them are showered with self-bestowed titles—Venerable Masters (both masculine and feminine), Great Gurus, Great-Masters of the Orient, Most Venerable High Priests abound. One spirit guide is even a Royal Highness. Other mediums hang the walls with Diplomas gained from strange secret-societies of the occult sciences to demonstrate their import-ance. A particular Venerable Mistress rides around in a chauffeur-driven limousine, sporting over her white uniform an impressive cape stiff with gold braid.

All of which offers a peculiar contrast to the extreme simplicity and humble mein of the spirit guides of old Negroes and Caboclos, and lends some point to the frequent complaint of mediums " interfering " with the purity of the spirit message. For the mediums, after all, should remain, as has been well said, merely horses upon which the spirits mount (and indeed, both in Umbanda and Quimbanda, are sometimes called " horses ").

But despite all these drawbacks, even though the qualities are difficult to find among many of their leaders, the sim-plicity and the humility *are* there, there in the heart of the movement, among the people who practice these cults in all sincerity and belief. And this, added to the fact that, whether you call it Umbanda, Macumba or whatever, such things are indelibly imprinted upon the Brazilian character, gives the cults themselves an especial vigour which is not easily matched.

One fact more has to be considered: we have been speaking of exceptions, but to the vast majority of people who seek help both spiritual and psychological, Umbanda does bring relief. Odd though it may seem, unbelievable though it may appear, it works. Undeniably, it works . . .

CHAPTER ELEVEN

Magic and the Two Mountains

WRITER Oliveira Magno, obviously an Umbandista, defines the difference between the two great Spiritist denominations in Brazil as follows. " Umbanda," says he, " is Jesus working; Kardecism is Jesus teaching."

Like most generalisations, this is something short of the truth, but like many generalisations, it is also near to it. To the legion of those in need of spiritual help, however, the distinction is critical. The gravamen of the problem revolves mainly around the actual nature of the spiritual work required and access to the spirit guides who perform it through their mediums (or " horses "). In Kardecist practices it is difficult if not impossible to speak directly to a guide through his medium. In those of Umbanda, it is the easiest thing in (or should we say out of?) the world.

All the seeker after help has to do is ask where there is a *consulta* (consultation), visit the Association on the appointed day, draw his number when he arrives (there is always a queue), and then speak to the guide he has chosen. Such consultations do exist in Kardecism, but they are rare. This makes a world of difference to the seeker as well as to the follower, who is by far outnumbered by the former.

(The distinction is drawn here between " seekers," the people who want only to avail themselves of the " facilities " of spiritism in order to alleviate their personal problems, and " followers," who regularly worship at the particular Association. It is because of the categoric insistence on all forms of charity by all denominations of spiritism that those who are not regular worshippers find themselves aided in this way: a situation without parallel in orthodox religions.)

The main attraction for both categories is of course contact with the divine: actual conversations with the emissaries of God, with the saints, with those who "know" and "understand" replaces the formal prayer to cold statues or in front of an altar. Problems, embarrassing or even trivial, can easily be revealed to the "old Negro" or Indian guide who talks in a fatherly way in simple, broken Portuguese, in a fashion that might seem to smack of the irreverent in a church. The humility and even wisdom which they bring to such troubles can be enthralling.

This direct contact with the divine, so easy in Umbanda, is one of the main reasons for its greater popularity in Brazil. Another is the *nature* of the spiritual work performed.

Kardecism does not admit the existence of magic. Everything is solved according to the laws of Karma; all evil provoked by evil spirits can be dissolved by summoning these spirits through a medium, "explaining" the situation to them, indoctrinating them with the message of the Gospels, and asking the spirits to translate them to a sphere where they can be "treated" and thus no more return to do evil on earth. Personal problems, of love or money or both, must be resolved by prayer to the spirits. And as far as help for specific problems is concerned, that is usually all.

With Umbanda things are different. Although the principle of Karma is invoked to explain the *reason* for the seeker's suffering, magic is not only believed in but constantly used. Working in principle only for good causes and against evil, Umbanda channels the white magic of its practices towards the defeat of black magic as well as towards the furtherance of the rightful objectives of those seeking its help.

A Caboclo may tell a seeker to light candles for the souls of the suffering and wear a special amulet for his own protection until the evil has passed; he may instruct his medium to call in other "horses" to summon the evil ones "closing the paths" of the seeker, and these other mediums may become possessed by such spirits, writhing in contortions on the floor while the evil spirits voice their animosity against the seeker. The spirit guide in command, as it were—who must be of a higher hierarchic order—can then exorcise them, cause them to be removed to a special sphere, as in Kardecism. But this intimacy with the guides, the possibility of themselves joining in the ceremonies and taking an active part in the ritual, inspires the seekers with confidence in the efficiency of the "treatment" and has a psychological impact carrying far greater weight than the intellectualised, apparently more passive attitude of Kardecism. And, not unnaturally, it exercises an unrelenting attraction on the minds of those in the humbler strata of society.

Yet, to take the case of São Paulo, intellectually the most advanced city in Brazil, despite the fact that Kardecism has its most active, organised and numerous nuclei of followers there, despite the fact that the area boasts the highest per capita income in the country, there too, in actual numbers, Umbanda still has far the more followers, according to a recent survey.

An interesting side-issue worth mentioning here is that, although as a rule Kardecism appeals mainly to the middle and upper classes and Umbanda to the lower, it is almost exclusively in urban centres that Umbanda flourishes. It is the more populated areas, the cities, the state capitals, that the problems of living and making a living become most acute; it is here that the complications and sophistications of modern existence, with all their strains and pressures, take the most toll. And thus it is here that, to many, the attractions of magic and the spirits exert a more compelling and satisfying influence, provide a better answer than either science or traditional religion are able or willing to offer.

"It would be an illusion," Freud said once, "to suppose that what science cannot give us we can get elsewhere." In which cases the spiritist and magic practices of Kardecism and Umbanda must be the most successful illusion of modern times!

But is magic an illusion?

And first of all what is magic? The antithesis of science, it has been said again and again. Science itself qualifies it simply as an expression of primitive religions and superstitions. Webster defines it as: " Sorcery, witchcraft, any apparently occult power." In the Oxford Dictionary it appears as " the pretended art of influencing the course of events by occult control of nature or of spirits, witchcraft; black, white or natural, involving invocation of devils, angels, no personal spirit." A French doctor named Encausse, writing under the pseudonym of *Papus*, described it at the beginning of this century in perhaps the most comprehensible and *au point* terms. Writing in his own *Elementary Treaty Of Practical Magic*, he said: " Magic is the application of human will dynamically projected to the rapid evolution of the living forces of nature."

This last definition is well illustrated by a recent controlled experiment carried out in an American university laboratory. A Protestant pastor blessed with extra-sensory perception (ESP) put fifteen corn seeds in each of two pots kept in identical atmospheric conditions. Over one he prayed and concentrated on the growth of the seeds. From this pot more than ten seeds sprouted, while from the other only three or four came—in other words, the seeds over which " magical " incantations had been made sprouted faster than those left for nature alone to develop. And the difference between ESP and magic is simply a matter of semantics.

César Lombroso, the world-famous Italian doctor and professor of psychiatry who was the founder of criminal anthropology, cites in *Hypnotism And Mediumship* an account by Louis Jacolliet, French consul in Bombaim, of a similar case of an Indian *fakir* who, under test conditions, made the seed of a papaya tree produce a twenty-centimetre seedling in two hours.

It is the Oxford definition that is the most pertinent in the case of Umbanda, however, for Umbanda truly is the art of influencing the course of events by occult control. But there is one vast difference between the magic of Umbanda and that of all the other practitioners in history, whether they be Caldeans, Assyrians, Babylonians, Persians, Hebrews, Mongols, Greeks, Egyptians, Japanese or even the modern covens of Brittany and England.

In all these cases, magic has been associated with witchcraft because it has been practised by sorcerers claiming to have themselves occult control of nature and the spirits, using them at will through magical formulas of evocation. But in Umbanda the medium is himself controlled by a spirit guide, who performs the magical acts without the conscious participation of the medium: it is the magical entities themselves who act.

It is interesting to note here that the most violent adversaries of the existence of magic, and therefore of its practices, have always been the Christians, especially since both Old and New Testaments are full of magical occurrences . . . although these are invariably attributed to " the devil " or to " angels."

" A man also or a woman that hath a familiar spirit, or that is a wizard, shall surely be put to death," says Leviticus severely (XX, 27). Moses, too, found it necessary to forbid such practices. Says he in Deuteronomy XVIII, 10-12: " There shall not be found among you any one that maketh his son or his daughter pass through fire, or that useth divination, or an observer of times, or an enchanter, or a witch, or a charmer, or a consulter with familiar spirits, or a wizard, or a necromancer. For all that do these things are in abomination unto the Lord." But he instances those " that *do* these things," not those that try to do them—a clear affirmation of the possible.

Hoseas relates magical practices (IV, 12) and Saul asked his priests to consult Jehovah through their Urim and Thummin, resorting to the Pythoness of Endor when they failed to obtain an answer. Yet who but his own father, Samuel, dead some time before, then appeared to predict his defeat?

All of which merely goes to show that magic and spirit communication are a constant in the history of all peoples. But the point at issue here is that in all these cases magic has always been considered an occult and extraordinary occurrence, the exception and not the rule, whereas in Brazil today it has become a commonplace, an ever-present factor in everyday life: what is new and different in " the new world of the tropics " is that it is practised quite openly and is accessible to all.

There is no better example to illustrate this than the annual December 31 ceremonies on the Rio beaches.

At midnight on the last night of the old year, hundreds of different Umbanda—and even Quimbanda*—Associations, as well as individual followers, take to the sands to make their offerings to Yemanjá, the Orixá of the seas, to ask for her protection in the coming year.

To assure themselves that they will get it, all manner of presents are taken, ranging from bottles of Champagne—the rich even take expensive imported French Champagne, in case it makes any difference!—to Cachaça, from flowers to beer, from cigars to a fiancée's corsage.

Some twenty years ago, the ceremony was performed on remote beaches by the worshippers only. But it spread and spread, more and more became involved, and finally the newspapers and magazines realised the news and feature potential there and began heavily publicising it. The Associations, sensing then their newly acquired importance, simply came right out into the open: instead of just making offerings, they transported their altars and images to the beaches, setting them up in style, and at the beat of the drums, the wail of the incantations, down came the Orixás, the Caboclos, even the Exús! Today there are candles, torchlights, much smoking of cigars, the insistent polyrhythms of dozens of drummers and chanting groups, the out-cries of "arriving" Caboclos as they

*It is in practice impossible to compartmentalise the two: though in theory Umbanda deals only in White Magic to combat the Black Magic of Quimbanda, there are occasional Quimbanda Associations practising White as well as Black Magic, and even Umbanda Terreiros who use Black Magic.

take over their "horses" and contort them upon the sand, the bulging-eyed gyrations of those upon whom the Exús become seated, and the non-choreographed rolling, dancing and uninhibited gymnastics of the many onlookers who came "just to see," perhaps to make a little wish, and, affected by the heavily charged atmosphere, hysterically joined in and outdid the worshippers in the violence of their reactions.

In 1964, newspapers estimated the number of people on the beaches of Rio de Janeiro on the night of December 31 at *more than a million!*

Intellectuals, who tend to exhibit similar reactions the world over, dismiss such excesses as an example of the lack of education of the Brazilian populace, an indication of under-development. But although the manifestations are un-doubtedly pure paganism insofar as they devolve upon placa-tory offerings to obtain the favour of gods, they do also testify to the psychological climate of the country in that they prove the unrelenting attraction to those involved of the spiritual, even if only in a primitive form. It is this climate, this *poten-tial* interest, this perhaps subconscious inclination, this in-stinctive acceptance of the spiritual that, more than anything else, makes the spiritist movement in its widest sense, with due allowance for its multiple aspect, the most powerful force in Brazilian religion today.

We are not so much concerned here to examine whether or not magic actually exists, whether it should be taken seriously, or even if it can be considered as a scientific possibility, as to illustrate the part it plays, for better or worse, on the Brazilian scene and in the psychological make-up of its people. The general attitude, in fact, may be summed up by the popular Spanish saying: *No creo en brujas—pero que las hay, las hay.* (Freely translated, this means: I don't believe in witches—but so far as their existence goes, oh, they exist all right!)

But there is more than the Yemanjá cult on the beaches to prove the draw of spirtism in Brazil today. It's not only the magical that will attract: the unmagical quietness of Kar-decism multiplies its followers too. Professor Candido Camargo, a sociologist from the São Paulo School of Politics and Sociology, recently made a survey of twenty seven cities in the state's interior under the auspices of the *Fédération Internationale des Instituts de Récherches Sociales,* of Freiburg, Switzerland. In São Paulo, the most advanced state, intellectually and economically, in Brazil, he found that " there is not the slightest doubt that, in *all* the cities surveyed, the spiritist book is more read than that of any other religious creed, political organisation or philosophical school." The survey also revealed an extraordinary growth-potential of Kardecism and Umbanda: no less than fifty five per cent. of those interviewed had been converted to one or the other brand of spiritism within the last ten years!

The Kardecists themselves, of course, object to any bracketing with Umbanda. A little piqued by the flourishing success of Umbanda on one side, a little status conscious on the other, the Kardecists openly attacked Umbanda as " an inferior African fetichistic cult." The mere ability to receive a spirit did not make the medium a spiritist, they said—and as for magic, well, it didn't exist; and if it did exist, it wasn't effective. But confirmation to the contrary came from an unlikely quarter: Friar Boaventura Kloppenburg, whose mission was to attack all branches of spiritism, admitted on p. 66 of *The Catholic Position Towards Umbanda* that " in our opinion there *are* true cases of magic. It was not possible for us to deny the reality of certain effects which we personally examined." Which is a fine testament to Dr. Kloppenburg's integrity and objectivity as a researcher.

But the Kardecists continued to strafe the Umbandistas until their great spirit guide, " Emmanuel," through medium Francisco Candido Xavier, took a hand. " We must consider that the spiritist phenomenon is there (in Umbanda), a genuine expression of the Truths that we are receiving from above," he told his followers. " The work of Umbanda, when orientated towards charity, is also laudable." Calling upon them not to forget to seek goodness in all spiritual activities, the spirit guide's message then likened spiritism to a state, of which Kardecism and Umbanda were different provinces.

" If we, under pretext of being pure, of being better orientated than others, forsake our brothers who need our goodwill, naturally our service will be basically wrong . . . we see no reason to be scandalised by the Lines of Umbanda, but they are an imperative . . . of better understanding and a greater demonstration of love on our part."

For the Brazilian Spiritist Federation the message, despite its faintly patronising tone, meant the end of hostilities. The message was published in their official gazette in July, 1953, and they have obeyed it. Not all the Kardecists were equally convinced, though, and when, in June, 1956, Fr. Kloppenburg held a conference on Umbanda, which he presented as a form of spiritism, a number of the more prominent dissenters issued a statement. After defining spiritism in terms of Kardec's beliefs, the moral betterment of man through Christ's teachings, and reincarnation of the human soul, the statement said: " No relation exists between spiritism and those cults or religions which include in their principles (a) rituals of any nature; (b) sacrifices, even if only symbolic; (c) priesthood, with any type of hierarchy; (d) formulas, invocations, promises or written indications of any nature intended to solve problems of material life; (e) payment for spiritual services; (f) worshipping of images, symbols or idols; (g) practice of witchcraft, magic or necromancy." In other words, without specifically naming it, this could, with the exception of (e), be held almost as a definition of Umbanda.

Many Kardecist Centres in São Paulo, where the movement is most dynamic, most against any association with Umbanda, and where the Federation is bitterly hostile to the latter, display similar statements. Perhaps not unreasonably, the Kardecists, whose practices are only now being tolerated by society, are wary of being lumped together with the " low " spiritism and humbler social status of Umbanda.

Unlike the Brazilian Federation in Rio, which mainly confines itself to publishing religious books and whose premises are normally only sparsely attended, the São Paulo Federation caters for 10,000 people a week, holds four-year courses for the graduation of mediums, instigates many conferences always packed to capacity, performs spiritual works throughout the week and programmes a vast schedule of social assistance. The middle and a section of the upper middle class participate actively and the higher echelon followers include college and university professors, doctors, engineers, military officers both active and retired, public servants and businessmen. They have thus much to lose in the social discrimination which results from association with Umbanda.

Professor Camargo underlined this in his survey of São Paulo when he complained of the difficulty of making a demographic analysis through sample interviews, " which are technically very difficult to obtain because the spiritist does not yet enjoy sufficient prestige in global society and tends normally to hide his religious preference." The Kardecist feels truly that he is intellectually and socially superior to the Umbandistas, placing both their rituals and the very conception of their beliefs on an inferior level of religious evolution.

All the emphasis of this attitude falls once again on the historical reluctance of both science and society to accept the practices of magic.

Perhaps the point becomes sharper if we examine the actual way in which the sessions proceed. Unlike the Umbandistas, the Kardecists use no special clothes at their meetings, no candles, no handclapping, no incense, no chants, no incantations or rituals of any kind. Soft music, perhaps the Schubert or Gounod *Ave Maria,* may play in the background, but all they need to start a session is a group of willing people with one or more mediums among them, a table to sit around, a glass of water, a copy of *The Gospels According To Spiritism,* concentration, goodwill and faith. Which is why there are virtually hundreds of thousands of " home circles " spread around the country. The meeting will begin with a prayer, continue with a reading from the book, another prayer, and then, slowly or rapidly according to the individual, the medium (or mediums) may become controlled by their guides. There may be a message, generally of high moral content, and then the same medium or other mediums may receive inferior spirits accompanying those present, or those whose names have been given by members of the circle. When an inferior spirit controls the medium, it is "indocrinated," usually by the person presiding at that particular session. Many inferior spirits do not yet know that they have discarnated (according to the Kardecists), and in this way they are told of their real situation and removed to the proper sphere, thus freeing those living here and present at the session from their perturbing company.

In general, though, the Kardecists are more independent from actual contact with the guides. Great emphasis is placed on moral and spiritual betterment through study of Kardec's doctrines and the modern teachings of "Emmanuel" and "André Luiz" via the writings of Chico Xavier. And thus it is perfectly feasible for a home circle to function without especially experienced practitioners.

The motivating force drawing most people to spiritism in the first instance is undoubtedly therapeutic—to obtain cures denied by orthodox medicine. The principal media through which these are obtained are the so-called "fluidified water," magnetic "passes" whereby mediums wholly or partially under the control of guides remove "negative" magnetic particles from the body and replace them with "positive" particles, homœopathic prescriptions, and "invisible" operations. "Fluidified water" is that which has been submitted to the outstretched hands of the medium, through which the spirits pass into the water other fluids of a magnetic, spiritual nature specifically designed to cure the body's ills or at least alleviate them. The technique, of course, appears totally removed from any known principle or scientific nomenclature, but that is not to say that it does not work.

Details of many of the practitioners effecting these cures have been given in previous chapters. But with Kardecism, once the cure has been obtained, and the seeker thus convinced of the efficacy of the creed, then he adopts the principles of the movement and endeavours to embody them in his own attitude; life is given a reason and an objective, which the Kardecist is set upon *living* himself, independent of direct contact with the spirit world.

Need for healing is also what initially draws the seeker to Umbanda. But the methods are wholly different. Before any spiritual work can begin, the Terreiro, the " plot of land," as the place of worship is called, whether it is one or not, must be prepared according to the ritual prescribed by the head spirit-guide, the House of Exú duly inaugurated, to keep him from interfering in the session, and so on. Then the spirit healing, when it does start, is far more " extrovert," far more ritualised than in Kardecism. Also, since there is no codified procedure in Umbanda, it will vary from Terreiro to Terreiro according to those in charge. The Indian and Negro guides prescribe mainly herbal remedies, though at times homœopathic or even allopathic specifics may be used. But when Umbanda is practised by the more ignorant, all illnesses may be debited to spiritual entities or said to be caused by the failure of the sick person to comply with his duties towards his Orixá. Yet it is undeniable that, in spite of some serious shortcomings, Umbanda does achieve remarkable cures.

The great difference is that, once cured, the seeker cannot (as he would in Kardecism) feel allegiance to the movement *as a whole,* for with Umbanda there is no movement as a whole. His allegiance is therefore merely to Caboclo So-and-so or Preto Velho (" old Negro ") Somebody-else. And his evolvement will therefore depend entirely on the level of the Association and its practitioners and guides to whom chance drew him in the first place.

While accepting the implication that Kardecism is therefore a far more " mental " and intellectual experience than Umbanda, we are by no means bound to assume that each is inimical to the other. For the " banishing " of Caboclos from any Kardecist sessions where they might appear and control the mediums (as is insisted upon at some circles) seems hardly logical in the light of Kardec's views on reincarnation: who can affirm that the spirit, before he became the Indian he was in his last incarnation, was not a doctor or an architect or a scientist, reincarnated as an Indian as a punitive measure? Indeed a striking illustration of this was vouchsafed to Wantuil de Freitas, president of the conserva-

214

tive but powerful Brazilian Spiritist Federation. Succumbing at last to the constant importuning of friends, he visited an Umbanda session where the " Old Negro " guide warned him to check a certain point in connection with the deeds of his land. De Freitas dismissed the warning as nonsense. The next week, at his customary Kardecist home circle, the spirit guide, after his usual sermon on a high-flown point of doctrine, addressed De Freitas and said: " You had better look up those deeds I warned you about last week . . ."

The primitive, backward " Old Negro " and the highly-evolved, cultured Kardecist guide were one and the same: the identical spirit was presenting himself in different " clothing," corresponding to different incarnations, according to the intellectual level of his different listeners. And, of course, there *was* a mistake in the deeds which required attention!

Although Kardecist hostility towards Umbanda is largely of class and racial origin, a kind of racial discrimination transferred to the spiritual sphere, the attitude itself is mainly institutional: a large number of individual spiritists disagree, seeing in Umbanda simply a lower form of evolution, a more primitive form of spiritism which they are perfectly able to accept as a useful vehicle to attract the lower strata of the people to the movement as a whole. " One, Kardecism, is 'table Spiritism,' the other, Umbanda, is 'Terreiro Spiritism '," was how one uncommitted Kardecist put it. For the majority of mediums, it is simply a matter of their guides: if the guide is a Caboclo or " Old Negro " then they say they belong to the Line of Umbanda; if the guide is neither, then they belong to " table Spiritism." Certainly (with the exception of Candomblé, which is sometimes confused with Umbanda) the Umbandistas themselves regard themselves as members of the spiritist religion, of which Kardecism is a part. There are Umbanda Associations which study Kardec's Gospels, others which work according to his principles, without chants, drums or ritual, and with their mediums sitting around a table.* Kardecists have explained to Umbanda meetings that it is possible to " receive " spirit guides without the

*This is usually called " White Umbanda " or " Table Umbanda."

use of Cachaça and drums. Similarly, some Kardecist circles have "borrowed" things from Umbanda, such as the wearing of white clothes for spiritual work and the use of incense. These movements, upwards from Umbanda, downwards from Kardecism, led Professor Camargo to conclude that, in fact, there could be said to be in existence a "mediumistic continuum."

An eloquent example of this in practice is the Centro Espírita Tupiára in Rio. The founder and head medium, José Hermann, recently deceased, "received," besides Tupiára, the chief spirit guide, an " Old Negro " guide called Pai Manuel, a Hindu and several former doctors. The centre dispenses spiritual help, each in his own way, from Tupiára and Pai Manuel on certain days in the month; on others, the spirit doctors, working through the same medium, perform innumerable "invisible" operations on cysts, appendicitis, tumours, tonsils, ulcers and even cancerous tumours—with a very high percentage of success. The point here is that while the work of Tupiára and Pai Manuel are in the Umbanda tradition, complete with the usual rituals, chants, drums and cigars, the "invisible" operations are pure Kardecism. For these, unlike those of Zé Arigó, who actually cuts into the flesh, are performed on the peri-spirit and later *reflected* in the flesh. And to this "syncretism within syncretism," this *mélange* of Umbanda and Kardecism through the same medium, more than 65,000 people flock every month . . . more than to any other Spiritist Association in Rio!

Another Rio Umbanda Association, the Centro Espírito Caminheiros da Verdade (Walkers of Truth), is led by a fifty two year old ex-army officer, João de Almeida, who used to run a Kardecist circle. " Our sessions were always nearly empty," he says. " We were preaching to the flies. Then one day Caboclo Guaraná visited our medium, lauding Umbanda. So I decided to change our Line to Umbanda, and in no time people started flocking to our hut. In less than ten years we have been able to build this four-storey building, each floor of more than 2,000 square metres in area . . ."

From the "consumer's" point of view, one of Professor Camargo's interviewees puts the thing in a nutshell. "Around the 'white table' (of Kardecism)," says he, "the concentration is more profound. Umbanda is a much more rustic and violent spiritism. In Kardecism, the cure may take more time, but it is much more positive. While with Umbanda a problem may be rapidly solved but in the long run be less positive." In other words, in Kardecism an *internal* change is sought and occurs, while in Umbanda, although problems are more directly dealt with, this internal change, which is permanent, does not always happen.

Whichever denomination is followed, however, the driving force behind both is charity. From a 300 bed hospital in the southern capital of Porto Alegre to a São Paulo "transitory shelter" serving 1,200 meals daily and housing 100 families in 3,733 square metres of constructed area; from an orphanage in Rio to a mental asylum in the interior state of Goias, spiritists everywhere, of every shade, are actively living Christ's parable of the Good Samaritan (Luke X, 25-37). And in Brazil, where the rich walk side by side with the poor even in such districts as Rio's Copacabana or São Paulo's Jardin Europa, to say nothing of the interior, where poverty is the rule, there could not be a better field for organised charity. And there is not a Spiritist Centre of either denomination that does not have some sort of social assistance, no matter how small or how poor it may be. "Spiritism without charity is inconceivable: it just is not spiritism," says Commander Edgar Armond, president of the São Paulo Spiritist Federation.

But more eloquent than any description, more telling than ten thousand words, are the official figures compiled by the government's Geographic and Statistical Institute.

The official statistics, and they are not up to date, list Catholics as making up more than 90 per cent. of Brazil's population. Yet Catholic social assistance establishments make up only 42 per cent. of the country's total. Spiritists, listed as only 1·5 per cent. of the population, contribute no less than 36 per cent. of the total of social assistance estabishments. As we have seen, there are far more spiritists in fact than reflect in the statistics. But if we accept one informed estimate and assume that the true number of spiritists is around 12 per cent. of a population approaching eighty million, then we have to conclude that each spiritist contributes eight times as much towards this work as his Catholic counterpart. And even this figure is a conservative one, since the state has always assisted Catholic enterprises quite lavishly, while, with rare exceptions, spiritists have generally been discriminated against. The spiritist places, in other words, are mainly the result of private efforts; the Catholic ones private efforts highly inflated by government aid.

For the purpose of analysis, the statistical department divides assistance establishment into hospitals, clinics, orphanages, shelters, schools and "others". This throws into even greater relief the nature of the spiritists' private effort when we see that more than half of the establishments listed in the Catholic social assistance figures are in fact schools, the building of which is especially easy for them, since Catholic institutions are particularly suited to this, ample financial support being forthcoming both from private and from state sources. For social and political reasons these resources are not available to spiritists, who have thus to count on themselves alone. If the schools were subtracted from the total number of social assistance establishments founded by both Catholics and spiritists, the latter would then be responsible for 48 per cent. of the total—almost as much as Catholics and Protestants together!

Spiritist orphanages number 71, Catholic 73 and Protestant 25, while the relevant figures for shelters are 125, 81 and 25, which would seem to imply the spiritist emphasis on assistance to the poorest section of the population, the one most in need and least capable of offering any sort of religious, social or political compensation. But this, indeed, is what one would expect from a movement whose *raison d'être* is charity.

One of the most admirable features of spiritist assistance, to those who receive it, is the absence of proselytism. To the spiritist there is nothing to proselytise about: to do charity is to practice his religion. Spiritism does not offer personal salvation; it denies its existence. All emphasis is placed on personal responsibility—today you reap what you sowed yesterday, and tomorrow you will reap what you have sown today; no miracles, but divine justice.

Mention has been made of the higher standards of social and economic life in the state of São Paulo, a phenomenon reflected in a correspondingly higher status for Kardecists there. As a final look at statistics, let us consider the figures relating to the expansion of spiritist social assistance foundations in that state since 1950.

	1950	1951	1952	1953	1954	1955	1956	1957	1958
Schools	9	16	21	22	22	33	36	39	43
Hospitals	1	3	3	6	6	7	7	9	13
Shelters and									
Orphanages	11	18	24	24	63	71	76	77	77
Libraries	59	68	71	83	71	82	92	101	?

Statistics in general are not one of the more highly developed activities in Brazil, indeed it has been said that while statistics are normally analysed, in Brazil they are merely doubted. Nevertheless, the above figures do show a trend and testify to the enormous vitality and expansion-potential of the spiritist movement, which is overwhelming.

A little too overwhelming for some, perhaps.

In 1962, the official annual statistics book published by the government's National Institute of Geography and Statistics divided the social assistance establishments into categories according to religion—Catholic, Protestant and Spiritist. The following year, this was not done, and in 1964 a new section headed *Charitable Institutions* was introduced. This lumped all existing institutions in the country together under the same heading, the statistics subdividing people according to religions confining themselves solely to religious activities.

While it is not for a moment suggested that there is any hint of religious discrimination here—that would be impossible: the constitution forbids it—the enquiring mind nevertheless cannot escape the base thought that, by thus separating social assistance from religious activities, the statistics office does happen to have been the means of avoiding what might have proved a painful comparison.

And the moon glows and shines over two mountains . . .

CHAPTER TWELVE

The Rising of the Moon

T O sum up: the Portuguese and the African Negro came from afar to meet in Brazil and together with the Indian form there a new people, a new civilisation with a different personality. In a unique way, different ancestries and levels of culture found in Brazil the catalyst which formed them into an amalgam that carries within itself the fundamental elements of spiritual greatness: the Brazilian people.

No other people has such deeply inbred religious feeling completely above all doctrine and dogma; no other people has such simple, sincere and friendly feelings towards its fellow men, whatever their race, creed or colour, and no other people whose culture is of Western extraction has such a flair for magic and the supernatural.

Several factors contributed to this. The colonists were initiated in magic practice by the Moors, the Mediterranean African Negroes and the European alchemists, while remaining themselves at the same time stoutly Catholic. This paradoxical combination of influences was enriched further in the colony, where the influence of the Church was diluted by distance and the eclecticism of the cultural scene increased by miscegenation, first with Indian, then with African women. The humility and simplicity of the Negro in his religious devotion was passed on to the Portuguese through African nurses and mistresses, the resulting blend being a mixture of Catholicism and fetichism, a strong belief in the " interference " of spiritual entities in material life coupled with an equally strong accent on the observance of Catholic liturgical ceremonies and feasts. Such a loose arrangement between church doctrine and animist practices favoured the birth of a new form of religious movement. When the original Afro-Catholic syncretism had been established, it was amended by a further amalgamation with the code of higher spiritual practices founded on logic and tested by paranormal phenomena advanced by Kardec, and at the same time another spiritist wave upsurged as the result of a syncretism between *Indian* and African practices, Catholicism and spiritism. This was Umbanda.

Worshippers flocking to the altars of these movements and their derivatives are calculated to total more than ten million. That is an estimate: the figure may be more; it may be less. What is certain is that, according to government statistics, the number of officially registered spiritistic churches (regardless of their native or jargon names) alone makes the Brazilian spiritist movement as a whole the strongest in the world.

Yet once again we find ourselves using the term " as a whole ", and in truth it must be repeated that it is not possible to regard spiritism as a whole. The picture is far too blurred; the impression of confusion is inescapable.

Umbanda and Kardecism both term themselves spiritism —yet in their open, visible practices, they could not be more different. While the former is all music, rhythm, dancing, incense and noise, the latter is all silence, contemplation, stillness and prayer. But both of them are bent to precisely the same end: contact with the divine. Similarly, the guides in Kardecism are intellectuals, those in Umbanda peasants; the Umbandistas make use of magic, the Kardecists deny it. And off to one side, different from either, lie the innumerable practices retaining African traditions, such as Candomblé in Bahia, each of them advancing different explanations, different routines for dealing with the same problem. But these, too, have as their *raison d'être* the contact of the divine.

What is lacking is a structure, a framework within which all these conflicting yet related practices could be accommodated. If the divine is indeed factual, there must be an explanation embracing all of them, in all their aspects, and rejecting none, which yet accords with the laws of science. An attempt to provide such a panacea began in 1958 when, against all the tabus, a new Temple was founded in one of the smartest districts of Rio. Between the diamond-hard, sculptured apartment houses, across the road from the beach and the glittering sea, a 20-foot neon sign proclaims to the 50,000 cars a week swishing past along the promenade that this is the

TEMPLE OF UNIVERSAL RELIGION.

Underneath the main lettering, a smaller sign reads: *Religion at the service of Science.* Inside, each Tuesday evening, more than 500 people await their turn to enter a room 30 feet by 10 feet in which some thirty mediums, all dressed in white, sit around a long table holding hands to establish a " current ". Under the direction of a young man standing at the head of the table, the mediums " receive " spiritual entities such as Caboclos or " Old Negroes "—those thought to be the exclusive preserve of Umbanda—yet the method of reception is as that recommended by Kardec: concentration, soft music, stillness, and so on. Inimical to a Kardecist circle, however, would be the white uniforms, the incense, the presence of Indian guides and, last but not least, the purpose of the meeting: the elimination of black magic, the " evil eye ", bad influences and " bad spiritual company ".

At a typical meeting, participants may give public testimony of the results they claim from previous meetings—a husband who had left home has returned, a job sought has been found, a lady unable to sleep for years relates, weeping, how doctors and pills were useless but that after only a few weeks of attendance she now sleeps soundly without pills. The trivial confessions are scarcely different from those to be heard at any spiritist centre. It is the approach, here, that is revolutionary. But let us allow the founder and head of this simple, humble, no-divinities-present temple to give its view of religion, science, spiritualism and their meaning today in his own words. Says he:

" The sickness of our age is anxiety and fear. The famous

223

columnist Walter Lippmann has written that this is caused
' by the impact of science upon religious certainty and techno-
logical progress upon the settled order of family, class and
community. The 'virtual despair' (Senator Goldwater's
expression) comes from being uprooted, homeless, naked,
alone and unled. It comes from being lost in a universe where
the meaning of life and of the social order is no longer given
from on high and transmitted from the ancestors, but has
to be invented and discovered and experimented with, each
lonely individual for himself. The modern sickness is the
despair which James Thomson called 'the insufferable
inane'. It is found among the rich and the poor, among the
grandees and the groundlings, and it has nothing to do with
an unbalanced budget, a swollen bureaucracy, with communism or anti-communism, with the New Deal or the New
Frontier.

"'. . . the poignant question, which is as yet unanswered,
is how, with the ancestral order dissolved and the ancient
religious certainties corroded by science, the modern man can
find meaning which binds his experience and engages his
faculties and passions. . . . It is the unease of the old Adam
who is not ready for the modern age.'

"Let us examine this problem so well judged, so truly
pinpointed and so ably expressed by Mr. Lippmann. Mankind has acquired knowledge in its history by observation
and measurement, prying and probing into the laws of
nature. Yesterday we took a horse-drawn carriage as transportation; today we fly in a jet plane. Yet in each period of
history we have lived by a set of values *based on the knowledge so far acquired at that time*. Those who were, as we
say, ahead of their time, always had a difficult time and a
great deal of trouble proving their point—when it meant
disproving concepts prevailing at the moment. Today this
distrustful attitude is largely past: to the contrary, we believe
that the scientist can do anything, given enough money! New
discoveries stream in every year, new processes are invented,
and although we follow man's conquest with a certain awe
and admiration, these things have begun to be taken very

much for granted. No one any longer doubts, or even marvels at, the fact that man really is going to reach the Moon this century: the only interest left is the competitive one of who gets there first. . . . There are no doubts about material matters and no limits to man's audacity in probing the secrets of the Universe.

"Yet in matters concerning man's inner self and his destiny, how different things are! For our attitude differs drastically in matters concerning religious beliefs: reason and logic, observation and measurement are substituted or superseded by what we have chosen to call ' divine revelation ' and its main dynamic: the miracle.

"Western religious thought is based on two sets of ' divine revelations '—the Old and the New Testament, on which all theological works are based. And what are the main tenets taught by these books? That there is a life after this one; that what is important is how we fare in that life because it is eternal while this one is ephemeral; that there is one God and that He created everything; that our eternal destiny depends on how we behaved in this life—we may merit eternal happiness or eternal unhappiness in ' heaven ' or ' hell ' respectively; that to save humanity God sent his only begotten Son, Jesus Christ. And that our souls are salvageable either by following the Catholic path (the Church acting as representative of Christ), going to Mass, Holy Communion, Confession and so on, or by accepting the precepts of one of the many Protestant denominations.

"The centre of all these ' divine revelations ' is obviously neither logic nor reason, neither progress nor evolution, but the miracle concept. Moses talked to Jehovah on Mt. Sinai and received the cornerstone of Western *mores*: the Ten Commandments. How? Through a miracle. The Messiah, the Saviour, the Son of God was born from a woman's womb. Yet the woman remained a virgin and has the rather odd title of Mother of God. How? By a miracle. The God-Man or Man-God was crucified and rose on the third day from the dead, to ascend thirty days later to Heaven itself, His body disappearing into a cloud. How? Again by a miracle.

"The fact that anguish and neurosis are the maladies of our age clearly indicates that such concepts are no longer satisfactory; what the churches, Catholic, Protestant or Jewish, have to offer is failing to reach man's innermost feelings. Nor are increased church attendances the answer. The point is that few really believe in these concepts any more. Faith in what Dr. Paul Tillich, one of our foremost theologians, calls ' the divine paradox ', the presence of God in an actual human body, revealing only in suffering His true majesty, no longer seems able to grant man that most precious of all personal treasures: peace of mind.

"Says Dutch theologian Albert van den Heuvel, head of the World Council of Churches: ' Man in growing up has more and more chased the various gods out of their positions of control of human destiny. Mankind will not go back to the Old Testament for governing principles of how the world was made, but we will go on to trace its physical mysteries with X-rays and microscopes.' What he did not say was that the world we live in is also at odds with Resurrection, with ' eschatological mysticism ', with the concepts of heaven and hell, with eternal life, with the miraculous birth of Christ and His miraculous uprising from the dead. ' The existing pattern of the Church is no longer in touch with real life,' says Dr. Harvey Cox, of Andover Newton theological school.

"And what does the Church advance as an answer? Secularisation. ' The Church should serve society, which also predetermines its form and shape. In the new world, the Church should really live the contents of the Gospel, living out its messianic ministry, communicating with society, gearing itself to its needs,' says the theologian van den Heuvel. It should be ' not the repository of the saved but a community of people, no better than anybody else, but who are trying to be the light of the world,' writes Editor Stephen Rose of the Chicago monthly, *Renewal*. ' Theology is overdeveloped in systems and arguments and not rich enough in concrete applications to existential problems.'

"What about the ' divine revelation ', heaven and hell, and so on?

" ' Preserve an agnostic silence about them,' says John Robinson, the Suffragan Bishop of Woolwich, ' since they cannot be painted with the assurance or the detail of the wide canvases beloved of our forefathers.' Followers of Dr. Tillich simply ignore dogmas that do not relate to modern man's ultimate concern. Many cry out ' Demythologise!', others crave to do away with ' the devil ' and his court. In other words, all churches and their thinkers have come to realise that there must be a change, a ' renewal ' if the church is again to have any meaning to modern man.

" It must be emphasised that this ' renewal ' is still as yet an intellectual movement within the churches themselves. To the majority of Christian churchgoers, themselves a minority, religion still implies sacraments and the Bible, believing in the truths of divine revelation, and so on. The miracle-angled belief in the ' divine paradox ' still prevails.

" But the reason for the widespread anguish and despair felt in the most affluent society in history remains the inability to answer the three vital questions of our existence : Where did we come from? What are we doing here? Where are we going?

" Western thought, philosophy, religion and theology all stem from the old Hebrew cosmology as outlined in the Bible. God created it all, and man is the next highest being after Him. With man the centre of such a system, it is basic that Earth is the centre of life in the Universe, and even if these concepts are worded differently today as a consequence of the findings of modern palæontology, Western thought remains steadfastly tied to two basic concepts: human life exists only on this planet; and each individual has only one life to lead, starting at birth and ending at death. After that, there is the eternal, rewarding life of the soul. Perhaps.

" This concept of our place in the Universe is not the result of scientific development of knowledge, through the accumulation of data by observation and measurement: it was derived from what astronomer Fred Hoyle, one of the most brilliant minds of the century, describes as an ' arbitrary starting point '—the so-called divine revelations.

"Says Hoyle in *Frontiers of Astronomy*: 'This procedure is quite characteristic of primitive peoples who, in attempting to explain the local behaviour of the physical world, are obliged in their ignorance of the laws of physics to have recourse to arbitrary starting conditions. These are given credence by postulating the existence of gods—gods of the sea who determine the arbitrary starting conditions that control the motions of the ocean, gods of the mountains, gods of the forest . . . and so forth. . . . There is a strong hint that what modern man is trying to do with the Universe is no better than what primitive man did with problems whose nature we now find simple.' Hoyle was speaking of 'the big bang theory' and others prevailing in modern cosmology. Yet his words could not be more apposite to describe our general attitude towards what we may call spiritual cosmology: we still think in terms of the Hebrew sages of old simply because the 'arbitrary starting conditions' contained in the Bible have been defined as divine revelations or miracles, and are therefore not subject to tests or observation. In other words, there is a gap of three thousand years between our scientific thinking and our religious thinking, centred around the old miracle concept.

"The Temple of Universal Religion is an attempt to close this gap.

"What we have to offer and what we base our actions upon is a working hypothesis in the scientific sense, whose value—as with all scientific theory—depends upon the possibility of disproving it. As T. Gold of Cambridge put it: 'For a theory to be valuable, it must be vulnerable.' The hypothesis is offered as an instrument with which we may attempt to answer those three vital queries of our existence."

And here we must come out from behind the quotation marks, reveal that the writer of this book is in fact the founder and head of the Temple of Universal Religion, discard the editorial plural and adopt the first person, and take responsibility for the hypothesis mentioned above.

What follows is necessarily only a general outline: to expound a detailed and scholarly apologia for the theory would itself require a whole book. It may therefore be convenient if I state the basic principles of the Temple of Universal Religion, expanding them where it seems necessary with supplementary material.

1. *God is supreme love and supreme wisdom. He expresses Himself through energy that sustains the Universe and is a constantly creative force.*

It is the continual emission of energy from God, which adopts many forms and types, that explains the " continuous origin of matter ". God is neither a fixed point nor a personality, nor (as the Bible would have us believe) does He ever rest. Nothing is at rest. The atom is not at rest: there is always at least one electron moving around a proton at incredible speed in any atom. If God " rested " for a billionth of a second, the entire Universe would disintegrate.

2. *The Universe is expanding, and everything that exists is ruled by the law of evolution.*

The expanding Universe—what Hoyle calls " a decisive reorientation on man's outlook . . . one of the most important scientific revolutions of thought of all time "—is, I think, a sufficiently proven scientific fact to be accepted without qualification. As to how it was created—you can choose the " big bang " theory, the theory of the continuous creation cosmologists, or the most recent hypothesis of Professor William H. McCrea of the University of London's Holloway College, that matter is created in the dense centre of galaxies. The fact is that matter *is* created and science cannot tell how as yet. This is as far as science can go.

Accepting the expanding Universe theory, it can be seen that life on earth follows similar dynamics of expansion which we call evolution. All animal life stems from the original one-cell organism, the amœba, which developed by evolution from the primordial protein cell. Both the super-small and the super-large have one thing in common therefore: dynamic evolution and dynamic expansion. Indeed, Hoyle has spoken of " so far unperceived connections between the physics of the ultra-small and the physics of the ultra-large."

We thus get a picture of a Universe continuously dynamic throughout its vast range.

3. *There are several degrees of condensation of energy. The spiritual world is less condensed than its respective material world. There are an infinite number of worlds and consequently an infinite number of different stages of spiritual and material evolution.*

A basic principle here is that material energy, the one that is known to science, is only a condensation of spiritual energy. The dynamic constitution of material laws, or the laws of nature as they are called, are therefore a consequence of spiritual laws. If one imagines the unbelievable energy that has been found to exist in quasars, for instance, and then reflects that this is but the condensation of the spiritual energy which originated them, one begins to comprehend something of the power of the latter.

The problem is how to explain the condensation of spiritual energy into material energy, how Supreme Love can condense itself down the scale, as it were, until it shows in the ultra-small atoms that form the primordial cell, then to develop again through millions of years of evolution to form *Homo sapiens*. This is a problem our present stage of intelligence is just not sophisticated enough to understand. But science is progressing at a fantastic pace. . . .

4. *Man is a particle of the Supreme Energy, created with undeveloped faculties which are developed through evolution, directed by his free-will.*

The question is often asked, and has been referred to in an earlier chapter, why, if everything is an expression of Supreme Love, there should exist poverty, misery, hunger and evil generally? If there were a God, how could he permit such things? This is not, as might at first appear, another divine paradox. The answer is: man's free-will. Could there be any real love without free-will? Or, in other words, would an *imposed* love in any sense at all be satisfactory? Of course not: the only validity love can have is if it is *felt* and freely

230

given; without that, by definition it is not love at all! So once we accept that "love makes the world go round", quite literally, it follows that the dynamic principle must stem from free-will, free initiative. In matter, this free-will is expressed through evolution, intelligent evolution, which shows a purpose in everything. "The Universe begins to look more like a great thought than like a great machine," Sir James Jeans said in *The Mysterious Universe*.

Our galaxy is about 6,000 million years old. Life on Earth as we know it took some 1,000 million years to evolve, man as he is today around 50,000 years. The free-will or evolution accomplishing this adds an extra dimension for man: the soul. My working hypothesis is that the soul is an individual particle of spiritual energy, endowed with intelligence in a completely primitive stage. It was created by God (to use an image that is intelligible) much as, in matter, the primordial cell was created. How, we cannot say: like the scientist who says, "When a neutron changes to a proton by a β-process an electron is disgorged . . . the electron originates", we just have to say, "it happens, according to an α process" . . . .

The energy with which the "primordial" soul is initially charged might be expressed by the formula $(E = alw) \infty$, where a is the age of the spirit, l is the love it can develop, and w the wisdom it can acquire. In other words, it has a beginning, but there is no end to the possibility of its evolution, which is infinite (or eternal).

This particle, through electro-magnetic energy continuously spurred by the intelligent principle, starts building round it a physical body in accordance with the conditions of the planet where the process takes place. Here it has so far progressed from the primordial cell to the present body of man (an evolution reflected and repeated in the nine months gestation, from cell to complete foetus, in every pregnancy). By whose influence? What makes this cell adopt the forms it does if not the intelligent principle, acting through DNA and exercising the knowledge acquired through millions of years of development? Each particle, each portion of spiritual energy is individualised and follows its own path, determined by free-will: the amœba reacts towards light, the fish decides to try and move on land and becomes the reptile, the amphibian takes to the air, the ape decides to build itself a shelter against the cold . . . and so on until evolution produces an Einstein or a Beethoven. And the more intelligence is developed, the more choice the free-will can exercise. Consideration of the billions of galaxies will show the limitless possibilities of evolvement their opportunities offer.

In modern man, the soul could be termed a closed-circuit of electro-magnetic energy, generated by what we call the mind. At first a particle charged with infinite energy, the mind must develop through evolvement. And for this it also has to develop free-will. Like a modern computer, the power station we call the mind learns, in the course of evolution, to accumulate data, and this accounts for the kind of process I have outlined above. But once the physiological evolvement of a species is complete, the computer has the data registered and repeats it mechanically at each new birth. From then on, the intelligence itself can be developed.

This is where consciousness begins. And at each new experience the computer registers more data and the opportunity to exercise free-will becomes proportionately greater. Each mind, each " power station " emits its own energy with its own wavelength. It is as though each of us were a private and separate radio station capable either of transmitting or receiving. How does this operate?

We know that the body acts according to " orders " telegraphed by the brain in the form of electrical impulses passing through the nervous system. What happens with thoughts and feelings is analogous. Each produces an impulse which in turn produces a wave of a certain type and length —thus the feeling of love produces the highest type of energy, with the fastest and subtlest wavelength, leaning towards the ultra-violet. Hatred, on the contrary produces a lower type of wavelength, tending towards the red end of the spectrum.

Since every feeling, thought and emotion thus has its physical expression in the kind of wave it emits, we dare to

232

affirm here that, apart from God, the intelligent principle itself, there is nothing that does not come under the heading of *physical* phenomena, nothing which has to be left in the realm only of philosophy, nothing which will not obey specific physical laws, not all of which have been discovered yet, of course. For I must emphasise again, the difference between what we call spiritual energy and material energy is nothing more than one of degrees in condensation.

Wladimir Leonidovitch Durov detected thought waves of the length of 1·8 millimetres during telepathic experiments in 1923. Parapsychologists are treading the same path today. And if in fact each thought and action (which is only the evolution of a thought, after all) produces its own electric wave with a wavelength and colour according to the kind of energy emitted by the original impulse of free-will creating it, then the traditional esoteric notion of the aura, whose colours vary according to its owner's personality, does not seem so far-fetched as once it did. "Life is an electrical phenomenon mediated by an infinite variety of chemical permutations," Dr. E. E. Suckling, Associate Professor of Medical Physics at the Downtown State Medical Centre, State University of New York, has written. I do not dispute it, but the definition can now be expanded into the "spiritual" sphere.

5. *Man's evolution is processed through constant incarnations which are but condensations and discondensations of his original energetic nature.*

The concept of reincarnation has always caused a certain repugnance to the Western mind, though over one billion people in the Orient have accepted it as a natural law for centuries. Partly, the reason lies in the possibility of "social degradation" in one incarnation as a sort of "punishment" for misdemeanours in another; partly it is the idea that a person now of a high status may not always have been so, both of them conceptions inimical to the highly developed Western ego! But the main stumbling block has always been the lack of remembrance of any past existence.

I unhesitatingly postulate that the *possibility* of reincarnation is verifiable through scientific method and therefore include it in our "working hypothesis", where it is vulnerable and welcome to observational attack. It is my conviction that the concept would manage to survive true scientific probing.

The main argument in favour is based not so much on proof as on logic and reason, much as the scientists affirm the supposition that intelligent life as we know it is not confined to this one planet.

I believe that, as DNA and the genes have "registered" in them all the process of evolution, so the intelligent and spiritual evolvement of the individual is imprinted in his "spiritual memory" The only difference between us here and "them up there" lies in the degree of condensation. If this is so, then why do we not remember our former incarnations?

Compared with the 50,000 years of our existence, our intellectual development is recent. The discovery of atomic energy is only about 30 years old; the formula that made it possible was first expressed by Einstein 60 years ago. And what is 60 years, what are 50,000 compared with the billions of light years that separate us from the quasars? But, during the tiny period of time in which our intelligence has begun to advance at last, our ethical and moral standards have already been left behind. Our capacity for producing and arranging thoughts may have improved; our capacity for love has not. All religions have failed, all social institutions and political structures have failed; we fought each other in the caves—and we are still fighting. . . . And this "backlog" of progress in love has inhibited the blossoming of higher sensitivity in the area of our cerebral cortex where all past experience, and thus all past incarnations, are registered. We have not, in short, yet evolved to the stage where our brain can "remember" all these past experiences, these former incarnations.

It is perhaps worth dwelling for a moment, though, on a discovery of Dr. Wilder Penfield of the Montreal Neurological Institute, reported in William L. Laurence's *New Frontiers of Science.* By stimulating the brains of human patients, Penfield, using tiny electrical currents, discovered " a new area of the cerebral cortex to which until now (1957) no function had been assigned ". Patients " suddenly re-lived, as though it was actually happening again, long forgotten episodes of their childhood. Many patients stated that the experience brought back by the electrode was far more ' real ' than remembering, yet they were completely conscious of the present. There was a ' doubling ' of consciousness and yet the subject was aware of which was the here and now.

" How is this record of the past stored in the brain?" Dr. Penfield asked. " One may assume that at the time of the original experience, electrical potentials passed through the nerve cells and nerve connections of a recording mechanism in a specific, patterned sequence, and that some form of permanent facilitation preserves that sequence so that the ' record ' can be played at a later time, in a manner analogous to the replaying of a wire or tape recorder. But this remains a supposition."

It seems a reasonable supposition that this discovery may well be the key to the secret of reincarnation. Any day now, a scientist might, even as it were by accident, activate through an electrode an area of the brain, perhaps adjacent to Penfield's, which could recall past incarnations.

6. *Each action or thought expresses itself through electrical waves produced by man's energetical potential. Moral law has its physical expression in the conception that for every action there is a reaction. Man receives himself the result of the waves he emits. The law of reincarnation can thus be expressed : We are today the result of yesterday; tomorrow we shall be the result of today.*

7. *Each man is fully responsible for his actions. His progress through reincarnations will be faster or slower according to his own choice.*

8. *There is no race, no religion, no people in any sense "chosen". Each of us originates from the same source— supreme energy—and is endowed with the same basic potentials. Creation being continual, there are older and younger spirits. This is one of the reasons for the different stages of spiritual evolution we constantly witness on Earth.*

9. *Miracles do not exist. Everything works according to laws which are perfect. It is up to us, through evolution, to discover them.*

10. *Jesus is the oldest and most evolved spirit that has ever incarnated upon Earth. He was born, and died, the same way as everybody else. His spiritual nature, or his discondensed body, continues to live, as is the case with any of us. The difference is in degree of evolvement. Universal Religion says to all men : Each one of you will become a Jesus one day, each one of you will be the carrier of a torch to light a lower sphere, a planet whose stage of evolvement will be similar to ours when Jesus came. Jesus himself happens to be millions of years ahead of us. The dynamics of the universe have it that those with more light guide those with less, so Jesus is truly our Lord, our Sun of love and wisdom. He reached this stage by evolution; and one day we shall reach it too.*

Where, a lot of people ask, do all the apparitions of Jesus come in? Evolvement is made possible through condensation and discondensation, also called reincarnation, because when the individualised personality in this spiritual, less condensed state condenses itself, it takes on flesh, incarnates. What Jesus did under special conditions was to condense his body to the point of being the same as ours, but only on special occasions and for a limited amount of time. Modern experiences of materialisation rest on the same principle. For even " the spirits " are material—though less condensed than we are.

236

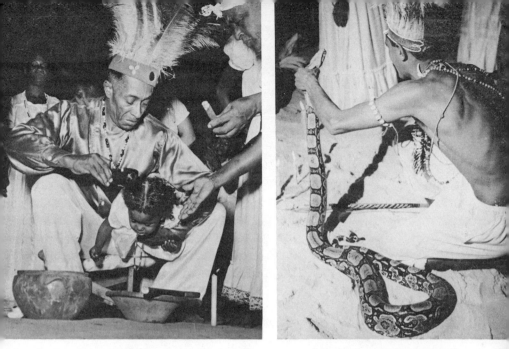

ABOVE, LEFT: A child is baptized according to one of the many Umbanda rituals. ABOVE, RIGHT: There are those who combine sensationalism with primitive forces, such as this 'horse' of an Indian spiritual entity who brought this python onto the beach of the prosperous district of Leblon on Yemanjá night. BELOW: Black and white children, side by side, intone Umbanda chants at the 'Tenda Caboclo Mirim.'

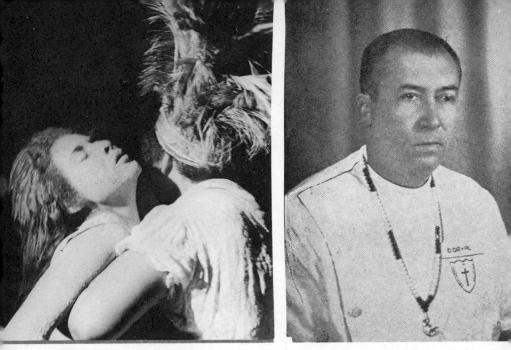

ABOVE, LEFT: A worshipper, a young girl, is lifted from the sand by an 'Indian guide' after falling into trance. ABOVE, RIGHT: Dorval Ketzer, the son of German Catholic immigrants, is the 'Spiritual Director' of an Umbanda Association, and is one of the more cultured and responsible leaders of Umbanda in Brazil. BELOW, LEFT: The Temple of Universal Religion, the centre of charity as well as spiritual activity. BELOW, RIGHT: The Founder of the Temple of Universal Religion and the author of this book is seen here at the door of the Temple at one of the annual Christmas distributions.

11. *Intelligence or intelligent life flourishes in as many billion galaxies as our imagination or science is able to detect. And many more. This planet is from one of the more inferior ones.*

12. *So-called spirit communications are nothing but the transmission of thought waves from the less condensed to the more condensed, through the perception of our nervous cells. Mediums have more sensitive nervous systems, capable of receiving and perceiving the faster wavelengths of the thoughts emitted by the spiritual entities. Just as, through evolvement, a previously " dead " area of the brain can now be stimulated to recall past material experience, and will one day no doubt be stimulated to recall past incarnations, so one day another area will be completely alive and sensitive to the presence and " speech " of spiritual entities. On that day, the question, Are you a medium? will become meaningless. Everybody will have the same powers as those we term mediums today, and the name will simply disappear. To ask the question would be like asking today : Are you a human being?*

Where does prayer fit into the picture formed by these twelve precepts? Prayer is the greatest, most effective catalyst of higher spiritual energy that we know. If it really " comes from the heart ", it concentrates unbelievable amounts of energy, which can be projected to a certain objective by higher spiritual entities, provided always that the motive is according to universal laws and stems basically from love.

To return to the subject of spirit communication, one of the main reasons why attempts to analyse this from a scientific viewpoint have failed lies in the fact that no two mediums are the same and thus no phenomenon ever exactly repeats itself. Observations with only one medium have been successfully attempted by several scientists during the past century, but they are vulnerable to the accusation of fraud. Yet if science were to apply its enormous knowledge of electronics, biochemistry and nuclear physics systematically to the discovery of the spiritual nature of man, accepting as a working hypothesis the tenets of Universal Religion, it could well make a breakthrough in the understanding of our nature and our predicament equal in impact to the discovery of how to split the atom.

On the Brazilian scene Universal Religion represents the first real effort of unification of the Spiritist movement, not through any kind of " Pope " or any imposed structure, but simply by harmonising the various currents of thought and of spiritual principle in conformity with the laws of nature, and not with preconceived ideas or ancient religious traditions, however valuable.

On the broader, world scene, Universal Religion presents a unified field theory capable of harmonising religion and science by giving them both a common ground and purpose. Dogmas and miracles are " out " and man emerges free to conquer the Universe through love and wisdom, not through missiles or bombs.

Religion, to have any meaning today, must take into consideration such diversities as the energy of the quasars, the millions of billions of possible worlds in the Universe, and the whole complex range of scientific knowledge here on Earth, as well as the moral and spiritual values by which the Intelligent Principle works. On a future world inhabited by a super-civilisation, religion will have an expression and a form beyond our present understanding. Yet the basic principles of Universal Religion will still apply, much as basic arithmetic still holds good despite the existence of computers. . . .

Let us end this study with a sentence of one of the most brilliant men of the century, Fred Hoyle:

" *It is true that we must not accept a theory on the basis of an emotional preference. But it is not an emotional preference to attempt to establish a theory that would place us in a position to obtain complete understanding of the Universe. The stakes are high and, win or lose, are worth playing for.*"